THE *UNAUTHORIZED* DAN BROWN COMPANION

THE *UNAUTHORIZED* DAN BROWN COMPANION

Edited by
JOHN HELFERS

This book is not approved, authorized, or licensed
by Dan Brown, his publisher or licensees.

CITADEL PRESS
Kensington Publishing Corp.
www.kensingtonbooks.com

CITADEL PRESS BOOKS are published by

Kensington Publishing Corp.
850 Third Avenue
New York, NY 10022

All Kensington titles, imprints, and distributed lines are available at special quantity discounts for bulk purchases for sales promotions, premiums, fund-raising, educational, or institutional use. Special book excerpts or customized printings can also be created to fit specific needs. For details, write or phone the office of the Kensington special sales manager: Kensington Publishing Corp., 850 Third Avenue, New York, NY 10022, attn: Special Sales Department; phone 1-800-221-2647.

First printing: June 2006

10   9   8   7   6   5   4   3   2   1

Printed in the United States of America

Library of Congress Control Number: 2005938605

ISBN 0-8065-2781-1

. . .

This book is dedicated to our mothers, for being there when we needed them, and to Dan Brown's millions of fans, bless them all. We are every bit as hooked on his books as they are—maybe more so.

CONTENTS

CHAPTER ONE

Dan Brown—The Man and His Fiction

For the record, Dan Brown didn't start out his life planning to be a writer. In the end, he became one almost by accident, thanks to a trip to the beach, Sidney Sheldon, and MTV. But that's jumping a long way ahead in the story.

Yet even though he didn't plan to be a writer, looking at Dan Brown's background, it's not surprising that he ended up on top of *The New York Times* best sellers list. In many ways, his upbringing shaped him into someone who almost had to put words to paper.

Dan Brown was born on June 22, 1964, in the small New England town of Exeter. With a population of less than 12,000, many of them employed by either schools or the history museum there, it was a town that placed a strong emphasis on education and academics. Dan Brown's parents were uniquely fitted to raise a best-selling writer. Brown's father was an award-winning professor of mathematics. His mother was a professional in the field of sacred music, who played the organ and taught.

And literary influences were all around him. Among the great authors and thinkers who have their roots in Exeter was writer John Irving, who had once lived just down the street from the Brown family home.

The town where Dan Brown was born and raised was steeped in history—it was one of the first four towns established in New Hampshire, dating back to 1638, and today it is the home of the American History Museum. Exeter thrived as a port and shipbuilding center from long before the American Revolution until the early 20th century, and it still retains a full measure of historic New England charm, something that undoubtedly left a strong impression on the young Dan Brown.

These days, the town is most famous for the school that both Dan Brown and his father taught at, the Phillips Exeter Academy. The exclusive boarding and prep school was founded there in 1781, and it has made the small town a hotbed of the literate elite throughout its history. With the school's sponsoring a full slate throughout the year of concerts, plays, and guest speakers, the small town offered learning opportunities in a broader range of disciplines and with an international flavor far in excess of the normal activities that would generally be available in such a tiny place.

The house Dan grew up in was filled to the brim with books, and family mealtime conversations ran the gamut from hard science to religion to music theory to art to politics. Dan soaked it all up. As soon as he was old enough, he attended school at Exeter, where he excelled in many areas. He graduated in 1982, and went on to Amherst College. He also studied art history at the University of Seville in Spain

Dan Brown wanted to be a singer and composer, and after college he headed to Hollywood, where he attempted to make it in the music business. Not one of the easiest fields to break into, it proved a tough nut to crack for the young man, even though he had the talent and the training to make good, thanks in no small part to his mother. Brown had only a small amount of success, despite his strong grounding in the field. For example, one of his songs was accepted and used as part of the 1996 Atlanta Olympic ceremonies. He also released four CDs of his music. People in the business believed he had a chance to break out, but all of Dan Brown's mentors agreed that it would mean remaking his image, stylistically and physically, in a manner that would play well on cable music channels or on stage as a touring musician, and Dan just didn't think he had it in him. He didn't like performing in front of audiences. He wasn't comfortable manufacturing a media-friendly image. And, as he put it in one interview, the world really wasn't ready for a guy like him to shake his booty on MTV. When Brown brought the question up—Who was the last slender, uptight, balding white guy who made it big in music?—only Barry Manilow seemed to fit the bill, and Manilow at least had all his hair.

In the end, Brown returned to Exeter in 1993, where he taught English and creative writing. His father had taught at the school for thirty-five years, and had won a Presidential Award for his work, so this was undoubtedly a comfortable niche for the son as well. Dan and his wife, Blythe, a painter and art historian, fit right into Exeter on their return to Brown's hometown. Dan Brown could have easily lived out his whole life shaping new generations of America's intellectual elite.

But that wasn't to be. In the end, it was a chance encounter on a vacation in 1994 that turned Brown toward writing. He came across an abandoned Sydney Sheldon book, *The Doomsday Conspiracy*, on a beach in Tahiti, and started turning the pages. It was, in many ways, a revelation to him. Thanks to his upbringing, Dan knew the classics backward and forward. He'd read virtually every great work in Western literature, from early masterpieces like *Beowulf* through Shakespeare through John Steinbeck. But he'd never really read a work of commercial fiction.

Before the day ended, Brown had finished the book, and he'd realized that he had found his future on that beach. He was going to write novels. He had a wealth of esoteric knowledge and the yearning to share it with readers everywhere.

Like the music business, publishing is a hard field to break into. For every ten thousand novels started by prospective writers, industry experts estimate, only fifty are ever completed and polished, and only one of those fifty manuscripts will sell to a major publishing house and be published. Of the roughly twenty thousand novels published in America in any given year, only a maximum of fifty-two will ever reach the top spot on *The New York Times*'s list, and usually fewer books make it, since the spot on the top of the list can be held by the same book for more than a single week, and that frequently occurs.

So, like most writers, Dan Brown was prepared to start small. He did a book of limericks. He wrote, with his wife, a humorous dating guidebook called *187 Men to Avoid: A Guide for the Romantically Frustrated Woman*. And, once again thanks to a chance encounter, he began his first novel. While Brown was teaching at Exeter, one of the school's students made a joking comment in an e-mail to a friend, about killing President Clinton. The next day, Secret Service agents showed up to see what was going on. Since no real threat was involved, just a couple of scared kids, the agents melted quickly into the background, but that event opened up a new window to the teacher and budding author. It was absolutely clear to him that there was a world of surveillance going on in the wings of ordinary everyday life. Just what, Brown wondered, was the government watching, and how?

He soon learned that the government was watching a whole lot more than most people suspected. The National Security Agency, or NSA, is fondly known as "No Such Agency" to those who work there and to the congressional oversight committee that oversees the organization. This inside gag is something that Dan Brown works into his fiction, but it's a true real-world punch line. Very few civilians have any inkling of how deeply ordinary communication is sifted by the spooks at the NSA. Cell-phone conversations, Internet chat rooms, e-mails, and all kinds of radio broadcasts are routinely checked for threats that can impact American security. These days, thanks to the Patriot Act and the war on terrorism rhetoric, most Americans are at least aware that their privacy is no longer sacred, even if they don't know exactly what the limits on privacy entail. But in the 1990s, that was big news.

And it was fascinating to Dan Brown as a budding novelist. He dug into research about the NSA: what it does, who works there, what kind of moral and ethical dilemmas their work brought them face-to-face with. He was able, thanks to the vast resources of the Internet, to contact a couple of former NSA agents who were willing to talk in a broad way about their work. He was also able, through the Freedom of Information Act and other sources, to get his hands on a number of descriptions of the kinds of gadgets that the NSA used to accomplish its mission.

All of it made a fascinating background for the story Dan Brown really wanted to tell, which was a bit of a romance, a bit of a thriller, and a bit of a morality tale about what happens when someone with too much power goes off the rails. He was able to incorporate memories from his time studying art in Seville by having a section of the thriller's plot take place in the streets of that city. The detailed research, the writer's wide breadth of knowledge, and his attention to detail added up to a manuscript and a story he was proud of.

In the end, like most budding novelists, he sent his manuscript to New York and hoped for the best.

He got it. An editor at Pocketbooks, a division of Simon and Schuster, made an offer on the book, and the company published it in 1998 under the name *Digital Fortress*. The novel generated some interest in Hollywood, and thanks to its subject matter it did very well among Internet booksellers. But on the whole it didn't make waves in the marketplace. Still, it was only the first book of three that Brown did while at Simon and Schuster, and he was about to get lucky again. After his first book, Brown was passed to editor Jason Kaufman, who would oversee his next two books, *Angels & Demons* (2000) and *Deception Point* (2001). Kaufman loved Dan Brown's work, and worked hard in-house to generate enthusiasm for the talented newcomer. But all of his efforts were not enough to bring Dan Brown to the attention of readers across America. The first three books by the new author tanked. Conservative estimates by retailers are that the total sales of all three books taken together didn't reach the twenty thousand-copy level. For major publishers in New York, those figures are extremely depressing.

For most authors, this kind of track record would have meant that their careers were over. Publishing is a ruthless business, and any author is only as good as his last book's sales. That should have made Dan Brown anathema in major-league publishing circles, because in this very small world most of the players know each other.

But Dan Brown had another piece of publishing luck. His editor was job hunting. Normally that's dreadful for an author—if his editor leaves a house, his books are "orphaned," passed on to another editor who doesn't have a personal stake in seeing the books succeed. The orphaned author gets relegated to the bottom of the pile of the new editor's responsibilities, and frequently the author's books and career vanish along with editorial attention.

But Jason Kaufman wasn't through with Dan Brown—not by a long shot. The editor was hired on at Doubleday, and one of the first things he did was bring Dan Brown's work to the attention of his new house. He brought in Brown's proposal for the book that would become *The Da Vinci Code,* and had his bosses and the company sales staff read *Angels*

& *Demons*. Jason's new house loved Brown's work and decided to take a huge chance on something that is even more risky than a new author— Dan Brown by that time was a has-been author with a dismal track record, even though everyone at Doubleday could see that the guy could really write.

Doubleday put together a hugely aggressive marketing plan. The publisher papered the country—booksellers, critics, anybody whose opinion could make a difference—with early reading copies of *The Da Vinci Code*. Doubleday worked with its clients to convince them to take what would seem to be staggeringly huge quantities of the new book by this almost unknown author. It wheeled and dealed to get the big chains to put the books at the fronts of their stores. It spent an unheard-of amount of money on advertising.

And this all paid off. The reviews of the book were dynamite. There was even a front-page rave in "Arts" section of *The New York Times*. People came out in droves to check out the book that was generating all this buzz. The book premiered as a number one *New York Times* best seller. It was like a dream come true for Dan Brown.

Usually, demand for a book dies down soon after it is released. But word-of-mouth on *The Da Vinci Code* was so strong that sales just kept on climbing. In addition, religious authorities were beginning to read the book and become alarmed at its content. Their shrieks of horror at the thought that Jesus might have married Mary Magdalene and had a child with her made news—front-page news—and television media headlines as well. This publicity drove sales to new heights, even though it was personally disturbing to Dan Brown.

Pretty soon the author was on the air everywhere defending his work, as well as pointing out something that was obvious to anyone who had actually read the book: *The Da Vinci Code* was meant to be a work of fiction, not a challenge to the whole Church and the tenets of Christianity worldwide. A firm layer of careful research backed up the story, but many story elements were there strictly to serve the fast-paced plot. Brown was in no way trying to upstage or destroy organized religion.

Raised as a Christian himself, with his summers spent at church camp and his Sundays spent singing in the church choir, Brown felt he was on reasonably strong ground in defending his tale. There was certainly enough evidence that many early writings by and about the women in the Church were suppressed by Church fathers when Christianity became the Holy Roman Empire's state religion—and there was also some evidence that the earliest Church fathers had done the same sort of suppressing soon after Christ's death. The artwork and sculpture pieces that Brown described in the book all existed, and though he was making his own interpretations of them to suit his plot, he was hardly pulling heresy out of thin air. But that was the real problem. In a way, the fact that his theories were so plausible and well researched was more threatening to Church authorities and religious conservatives than something outlandish would have been. Had the book been improbable or ridiculous, nobody would have paid attention. Had it sunk without a trace, as his previous volumes had, the author would have never heard from the all the people who now came out of the woodwork, each feeling attacked in some way or disturbed by the images and ideas contained *The Da Vinci Code.*

The backlash to his book surprised Brown. He had been writing fiction, not Sunday school texts, and the hoopla and fury of his critics were both unexpected and a bit frightening. His critics responded with vehemence and passion—and with a barrage of books debunking virtually every point he'd made in the course of his novel. He was even sued by the authors of a nonfiction work he'd cited as one of the sources for his theories on Mary Magdalene: a book called *Holy Blood, Holy Grail.*

Dan Brown fought back. The lawsuit was thrown out of court. The author participated in cable-channel documentaries about the facts behind his fiction. He appeared in live interviews during news broadcasts and on news magazine shows on network television. And every appearance seemed to generate more controversy—and to add yet another spike to the unprecedented sales of *The Da Vinci Code.*

Publishers took careful note—and re-released all of Dan Brown's previous books. In hardcover. And they sold by the millions. Each of them quickly climbed to the top of *The New York Times'*s list—often only to be denied the very top slot by the author's own still-hot volume: *The Da Vinci Code.* To date, *The Da Vinci Code* has sold more than seventeen million copies internationally, and more than twelve million copies in the United States alone. It has spent more than 150 weeks on *The New York Times*'s list. It may be the most widely read novel in history—even when the Harry Potter books are included.

And it's unlikely that sales have reached their peak. *The Da Vinci Code* has made the jump to the big screen, in a big-budget Columbia film starring Tom Hanks. Ron Howard directed, and veteran writer Akiva Goldsman did the screenplay. Dan Brown got six million dollars for the film rights. *The Da Vinci Code* has been probably the most anticipated film since the *Lord of the Rings* trilogy. And the film is most likely going to drive millions more people to pick up a copy of *The Da Vinci Code* to see what all the fuss is about.

As for Dan Brown, he's hard at work on a sequel, *The Solomon Key*, quietly researching American history and secret societies, particularly the Freemasons. A lot of nervous society members are worrying over what Brown will have to say about them when the book is finally available. If the experience of his previous volumes is anything to go by, they'll probably benefit from a wide discussion of the strong points of their organization along with the weak points, of what is mythology and what is fact. They'll pick up new members even as their detractors become more vocal.

And Dan Brown will smile all the way to the bank.

CHAPTER TWO

Conspiracy Theories— A Look at Dan Brown and His Debunkers

It's hard to get on a plane or train without seeing at least one person, and often more than half of the people in the conveyance, reading a Dan Brown book. Even when people aren't reading something by Dan Brown, they're likely to be talking about his books.

Perhaps because of that nearly universal conversation on the works of Dan Brown going on just about everywhere readers congregate, day in, day out, a whole lot of people are curious about the facts behind the fiction. And along with the wide audience interested in learning more, there are growing numbers of people determined to debunk every concept, every so-called fact, and every challenge to a deeply held belief presented in the pages of Dan Brown's thrillers.

The media has certainly joined in on the debate. These days it's hard to turn on a television set for any length of time without seeing a special presentation discussing or rebutting some point made in one of Dan Brown's books, particularly *The Da Vinci Code*. Discussions on Mary Magdalene, the Holy Grail and its true meaning, and the role of the Catholic Church are perennial themes on any number of cable channels; public broadcasting stations and even standard broadcast networks are getting into the act. They aren't alone. Preachers are holding seminars among their parishioners to discuss what they feel are the truths and the falsehoods behind the plots of the novels. Book groups across the nation are discussing every volume. Travel companies are organizing trips that take tourists through the locations in the Robert Langdon books, accompanied by docents to explain and interpret the artworks along the way. And all around the edges of these discussions, people who haven't read the books are curious enough, after what they've heard, to pick them up and begin the cycle anew.

It isn't just *The Da Vinci Code*. Brown's earlier bestsellers are generating their share of controversy, too, from the privacy issues in *Digital Fortress*, to the implications of extraterrestrial life and the machinations of high-level power brokers in *Deception Point*, to the war between the Catholic Church and the secret society of the Illuminati in *Angels & Demons*.

It's clear that Dan Brown has a real knack for finding a focus for his works that his readers—and just about every other literate person in the country—care about. His ability to mix cleverly researched conspiracy theories into his plots, for better or for worse, has opened public discussions on a number of hot-button issues that show no sign of stopping anytime soon.

A simple count of the number of books defending, debunking, or explaining the works of Dan Brown (you are holding one in your hands right now) reveals just how intense these discussions have become. More than four hundred books have been published to date to amplify, rebut, or challenge the four published novels that Dan Brown has written so far. That's over a hundred replies in book form to every novel Dan Brown has written. It's become quite a cottage industry.

But why are these novels generating so much controversy? Brown's works are fiction, not public policy statements. Even Dan Brown himself, while defending his research, is perfectly willing to concede that the main thrust of any of his books is simply to provide entertainment.

The short answer is that the conspiracies and plots that Dan Brown has set up are so interesting that it's impossible not to think about them. The author turns reality on its head so plausibly and so challengingly that it becomes impossible to finish a Dan Brown novel and not start a quest to find the truth behind the fiction.

But not everyone is comfortable with the challenge that Dan Brown's books provide to widely held belief systems. And some have more cause than others to take offense.

The Opus Dei, a Catholic society that Brown uses heavily as the source of some of his villains in *The Da Vinci Code,* has set up on its website a full and testy rebuttal to its portrayal in Brown's book—127 pages worth. Opus Dei wants it made absolutely clear that it is a benevolent lay society, that its members don't torture themselves on a daily basis, and that the cloak of secrecy that Dan Brown suggests they operate under is laughable, a total myth. In some ways, the vehemence of the society's response actually makes Dan Brown's version of events sound even more plausible—and accounts written by former Opus Dei members suggest that the organization isn't always as wholesome and as open as it claims it is. But there's a sort of affronted dignity, along with an air of exasperation in Opus Dei's protests, that makes their protests sound quite sincere.

Which is probably for the best—the Opus Dei villains in *The Da Vinci Code* are so scary that keeping them confined to the pages of fiction rather than out in the real world will undoubtedly allow millions of Dan Brown's readers to sleep better at night.

Catholic, as well as other Christian scholars and preachers of all faiths, have written hundreds of articles and scores of books furiously denying that Mary Magdalene ever had a physical relationship with Jesus, much less that she ever bore him a child. This is not surprising, since the chastity of Jesus is a concept that many Christian religions hold near and dear to the center of their doctrines, and any challenge to the established view is considered by them to be an all-out assault on everything that they believe in.

Most Christians refuse to believe in anything to the contrary.

And they do have a point when they refute the possibility that the Grail myth is a reference to a sacred bloodline descending from Jesus. The authors of *Holy Blood, Holy Grail,* which Dan Brown drew heavily upon in plotting *The Da Vinci Code,* conceded in their book that they didn't have a shred of concrete proof that Jesus and Mary Magdalene had married, much less that the couple had had a daughter named Sarah. All the evidence that they had amassed in years of searching was only good enough to support asking the question. It was not nearly enough to make the answer anything more than possible, much less probable.

What the naysayers and debunkers haven't considered, in their drive to discredit Dan Brown, is that for the first time in decades people are actually flocking to the source documents, from the Bible to the Apocrypha to early Church histories, to find out what their religion truly stands for, and to test what their personal beliefs really are. For the most part, readers of the books react by reaching out to their original faiths, and seeking clarity in what those faiths believe. And that has to be a good thing.

But, at some level, perhaps the works of Dan Brown really do pose a threat to the people behind the conspiracies the books present. Secret power structures simply work better in the dark, and Dan Brown's methodology as a novelist is to shine a big, bright light on the secrets he is exploring in his novels. He does the research, takes his share of liberties with the facts in the name of fiction, and waits to see what crawls out of the woodwork. So far, Brown has tackled government secrecy issues, the problems of technological encroachment on privacy, the existence and purpose of the Illuminati, the possible existence of life on distant planets and the lengths to which the government will go to influence debate on that subject, the reach and power of organized religion, and the true meaning of Christianity. All in all, it's not a bad range of targets for a mere four medium-length novels.

And Brown has done more than get people talking about these issues. He's stirred up a hornet's nest of critical examination from professionals and amateurs in every area he's tackled.

For example, *Digital Fortress* purports to give a glimpse into the secret world of the NSA. Though intelligence experts are divided on how close Brown came to the truth, recent events seem to point to the fact that the author was closer to that truth than most of us feel comfortable with. In the novel, a once-honorable man succumbs to the paranoia of power and begins to make unilateral decisions that he feels are for the good of the country. One of those decisions is to abuse the practice of surveillance by the NSA.

In a case where life seems to imitate art, after 9/11, President Bush quietly issued an executive order that gave the NSA free rein to spy on specific members of the American public without the usual need for wiretap permissions, subpoenas, or other general checks and balances that have traditionally been a part of domestic surveillance operations.

An important plot thread in *Digital Fortress* is the incredible tension between the need to protect the country from potential threats to its existence and the need of ordinary individuals to be safe from unnecessary government prying. In post-9/11 America, the issues Dan Brown brought up in the novel seem almost prescient. And reporters frequently point to Dan Brown's books as they speculate on the possible fallout of the President's decision.

Lawsuits filed by the American Civil Liberties Union have uncovered documents that seem to indicate that domestic spying has reached an all-time high, surpassing even the paranoid Nixon and McCarthy eras in the kinds of organizations and people that receive federal scrutiny. In these documents, recent targets of the FBI and NSA allegedly have included such groups as People for the Ethical Treatment of Animals, a Quaker church organizing an antiwar protest, and Greenpeace. Admittedly, some of these organizations have stepped over the line of full civil obedience in the past, but none of them could seriously be considered a threat to the security of the United States. One of the sweeping themes in Dan Brown's *Digital Fortress* is that when the government operates without a fail-safe lock on its powers, very bad things can occur. Recent events make it clear that the American government has a very strong interest in dismantling every fail-safe lock on restraint of its powers that it can. Dan Brown's hypothesis, that such abuse of power can only unleash disaster, has yet to be proved, but most of America is watching curiously, trying to decide if the Patriot Act and other associated governmental initiatives to remove safeguards have in fact made us safer, have merely eroded our privacy for no good cause, or have unleashed a power-mad monster on the American people.

So far, the jury is still out.

But by far the most controversial novels written by Dan Brown feature the entirely fictional character of Harvard's Professor Robert Langdon, an expert on symbology. (Interestingly, there is no such specialty at Harvard, though many Harvard professors are steeped in the subjects quoted by

Langdon throughout the book, from art history, to comparative religion, to mathematics and physics.) The fictional Langdon is called in as an expert consultant when truly terrible crimes are committed in a strange manner, leaving behind a layer of deeply symbolic clues. In the course of solving the crimes he is presented with, Langdon stumbles into massive conspiracies promulgated by huge and terrifying secret societies, and the equally secret organizations that exist to fight them.

In *Angels & Demons*, he runs afoul of the Illuminati. The name Illuminati is simply Latin for "enlightened ones," so it is not surprising that secret societies throughout history have identified themselves under the Illuminati banner. Underground groups of every kind, from persecuted Freemasons, Rosicrucians, remnants of the oppressed Knights Templar, members of the Skull & Bones fraternity, and even video-game villains fighting Tomb Raider Lara Croft have united under that banner.

More ominously, concerned members of the ruling elite, and churchmen concerned about the influence of freethinkers and secret societies, have, throughout history, written many hysterical screeds against organizations known as Illuminati. The anti-Illuminati books have accused that organization of everything from satanic masses and sacrificial burning of children on ritual fires, to orgies and torture. John Robison's *Proof of a Conspiracy Against All the Religions and Governments of Europe*, published in 1798, is typical of such books. In it, the author blames virtually every ill of society on intervention by the Illuminati, and gives descriptions of Illuminati rites that are terrifying enough to curdle the reader's blood.

Since the organizations bound under the name Illuminati are almost all societies that prohibit their members from discussing the rites and purposes of their groups, very little authoritative literature on what really went on in the secret societies exists. On the other hand, since all of the anti-Illuminati works were meant to be broadly distributed, the bulk of public knowledge about the secret societies comes not from the organizations themselves, but from their detractors, few of whom were committed to fair and balanced journalism, even by the standards of the times in which they wrote. So it's safe to say that the public picture of the Illuminati, no matter which group of them is pointed at by the finger of civic authority, is likely to be a bit hysterical and not very flattering.

In some ways, the Illuminati make almost perfect fictional villains. Just enough is known about them for us to be completely sure that they really did exist at various times through history, but not enough is known about them for us to understand fully what was going on behind the veil of secrecy drawn around them. Even many of the reputed members denied their involvement, and no one is sure what they were really up to. The imagination of the writer describing the group is the only limitation on how terrifying the picture of it is. In a way, any description of the Illuminati is likely to be fictionalized to some degree, whether the writer purports to tell the absolute truth, or is a novelist looking for a handy über-villain. In *Angels & Demons*, Langdon saves the Vatican from a terrible plot of the Illuminati to reduce the Holy See and a good chunk of Italy around it to a smoking crater.

But in *The Da Vinci Code*, Brown and Langdon take on the Church itself. In the novel, the Church will stop at nothing, absolutely nothing, to keep the secret of Christ's bloodline from the rank-and-file members of the laity. Langdon is on the run from the moment his inquiries stumble over the possibility that there is such a bloodline.

Church theologians are up in arms over *The Da Vinci Code* because it attacks on several levels what they see as their moral authority and the Church's core doctrines. As recent scandals in the Church have revealed, when Catholics don't trust their priests and bishops, the consequences for the Church as a whole are very serious. Pedophilia scandals recently embroiled a large number of bishops and cardinals worldwide in a kind of organizational cover-up worthy of a Dan Brown novel. It became clear to virtually everyone—Catholic, Protestant, agnostic, or atheist—that the Church had fallen into a pattern of hiding among the priesthood known pedophiles, as well as the crimes and sins they committed. The backlash from the public hit virtually every portion of the priesthood.

Some news sources alleged that as many as five percent of the members of the Catholic Church's hierarchy in America were tainted in one way or another by the scandals. Court judgments against the church have amounted to $661 million to date (winter 2005), with new cases being adjudicated as time passes. Many dioceses had to sell Church real estate and/or declare bankruptcy to continue to operate. At the same time that the Church was going through this financial and moral crisis, contributions and tithes by parishioners fell noticeably, thanks to the general lack of trust that believers felt in the business and religious practices of the Holy See and their local church officials.

This real-life crisis of the Church points out how vulnerable it is to bad publicity and loss of faith by its members. Dan Brown's *The Da Vinci Code* posits a Church-wide conspiracy involving dangerous secret societies, religious hit squads, Church-sanctioned murder, and cover-ups that extend across virtually the whole Catholic world.

Even though the book is clearly a work of fiction, under the current circumstances the Church is understandably sensitive to anything that could sully its image among constituents—though some Church critics contend that it would be hard for anything to do more damage than the daily reports in the media and the actions of the Church fathers throughout the pedophile scandals have managed to do so far.

But the Church has taken a lot of hard knocks lately, so it is on the defensive. And in many ways it is a lot easier to address a piece of fiction like *The Da Vinci Code*, a book that that can be easily rebutted, than it is to tackle the very real and public problems the Church is having today. With issues like pedophilia within the priesthood, the cover-up of that problem by Church bishops, the contentious discussions of the role of women in the Church, and the vast and unbridged distance that lay Catholics perceive exists between the rank-and-file Church and the Holy See, the Catholic Church hierarchy already has its hands full dealing with reality. Rebutting a mere novel, albeit ever so popular, has to be a lot more appealing than trying to tackle the raft of serious difficulties it already faces.

Like a sleight of hand, in some ways, discussions sparked by *The Da Vinci Code* among the faithful serve to take some of the heat off the Church's other problems.

The Da Vinci Code has also brought out Church apologists in droves because the book addresses an issue that most Catholics have very strong feelings about: the place of women in Catholic worship and the Catholic Church, both historically and today.

In 1969, the Catholic Church admitted that the Church's characterization of Mary Magdalene as a whore was not in any way supported by a close reading of biblical texts. Not only was she not a prostitute, she appears to have been a wealthy woman who was instrumental in the financial support of the early Church. She and Jesus's mother, Mary, were present at Christ's crucifixion, even though his male disciples had fled. And Mary Magdalene was, according to the Gospel of John, the very first person to see and recognize the risen Christ. She believed in the miracle of His Presence immediately, and carried word of it to his disbelieving male disciples, among them Thomas, who all refused to believe that Christ had come back, until the evidence before their eyes and their touch was overwhelming.

Mary Magdalene was clearly a strong and central figure in Jesus' life.

The wealth of modern scholarship on Mary Magdalene, both inside the Catholic Church and out, and the reassessment of her role in the Church serves to undermine the Holy See's proscription of the ordination of women as priests. Dan Brown's novel confronts this issue head-on.

If Mary Magdalene really was Christ's closest advisor, if she was given special knowledge that He shared with no other disciple, and if she was the first person to see the Lord after His Resurrection, all of which is confirmed in the various Scriptures, then why were women kept out of the Church's power structure from its earliest days?

Why was the sacrifice of women's lives for the Church throughout its history discounted in its temporal existence, even if the Church accepts that such sacrifice is rewarded in Heaven? It is true that many women have been granted sainthood. It is equally true that not a single woman has ever willingly been granted entrance to the priesthood, despite the apocryphal existence of women like Pope Joan.

The Da Vinci Code addresses these contentious issues at a time when the Church is getting more conservative in its world view, rather than less so.

Given the number of problem issues that the fiction of Dan Brown brings up for the Church (and for conservative Christians everywhere) to discuss, no wonder it is hard to pick up a religious publication that doesn't discuss Dan Brown or *The Da Vinci Code* somewhere in its pages. And with the movie out and a sequel on the way, it is unlikely that the dialogue will quiet down anytime soon.

CHAPTER THREE

Dan Brown and Technology: Fabulous Inventions— Do They or Don't They Exist in the Real World?

In the world of Dan Brown, the impossible seems possible, the unthinkable can end up as a comfortable pocket-sized gadget, and the unheard-of is explained away with a paragraph or two of technobabble. But how much of it is real?

As things turn out, almost all of it. Dan Brown does his research well.

Here are some of the scientific bombshells that the novelist drops in the pages of his books that exist in the real world:

The Acoustic Doppler Current Profiler

Featured in *Deception Point*, this device gave the characters a three-dimensional view of what was going on under water. The device not only exists, it is readily available commercially.

Also known as ADCP, the acoustic Doppler current profiler is an instrument that measures the speed of water currents by using sound, in particular the Doppler effect, which states that sound waves moving toward a specific point have a different frequency than sounds moving away.

Listening to a train or car pass by, with the characteristic shift in pitch just as the vehicle passes, gives the listener a quick rough experiment in observing the Doppler effect. When the sound changes, the object has gone from approaching the listener to moving away.

ADCP instruments are on the frontline of defending many nations from tsunamis. A network of the instruments along our coastlines is an important part of the early-warning system that enables emergency services to get people out of the way if a giant wave is approaching America's coastline.

One of the reasons that the Asian tsunami of Christmas 2004 was so devastating was that a good part of the Pacific Rim had chosen not to participate in setting up an ADCP tsunami early-warning system for their coastlines. The United States and Japan both have high-tech data collection stations and a net of buoys featuring the Doppler systems staged around their coastlines. These create an essential safety net. On coastlines with no warning system in place, people will die in the hundreds of thousands in low-lying areas, possibly in the millions, if ever a tsunami heads toward their coastline.

BrainStorm Software

Digital Fortress

While a few of the high-tech programming tricks featured in *Digital Fortress* were more fiction than fact, a great many of the programs weren't. BrainStorm, for example, exists, and is available for sale to ordinary citizens. It is a software program that helps organize a series of related thoughts and ideas into a logical structure or plan, then publish them to the Web for others to see. In the novel, Strathmore uses the program to run what-if scenarios.

CERN

Angels & Demons

The high-tech lab where Robert Langdon comes face-to-face with the reality of antimatter really does exist, and is a center for the study of particle physics—the world's largest. Scientists from around the world congregate there. The lab is located partly in Switzerland, partly in France near Geneva. CERN is an international organization whose activities are sponsored by twenty European countries.

The origins of CERN lie in 1951, when a council was created called the *Conseil Européen pour la Recherche Nucléaire* (CERN). In 1953, the Council decided to build a central laboratory near Geneva to concentrate on understanding the inside of the atom.

The laboratory has since gone beyond the study of the atomic nucleus to look for effects between the forces of nature that become noticeable only at very high energies.

To enhance collaboration on research documents pertaining to particle physics, Tim Berners-Lee invented the World Wide Web, a system of internationally distributed, hypertext-linked materials on the Internet, at CERN in the early 1990s. Web junkies around the world owe CERN a big debt of gratitude.

Cray Supercomputer

Deception Point

Seymour Cray was a Wisconsin-born architect and designer of large-scale computers, who founded Cray Research in 1972. He died in a car wreck in 1996, but his name lives on. These days, that name is synonymous with fast supercomputers. Now named Cray Inc., the company is located in Seattle, Washington, and still manufactures and supports the fast, high-performance computer systems known as supercomputers. They make a top-of-the-line Dell or Gateway or IBM system look like a cheap supermarket calculator. Of course, the cost of a Cray system is in line with its power.

Some complicated but necessary computer applications require a bigger, more stable platform than any desktop can achieve. Weather prediction systems, for example, like the programs that predict the paths of hurricanes, and the best of the programs modeling global-warming projections, are often done on Cray systems.

Earth Observation System (EOS)

Deception Point

The Earth Observation System (EOS) is a NASA program composed of a series of satellites and scientific instruments in Earth orbit designed for long-term observations of the interactions of Earth's environment, including land surface, biosphere, atmosphere, and oceans. The program is the centerpiece of NASA's Earth Science Enterprise (ESE).

Ground-Penetrating Radar (GPR)

Deception Point

These machines exist, and are being used all over the globe in an amazing number of applications. The machines are revolutionizing archeology and paleontology because they eliminate the need to dig endless test trenches before finding the appropriate buildings, dinosaur bones, or other target items. The units are especially useful in areas where the ground can't be disturbed easily, either because the area has been built up and is now home to apartment blocks, malls, and houses, or because the land can't be disturbed for religious reasons. When archeologists were looking for the remains of Hitler's bunker under what used to be an East Berlin parking lot, they found it with ground-penetrating radar.

The radars are starting to show up as pop culture icons—they were featured in *Jurassic Park*, where they made Dr. Grant a bit nervous as he contemplated whether science was going to make him replaceable. Little did he know that, in the universe of that film, cloning was about to make the radars look like Stone Age technology.

Ground-penetrating radar uses pulses of electromagnetic radiation to detect underground structures and objects. GPR is used in archaeological exploration; in construction to locate subsurface objects such as buried lines, pipes, and storage tanks; by law enforcement and rescue services; and by other commercial and scientific organizations.

J23

Digital Fortress

These guns are quite real and are even now being considered for use on jet airliners as a means of dealing with potential hijackers. The J23 stun gun that hits David Becker in the novel is an electroshock gun used to temporarily incapacitate a person by administering a high-voltage, low-current electrical shock. Intended to be nonlethal and avoid severe injury, the stun gun confuses the central nervous system, causing the recipient to experience great pain, paralysis, and/or muscle spasms. A half-second charge will cause intense pain and muscle contractions, two to three seconds will cause confusion and incapacitate the person, and over three seconds can completely disorient a person and put him out of action for up to fifteen minutes.

Large Hadron Collider

Angels & Demons

Speaking of CERN, the particle accelerators in *Angels & Demons* exist there as well. The Large Hadron Collider (LHC) is a particle accelerator and collider at CERN that is relatively new and very, very powerful. It is in a circular tunnel about 100 meters underground and 27 kilometers in circumference. The purpose of the LHC is to produce enormously high concentrations of energy in a minute space to resemble the state of the universe close to the Big Bang. It is intended to answer questions in physics such as what mass is, why elementary particles have different masses, what dark matter is, if there are extra dimensions, etc. Physicists around the world can't wait to get their hands on this baby and see what they can do with it.

Long-Range Stun Guns

Angels & Demons

These exist, but they are still very experimental. Most commercial stun guns work at close quarters and target one person at a time. Long-range stun guns, developed for the police and military for nonlethal crowd control, can incapacitate many people at a greater distance by sweeping a beam of electricity across them. These devices will also interfere with electronic ignition systems and stop vehicles.

To do this, scientists and manufacturers have to create an electrically conductive path between a gun and a target without using wires. Some long-range stun guns that have been developed or are still in development squirt tiny conductive fibers, ionized gas or plasma, or conductive liquid through the air at the victim.

But nobody, as yet, anyway, has a chestful of them that they can deploy at will.

Z-Particle

Angels & Demons

This is quite real, even though it defies all common sense—as do most of the workings of subnuclear particle physics. A Z particle or Z boson is an elementary particle that is identical to the photon in all respects except mass. Its mass is 100 times that of the photon, and it is one of the elementary particles that mediate the weak nuclear force.

CERN discovered W and Z particles in 1983 after building its particle accelerator. The Z particle was jokingly given its name because it was said to be the last particle to need discovery and because it has zero electric charge.

CHAPTER FOUR

Traveling with Dan Brown— A Guide to Some of the Real Locations and Attractions Seen by His Characters

Dan Brown's books may have left a number of people determined to debunk his every word, but people in the travel business aren't among them. Virtually every leisure-business operator who has access to even a single location that appears in one of Brown's novels is setting up tours and working out deals, and they are jumping on the Dan Brown bandwagon in every way that they can think of.

Heck, even places that don't appear in his books are trying to get in on the action. The state of New Hampshire's travel Web site and tourist documents all reference "Dan Brown, author of *The Da Vinci Code*," in their material, hoping that travel search engines will lead prospective vacationers to their sites. Dan Brown merely lives there, but judging by the number of times the state of New Hampshire mentions that fact, and also that it does so in the lead paragraph of these articles, the author has been very good for New Hampshire's tourism business.

For travel agents in Paris, Rome, London, Scotland, and other locations actually mentioned in the novels, the whole Dan Brown phenomenon has been a watershed event. From three-hour walking tours of Rome or Paris to fifteen-day luxury vacations that whisk travelers through everything from the Louvre to the Vatican and dozens of locations in between, Europe is hopping with tourists who have come to see for real all the places and masterpieces they read about in Dan Brown's books.

This trend has turned all of the churches, museums, and other public places mentioned in the books into jam-packed tourist meccas—to the point that many of these institutions have had to establish dramatic traffic-control measures. So, take heed. If you're heading off to see the sights, make reservations far in advance. You'll need them. Even the Dan Brown tours, which reserve blocks of the tickets to those sights as early as they can be gotten, are often sold-out far in advance. The day-trip tour folks tell us that any given tour is generally sold-out at least three days before it is to take place, and much further ahead around weekends and prime tourist months.

And, in a way, that's not surprising. After all, more than seventeen million people have read at least one of Dan Brown's best sellers. One of this author's hallmarks is his ability to make a setting sound almost irresistible.

In the opening scene of *The Da Vinci Code*, as one of the Louvre Museum's fictional curators is dying a horrible death in the Denon Wing after hours, Brown's description of the artwork that the man tries to use as a shield is so luscious that it makes most readers, even in the midst of the murder scene, take the time to make a quick mental note. "You know, I'd like to see that painting," they think. "In fact, I'd really like to see that whole gallery." Judging by the crowds waiting to get into the Louvre or the Vatican Museums on a daily basis—and numbers of tourists at both places are way, way up since the books became such big hits—a whole bunch of Dan Brown's readers have decided to act upon that urge. In fact, the lines are so long, the crowds show up easily in satellite imagery.

That's how popular Dan Brown is: the tourists his books send to museums every day form lines waiting to get in that are so large that you can see them from outer space.

So just where are the places that Dan Brown has sent his hordes of fans?

For the most part, they are in Europe, though America does have a small share in the tourist action. New York's Opus Dei building (at 243

Lexington Avenue) gets its share of visits from curious readers. On the whole, they are not made very welcome there, but it is worth a look if you happen to be in the Big Apple. The ediface is near established tourist magnets like the Empire State Building, in the city's Murray Hill district, on 34th Street and Lexington Avenue. It's a new structure—it only opened in 2001. You won't see an Opus Dei sign on the building. But the place exists, even though what goes on in it has very little to do with what Dan Brown described in his books.

The NSA is located at Fort Meade, Maryland, and has a fair share of top-level security around its headquarters, so it isn't on the tourist track, though it does have a nice Web site with pictures and mission statements for the curious to explore.

And all of the real Washington, D.C., locations are easy to find, though security is a lot tighter since 9/11. It pays to write your congressman in advance of your trip for tickets to any of the government buildings you'd like to visit, and you should be prepared to be searched, along with any belongings you're carrying.

But the big Dan Brown tourist bonanza is, as we said before, based in Europe, and people are visiting in droves. Here's a look at some of the best places to check out the scenery from Dan Brown's books:

In and Around Paris

The Louvre museum

This is ground zero for readers of *The Da Vinci Code*. The book begins and ends there, with numerous mentions of it in between. And the museum has more than its share of masterworks, including two Da Vinci paintings and the Caravaggio mentioned in the book's first scene, all worth seeing. The Louvre's gift shop sells copies of *The Da Vinci Code*, though in French rather than English. Members of the staff may sniff at the thought of American popular fiction, but they readily agree that anything that brings in people to look at great works of art has its good side. The beautiful glass pyramid entrance, designed by I. M. Pei, has 673 panes, rather than the 666 that Dan Brown claims, but it's still an imposing sight. Just be sure to use a tourist map to find the Louvre, rather than trusting in Dan Brown. The museum is southwest of Paris, not northwest, as the book claims.

Saint-Sulpice

This 17th century church boasts two Delacroix frescoes as well as one end of the Rose Line (see Concordance). It's worth a visit for more than the art and its associations with *The Da Vinci Code*. Among other events of interest, Victor Hugo was married there, and the Marquis de Sade was christened there. French film star Catherine Deneuve lives across the street, so you may even spot some celebrities as you tour the place.

Château Villette

The home of the fictional Sir Leigh Teabing is not open to the likes of the average tourist, though it can be rented if you have sufficient resources— more than $10,000 a day, with a week's minimum stay. The palatial digs have jumped on the Dan Brown bandwagon, and are offering more moderately priced stays for groups of guests—for about half that, you can join other fans for a stay at the Château, which serves as the base for a tour of the other French sights on *The Da Vinci Code* tour.

The Ritz

The Hôtel Ritz on Place Vendôme in Paris, was designed by Jules Hardouin Mansart and constructed in the early part of the eighteenth century as a private dwelling. Converted to a luxury hotel by César Ritz, it opened in 1898 and quickly gained a reputation for opulence, service, and fine dining.

Champs-Élysées

This most Parisian of streets is as lively and beautiful as ever, and still one of the best people-watching spots on the planet. Grab a table at a café, have a pastry, and be glad that no albino monks are chasing you.

In and Around Rome

A note to the unwary—Romans drive like Mario Andretti on speed, and the city shows it. No sidewalk is safe, and the handicap ramps at cross-ings, though protected by stout iron railings, have been hit so often and so hard that they are merely tangled heaps of iron that you have to hop through. While ducking the traffic, you also must be aware of the presence of hordes of excellent pickpockets, especially around tourist destinations. Be careful out there and don't let your guard down for a minute!

Vatican City

Covering 108 acres of walled land next to the Tiber River, this is an independent nation stuffed to the gills with architectural and artistic treasure. With Michelangelo and Bernini masterpieces, frescoes by Raphael and Fra Angelico, and enough of an aura of history to swamp the sensitive, it's a place that inspires imagination, even without Dan Brown's books to feed that fire. If you aren't going there on a tour, be aware that the daily tickets available for the tourist venues disappear fast—line up by at least 7:00 A.M. if you want to get in.

Castel Gandolfo

This papal summer retreat is not open to tourists, but the Church does open up the grounds, if you'd like a lovely stroll.

In and Around Edinburgh

Rosslyn Chapel

This beautifully carved 15th-century chapel is home to some of the loveliest stone carvings in all of Scotland. Given its Masonic imagery and its associations with the Knights Templar, the chapel would be a fascinating place even without the Grail mythology long associated with it.

CHAPTER FIVE

From Indiana Jones to Robert Langdon— Great Academic Heroes in Fact and in Fiction

Robert Langdon isn't the first man of letters and learning to show up in fiction in the unlikely role of action hero. In fact, he's just the latest in a very long line of characters who were better known for their brains than their brawn, but who still managed to save the world on a regular basis. If you've enjoyed reading Dan Brown's books, and you're absolutely starved for something to read before his next one comes out, you might look to these characters, who manage to strike a similar note as they go about their business of saving the world. There's probably a large element of wish fulfillment involved in the evolution of these well-known heroes and heroines. Most of the writers and creative people we know, when faced with the necessity of saving the world, would really prefer to have the Marines or the police handle the job, if possible. But the authors of this book believe that, deep down in their secret hearts, they really want the chance to show their stuff in an emergency. They just prefer to have an emergency that comes with creature comforts like indoor plumbing, air conditioning, and Internet access.

So here are some of characters who, like Dan Brown's leads, come from sheltered academic backgrounds, but go out to move mountains in time of need.

Indiana Jones

When the name of Robert Langdon comes up, generally the first comparison made is to Indiana Jones, and it's quite valid. Both characters are academics, well read and well respected in their fields, who spend their spare time consulting in ways that almost always end up with them up to their necks in situations of world-in-the-balance mortal peril. Another thing that distinguishes both of these heroes is that they do their daring deeds without a covert identity—they work in the open and under their own names, no matter how difficult the mess that they've managed to get into. Both characters have huge cult followings, and both tend to get the girl during every adventure. After all, if someone is going in for wish fulfillment, might as well go all the way.

The Scarlet Pimpernel

Heroic gentlemen of learning are nothing new in the world of literature. Baroness Emmuska Orczy's famous hero, the foppish Sir Percy Blakeney, spent his spare time rescuing the innocent victims of the French Revolution before they could be fed to the guillotine. Sir Percy ends up married to the most beautiful, most intelligent woman in the known world, and remains faithful to her. Robert Langdon has not, as yet, achieved a permanent partner, finding new romantic relationships in each of his books.

Ian Malcolm

Jurassic Park

A famous mathematician invented by author Michael Crichton to add tension and comic relief to his novel, Ian spends the bulk of the book telling everyone who will listen to him that nothing but disaster can come of such widespread abuse of science as cloning dinosaurs. He then has the joy of saying, "I told you so," in a hundred different ways when he's proved right. Like Robert Langdon, he's brought in as a consultant, and like Robert Langdon, from there on, absolutely nothing goes as planned. Unlike Langdon, Malcolm's record with the women in his life is hardly successful.

Dr. Benton Quest

Jonny Quest

Like Robert Langdon, Dr. Quest seems to find mortal peril in every job he takes on. Also like Langdon, the doctor makes a good showing against evil in the end. Unlike Langdon, Quest invariably fails in the fight, and must be rescued by his son and his sidekicks. Perhaps it's just as well that Langdon doesn't have children to steal the show.

Fox Mulder

X-Files

Fox Mulder has many of the same traits as Robert Langdon—including a whole lot of book learning, and a nasty tendency to wind up in trouble when he sticks his nose into a problem. Unlike Langdon, Mulder has an official partner to fall back on, the beautiful Dr. Dana Scully, and a whole organization at his back to come to his rescue when things get really, really bad. He also routinely carries a gun and a badge—both highly useful when times get bad.

Sherlock Holmes

The original academic consultant on all things symbolic, Holmes was brought in when Scotland Yard was at a complete loss, or when a private citizen needed help with a particularly knotty problem. Many of the cases Holmes consulted on had the same elements as those found in Dan Brown's books: mysterious drawings, secret societies, a master villain. The two men have much in common, including a slight similarity between the lead character and his creator.

Buckaroo Banzai

Buckaroo Banzai is essentially a Dan Brown hero taken to the furthest extreme. Rock star, surgeon, scholar, scientist, he's the guy you call when you really, really need to save the world. Though Banzai is played for comedy, there's more than a little of him in Robert Langdon. Watching

Langdon cope and triumph as every kind of danger and disaster his creator can think of is thrown at him makes us think of Buckaroo Banzai. That's especially true when we try to imagine what any of *our* college professors would do if mysterious assassins ever came after them. Suffice it to say that the world as we know it would no longer exist. For that element of being able to find the answer in the nick of time, and to employ it even when all around him people are throwing up their hands in despair, Buckaroo Banzai is probably the closest thing in all of the fictional world to a Dan Brown hero. Over the top, yes, but not by much more than one of Dan Brown's creations. And that's one of the reasons we love them so.

An A-to-Z Look at the World of Dan Brown's Novels

Assembled and Written by Pam McCutcheon

Aaronian, Richard

Angels & Demons

Richard Aaronian teaches at the Phillips Exeter Academy in New Hampshire, where he holds the Harlan Page Amen Professor of Science post. He is a famed ornithologist, and is well known among his students and peers both for the difficulty of his tests and the excitement of his field trips, which have opened the eyes of many of his students to the glories of fieldwork and the wonder of the natural world.

ABC News

Deception Point

Not that this needs much explanation—but Yolanda's workplace is one of the premier broadcast news organizations even in the age of the continuous news cycle, and ABC is still giving CNN a run for its money with its popular *Evening News* broadcast.

And its history is fascinating.

The American Broadcasting Company was founded in 1945, and began filling the airwaves in April 1948 as something of a shoestring operation. It couldn't afford to broadcast except in the New York area. Thanks to mergers and increased financing, ABC went nationwide in the fifties. It came into its own in the sixties with such programs as *Leave It to Beaver, Batman,* and *The Flintstones.*

ABC News came into prominence with the appointment of the late Peter Jennings as its news anchor during the Vietnam War—and gained widespread publicity thanks to the anchor's subsequent run-ins with the Johnson administration over the network's coverage of that war. Those run-ins reputedly resulted in Jenning's ouster from the anchorman's chair for well over a decade. Another longtime and influential member of the ABC news team is legendary producer Roone Arledge, who revolutionized the coverage of sports in America with such long-standing staples as *ABC's Wide World of Sports* and *Monday Night Football.*

Though, to date, several attempts by ABC to launch a full-time cable news network have failed, the organization is still widely respected in the news field, and may yet succeed in taking on the 24/7 world of news in the 21st century.

Academy of St. Martin's in the Field

Digital Fortress

Founded in 1959 by Sir Neville Marriner and the then-Master of Music, John Churchill, this chamber orchestra spearheaded the 1960s Baroque revival in Europe and America. Renowned for their mastery of Bach, Pachabel, and other greats of classical music, the orchestra is the most widely recorded on earth, and is familiar to a wide audience thanks to its work in numerous big-screen productions, including the movie *Amadeus.* The Church of St. Martin's in the Field has a long and glittering musical reputation—Handel and Mozart are among the greats who have performed in its environs.

Acclamation by Adoration

Angels & Demons

Essentially a practice abandoned by the Holy See in Rome hundreds of years ago, this is a method of electing the Pope. What Brown refers to as acclamation by adoration occurred when, as the assembled College of

Cardinals met after the death of the Pope, a number of cardinals fell over and prostrated themselves in front of the single cardinal they wished to select as the new Pope, rather than going through the formal process of balloting. Since the Papal election is supposed to be done without any prior discussion or prearranged negotiation, this form of Papal selection is supposed to be a direct result of the action of the Holy Spirit upon the assembled priests.

Though the spontaneous movement of a large number of powerful Church clerics can, in theory, be so powerfully influenced by God as to overwhelm all of them at once to bow down before a single man during a Papal election, more often in Church history the evidence indicates that the process was, despite the rules, the result of careful arrangements made beforehand.

In practice, it seems that a great deal of back-room politicking generally had to occur in order for election by acclamation (rather than a formal balloting process) to be successful. Election by acclamation also left open the possibility of imprecise accounting, and offered opponents of the new Pope an opportunity to contest the election and set up opposition papacies, or "antipopes." Dueling popes were a feature of the Church during certain periods in its history—and they generally excommunicated each other as their first official act.

For obvious reasons, this lack of clarity was bad for the Church. Gregory XV laid down new rules after his own election by acclamation in 1621 that made this form of papal election obsolete.

Acoustic Doppler Current Profiler

Deception Point

Also known as ADCP, the acoustic Doppler current profiler is an instrument that measures the speed of water currents by using sound, in particular the Doppler effect, which states that sound waves moving toward a specific point have a different frequency than sounds moving away.

Listening to a train or car pass by, with the characteristic shift in pitch just as the vehicle passes, gives the listener a quick rough experiment in observing the Doppler effect.

The ADCP measures the Doppler effect in a column of moving water. Using one of these instruments, it is possible to measure accurately the speed and direction of water from anywhere the instrument can be mounted. For example, an ADCP anchored to the seafloor can measure water speed not just at the bottom of the ocean, where the instrument is located, but also at equal intervals all the way up to the surface in the column of water in the path of the instrument's sound beam. Trailing an instrument on a buoy can give a continuous picture of the water currents surrounding the buoy, even if the ocean bed is too deep to anchor an ADCP to it. The instrument can also be mounted horizontally on seawalls or bridge pilings in rivers and canals to measure the various currents as they pass through from shore to shore. The instrument can even be affixed to the bottom of a ship to take constant measurements of the water movement around the vessel as it moves.

The ADCP works by sending out constant pings of sound at a regular rate and fixed pitch. These sounds are reflected back to the instrument at different pitches from flotsam, bubbles, wildlife, or any other obstructions in the water. Depending on how the water is moving in relation to the instrument, the pitch in the reflected sound returned to the instrument varies. Currents coming toward the ADCP send back echoes that are higher than the original "ping." Currents moving away from the instrument send back echoes that are lower in pitch. By measuring these shifts in frequency, the instrument can tell—from the time it takes the echo to return to the instrument—how far away the water area being measured is. The change in frequency tells in what direction the water is moving and how fast it is going. Collating all the data from the reflected pings gives a three-dimensional picture of all the water in the column being measured.

Babel

The Da Vinci Code

Babel is the Hebrew name for Babylon. In the Bible, after the Deluge, Noah's descendants attempted to build a tower to heaven in Babel (the Tower of Babel). To punish them for their presumption, God confused the language of the builders so they could no longer understand each other.

As Dan Brown mentions in his book, biblical scholars were baffled for many years by the prophet Jeremiah's reference to the city of Sheshach since it was mentioned nowhere else in the Bible and couldn't be found in contemporary documents. However, when a using a simple letter substitution method, Sheshach is actually a cipher for Babel.

The Atbash Cipher method lays the Hebrew alphabet out twice, in opposite directions, each letter from the top row substituting for one on the lower. Doing this, the letters Sh-Sh-Ch become B-B-L, the Hebrew spelling of Babel.

Since the decoding of Sheshach, scholars have found several other simple substitution methods used as ciphers in the Bible, including the Atbash Cipher (aleph for het), previous letter method (beth for aleph), and next letter method (gimmel for beth).

Back door

Digital Fortress

A back door, in computer programming terms, is an alternate, secret way into program software or an encryption algorithm, usually put there by the author of the program to bypass security controls.

Baldwin II

The Da Vinci Code

King Baldwin II (?–1131), also known as Baldwin of Le Bourg, was the second count of Edessa (1100–1131). He accompanied Godfrey of Bouillon, his cousin, on the First Crusade and was captured and imprisoned for a couple of years by the Muslims. He succeeded another cousin, King Baldwin I, to the Latin throne of Jerusalem where he became its third king, ruling from 1118 to 1131.

In 1118, Hughes de Payens asked King Baldwin II for quarters in the royal palace in Jerusalem for himself and a few companions to found the Knights Templar. Baldwin wholeheartedly supported their request, and the same year also added a military mission to the charitable order of Knights Hospitaller (founded in 1113).

Balearic Islands

Angels & Demons

The Balearic Islands (*Illes Balears Catalan*) are an archipelago in the western Mediterranean Sea, floating between the eastern coast of Spain and the North African coast. A province of Spain, their capital is Palma de Mallorca, and the four main islands of this autonomous community are Mallorca, Menorca, Ibiza, and Formentera. The islands are a popular summer tourist and party destination, and also boast Gothic cathedrals, Stone Age ruins, fishing villages, and orange and olive orchards.

Balearic Sea

Angels & Demons

Sometimes called the Catalan Sea, the Balearic Sea is one of several seas that comprise the western basin of the Mediterranean Sea. It lies in the northwestern portion of the Mediterranean, between the Iberian coast, the Balearic Islands, and Sardinia and Corsica.

Bang-stick

Deception Point

In *Deception Point*, Dan Brown has Michael Tolland use a bang-stick, which he also calls a Powerhead Shark-Control Device, to defend himself against attack by Delta-Three. However, these are two different types of devices, often confused.

Though both use gunpowder cartridges, the Powerhead Shark-Control Device is a spear gun that employs a propellant to fire a sharp projectile into the shark. The bang-stick, or bang stick, is actually what Tolland used. A bang-stick has a shotgun round placed on the tip of a pole and is employed by jabbing the end of the stick into the shark. The concussive effect of the exploding gases causes sufficient damage to seriously injure and deter a shark. Or, as in the book, a human assailant.

Baphomet

The Da Vinci Code

Baphomet is an idol or mystical figure that Dan Brown mentions as a pagan fertility god. Though the Knights Templar were accused of using licentious rites to worship this idol in the fourteenth century, their "confessions" were achieved as the result of torture by the Inquisition, and were later recanted. The Inquisition used the Templars' so-called worship of Baphomet, along with their torture-induced confessions of spitting on the cross and denying Christ, to declare the Knights Templar heretical.

The origin of the word Baphomet is believed by some to be a corruption of Mohammed. Or, using the Atbash Cipher, the letters of the decoded word spell Sophia, the Gnostic goddess. Interestingly enough, Gnostic texts often equate Sophia to Mary Magdalene.

Not only is there some confusion as to the word's origin, there is also great confusion as to what Baphomet actually looks like. The idol is depicted in many ways in Church texts, variously represented as a goat's head drawn within a pentagram, a severed bearded head, an idol possessing two or four heads, a cat idol, or a grotesque creature with the head of a goat, cloven hooves, and the body of a nude woman. In short, the varying depictions indicate that there is even less consensus as to what Baphomet looks like than there is as to Baphomet's origins.

Barrio Santa Cruz

Digital Fortress

The neighborhood (or barrio) of Santa Cruz, where Brown's character David Becker attempts to evade his pursuer, is the former Jewish Quarter in the historic center of Seville, Spain. Delightfully picturesque, the area features narrow winding cobbled streets, ancient whitewashed houses, old palaces, churches, hidden passageways, beautiful patios, and multitudes of flowers.

Surrounded by Calles Mateas Gago, Santa Maria La Blanca/San José, the Jardines de Murillo and the Alcázar, the barrio of Santa Cruz gives the observer unique insights into the Andalusian culture.

Bartók, Béla

The Da Vinci Code

Béla Bartók (1881–1945) was a Hungarian composer who collected Hungarian folk music and later taught piano at the Royal Academy in Budapest. His first success as a composer came with his mime play *The Wooden Prince*, and he achieved acclaim for his operas and ballets. He was best known, however, for his compositions for piano, violin, and orchestra.

Dan Brown mentions Bartók as one of the most famous examples of a composer who consciously used phi (see Phi), or the golden ratio, to determine the point of climax for his works.

Bas-relief

Angels & Demons

Bas-relief, sometimes written as bas relief, comes from the Italian *basso rilievo*, meaning raised contrast. It is a method of sculpting in which the surface of a flat piece of stone or metal is carved away, allowing the resulting image to project slightly above the flat surface below it. Used extensively in ancient times, it is still employed today. You will find bas-relief most commonly used on architectural surfaces, rather than as free-standing sculpture.

Dan Brown's second Altar of Science for Air, the West Ponente, is a bas-relief sculpture.

Bastion host

Digital Fortress

This is one of the security measures Jabba uses to protect the NSA computer. A bastion host defends a protected inner network from attacks that might come through an outside network, essentially performing as a firewall.

Bathynomous giganteus

Deception Point

A species of aquatic crustacean commonly called a giant isopod (louse). It is the largest known species of isopod, up to forty five centimeters long, and can be found in great numbers in the deep, cold waters of the Pacific and Atlantic oceans.

In *Deception Point*, Rachel and Michael realize that the fossil species in the meteorite is actually a bathynomous giganteus, not the alien life they were led to believe.

Baudelaire, Charles Pierre

The Da Vinci Code

Charles Pierre Baudelaire (1821–1867) was a French poet, critic, and translator noted for macabre imagery and evocative language. *The Flowers of Evil*, the only volume of his poetry published in his lifetime, was condemned as obscene for its themes of sex and death, and Baudelaire, his publisher, and the printer were convicted for creating an offense against public morals. Since then, Baudelaire has been hailed as a master and has had a major influence on other Western poets.

Dan Brown mentions in passing that Baudelaire was baptized in the Church of Saint-Sulpice.

Bavarian Illuminati: New World Order

Angels & Demons

The Bavarian Illuminati game is published by Steve Jackson Games and consists of cards, a rule book, and money chits that two to six players use to grab control of secret conspiracies to battle for world domination. The Bavarian Illuminati: New World Order is a collectible trading-card version of Illuminati. Hundreds of different cards are available, as well as two expansion sets. It won the Origins Award for Best Card Game of 1994.

Bazooka

Angels & Demons

A giant, portable rocket launcher. Held on the shoulder, it consists of a long, lightweight metal smoothbore tube for firing armor-piercing rockets, usually operated by two men. Often used by mobile suits to attack tanks, ships, and fortifications, it is a short-range weapon with low accuracy. Though it was widely used in World War II and the Korean War, it has since been replaced by recoilless weapons and antitank missiles.

BBC

Angels & Demons

Dan Brown's fictional journalist Gunter Glick and camerawoman Chinita Macri work for the British Broadcasting Corporation (BBC). Founded in 1927 by a royal charter from the Crown, the BBC is the national broadcaster of the United Kingdom, producing programs on television, radio, and the Internet. It is publicly funded by levying license fees on television-set owners.

Beal Aerospace

Deception Point

Dan Brown's book, published in 2001, mentions Beal Aerospace as one of the private aerospace companies that offered bribes to Senator Sexton to put space exploration in the hands of the private sector. Though this Texas-based company did exist, it ceased operations in October 2000. The company's objective was to build and operate a privately developed orbital launch vehicle, but it ran into a series of problems, mostly political, when it tried to compete against NASA. No wonder Dan Brown put Beal Aerospace in this role.

Beechcraft Baron 58

The Da Vinci Code

The Beechcraft Baron is a leader in the piston twin-engine class of business aircraft. The Beechcraft Baron 58 is a stretched version of the 55, and first entered production in 1970. It remains in production today by the Raytheon Aircraft Company, which produces about forty per year. This is the aircraft that Bishop Aringarosa chartered in the novel.

Beethoven, Ludwig van

The Da Vinci Code

Ludwig van Beethoven (1770–1827), a German composer of classical music, was one of the greatest and most influential composers who ever lived, radically transforming nearly every musical form in which he worked. He is best known for his powerful, stormy compositions, and the ominous four-note beginning to his *Fifth Symphony* is one of the most famous moments in all of music. Though he became deaf at twenty-eight, he continued to compose and conduct.

As Dan Brown mentions, Beethoven used phi, or the golden ratio, in composing his *Fifth Symphony*. However, though Dan Brown claims Beethoven was a Freemason, this can't be substantiated. Beethoven didn't belong to a lodge, but he had many friends, patrons, and publishers who did. For this reason, many believe that he was a closet Freemason, since active participation was forbidden in Vienna at the time.

Bell Laboratories

Digital Fortress and Deception Point

Bell Telephone Laboratories, Inc., or Bell Labs, was founded in 1925 by Walter Gifford, president of AT&T. Owned jointly by AT&T and Western Electric, Bell Labs took over the research division of Western Electric's engineering department and became a subsidiary of AT&T after the divestiture in January 1983.

Performing research, systems engineering, and development, Bell is one of the most renowned scientific laboratories in the world, developing a wide range of technologies from telephone switches to the transistor, and creating the theoretical basis for today's telecommunications.

Beretta

Digital Fortress

The *Fabbrica d'Armi Pietro Beretta* is an Italian gun-manufacturing company that was founded in 1526 when gunsmith Mastro Bartolomeo Beretta received a large order for musket barrels for the arsenal of Venice. One of the world's oldest corporations, it has been owned by the same family for nearly five hundred years.

Today, the company is run by Ugo Gussalli Beretta and his sons. Though Ugo is a direct descendant of the original Beretta, the traditional father-to-son dynasty was broken when he took over. Since his two uncles had no children, his uncle Carlo Beretta adopted Ugo Gussalli to give him the Beretta name.

Beretta has a broad product range, from three different types of shotguns and rifles to submachine guns, revolvers, and pistols. They are used by civilians, police, and military forces all over the world. It's no wonder that Dan Brown puts a Beretta in the hands of his character Strathmore.

Bergofsky Principle

Digital Fortress

The Bergofsky Principle, as Dan Brown's character states, maintains that every code is breakable, that if you try enough keys, you are mathematically guaranteed to break any code . . . eventually. Mr. Brown may have access to research we don't, but we can't verify that the Bergofsky Principle exists. However, it is an excellent literary device to establish this principle as fact when it is necessary for the plot.

Bering Sea

Deception Point

Discovered by Danish navigator Vitus Bering, the Bering Sea (or Imarpik Sea) is a body of water in the far northern Pacific Ocean, bordered by Alaska, Siberia, and the Aleutian Islands. It is connected to the Arctic Ocean by the Bering Strait and covers about 878,000 square miles. The Bering Sea is one of the world's major fisheries, but can usually be traversed by ship only from June to October.

Bermuda Triangle

Deception Point

The Bermuda Triangle is a triangular-shaped area of the Atlantic Ocean (approximately 1.5 million square miles) bounded by Bermuda, Puerto Rico, and the southern tip of Florida. It is said that a number of ships and aircraft have vanished in this area, leading many to speculate that paranormal forces are to blame.

There is no scientific evidence to prove that unusual phenomena were involved in the disappearances, though Dan Brown mentions that some have speculated that megaplumes (see Megaplume) may be blamed for some of the missing ships.

Berners-Lee, Tim

Angels & Demons

In Dan Brown's novel, Langdon is surprised to see a plaque that credits CERN and Tim Berners Lee [sic] with the invention of the World Wide Web. Tim Berners-Lee did indeed receive the Ars Electronica Award for invention of the World Wide Web, but Langdon's surprise may be due to the fact that many confuse the World Wide Web with the Internet, which was developed and funded by the United States government.

To differentiate between the two: The World Wide Web is made up of a series of Web servers around the world that store Web pages—the content. The Internet is the vehicle that allows users to contact the Web servers to retrieve the content on the World Wide Web.

Tim Berners-Lee graduated with a degree in physics from Queen's College at Oxford University, England, in 1976, then worked with Plessey Telecommunications Ltd., D.G. Nash Ltd., and as an independent consultant. While consulting for six months at CERN (see CERN), he wrote a program for his own private use that formed the conceptual basis for the future development of the World Wide Web.

Later, Berners-Lee took a fellowship at CERN, then proposed a global hypertext project to be known as the World Wide Web in 1989, developed it in 1990, and made it available on the Internet in 1991. The first Web site that Berners-Lee built, and therefore the very first Web site, was put online on August 6, 1991, at info.cern.ch/. (It has been archived.)

Bernini, Gianlorenzo

The Da Vinci Code and Angels & Demons

Gian Lorenzo (or Gianlorenzo or Giovanni) Bernini (1598–1680) was appointed official artist to the Papal Court and the Barberini family by Pope Urban VIII (Maffeo Barberini). Though known primarily as a pre-eminent sculptor and architect in the Italian Baroque period, Bernini was also a poet, painter, and draftsman, and designed stage sets, fireworks displays, and funeral trappings as well.

Bernini designed many churches, chapels, tombs, statues, and fountains. Some of his most famous works, including those mentioned in Dan Brown's novels, are the *Ecstasy of St. Teresa*, the Fountain of the Four Rivers, *Apollo and Daphne*, the piazza and colonnades of St. Peter's Square, St. Peter's Chair, the Royal Stair in the Vatican Palace, the bronze baldachin over the high altar of St. Peter's Basilica, Pope Urban VIII's tomb, several palazzos, and the artwork inside the Chigi Chapel.

Another of Bernini's famous sculptures which is not mentioned in the novel is known as *Bernini's Elephant*. It is located in the Piazza della Minerva, and was commissioned by Pope Alexander VII to create a support base for an obelisk. The elephant sculpture was executed by one of

Bernini's assistants and features a smile. Why? If you take a look at the rear, you will see that its muscles are tensed and its tail is shifted to the left . . . as if it were in the act of defecating. The elephant's rear is pointed directly at the former offices of Father Domenico Paglia, a Dominican friar who was one of Bernini's main antagonists. That's one way to get in the last word. . . .

Dan Brown speculates that Bernini was the hidden, unknown master of the Illuminati, using his sculptures and architecture to create the Path of Illumination. This, of course, cannot be proved.

Bibliothèque Nationale

The Da Vinci Code

The Bibliothèque Nationale de France is one of the foremost libraries in the world. It originated in the fourteenth century with collections of writings made by early French kings and has been the legal repository of all books published in France since 1537, including governmental archives. This is where *Les Dossiers Secrets* were deposited in 1956.

Big Bang Theory

Angels & Demons

The Big Bang Theory is a cosmological theory for the origin of the universe, holding that it began some thirteen to twenty billion years ago (estimates vary), when all matter and energy concentrated to very high density and high temperature, then exploded. The present universe is still expanding from that event.

The theory was first proposed by the Belgian astrophysicist and Catholic priest Georges Lemaître. Though this was a radical departure from scientific theory at the time, it has since become accepted as the most probable explanation for the origin of the universe. In addition, it is not inconsistent with the Catholic Church's theological position that time itself began at creation.

Big Ben

The Da Vinci Code

Big Ben refers to the Great Bell of Westminster, part of the Great Clock of Westminster, which is located in the Parliament Clock Tower of the Westminster Palace in London. It was installed in 1856 and named for Sir Benjamin Hall, the commissioner of works at that time. The name Big Ben is often used to refer to the huge clock in the tower, which is one of the most famous landmarks of the city.

Biggin Hill Airport

The Da Vinci Code

Biggin Hill, in Westerham, Kent, is an airport in South London where a flight can be chartered to anywhere in the world. It opened in 1917 as a communications base, added flying in the 1920s, and launched Spitfires and Hurricanes for the Royal Air Force during the Battle of Britain in the 1940s. Today it is the point of arrival for many business visitors to London, and the home base for many corporate, private, and charter aircraft owners.

In the novel, this is where Sir Leigh Teabing keeps a hangar, and where four central characters arrive in England without fanfare, passports, or legality.

Biggleman's Safe

Digital Fortress

In *Digital Fortress*, Susan and Strathmore discuss the Biggleman's Safe concept, saying it is a hypothetical scenario in which a safe maker created blueprints for an unbreakable safe, then put the blueprints in it to keep them secure. Though we cannot find any other references to this concept, Dan Brown uses it to illustrate how Tankado protected his "unbreakable" algorithm—by encrypting the algorithm with itself, in his own electronic Biggleman's Safe.

Bioentanglement physicist

Angels & Demons

In the novel, Vittoria Vetra works as a bioentanglement physicist. In quantum physics, entanglement is the theory that, under certain circumstances, particles that appear to be isolated are actually instantaneously connected through time and space. Living cells also display properties associated with quantum entanglement, which means they could be interconnected without being physically near each other. This is probably what Dan Brown means by bioentanglement, though it doesn't seem to be an established science (or profession) as yet.

Bioluminescent dinoflagellates

Deception Point

Found in both fresh and salt water habitats, dinoflagellates are single-celled algae that sometimes bloom in concentrations of more than a million cells per milliliter. About half are bioluminescent and emit short flashes of light as a means of defense.

The melted water above the meteorite in *Deception Point* contains these tiny flashes of light. This is the trigger event that leads to Ming's death and is the first indication for the other characters that the meteorite might not be what it seems.

Biomimics

Deception Point

Biomimics, or biomimicry (from *bios*, meaning life, and *mimesis*, meaning to imitate), is a science that takes inspiration from nature and mimics natural processes with technology to solve human problems. For example, a solar cell was inspired by a leaf, Velcro was invented when a man noticed that burrs with tiny hooks naturally attach themselves to the loops in fabric, and Dan Brown's Delta Force used tiny microbots that simulated the flight of dragonflies.

Bishop's ring

The Da Vinci Code

When a bishop is consecrated, he receives a ring representing the authority of his office and symbolizing that he is wedded to the church or his diocese. The ring first appeared as a symbol of Episcopal authority in the third century, and was mentioned as an official part of the bishop's regalia in the early seventh century. It was also used as a seal in hot wax to authenticate documents.

Usually made of gold with an amethyst, the ring can be very elaborate, making it extremely valuable for both religious and monetary reasons. This is why Bishop Manuel Aringarosa in the novel is so upset at losing his.

Black-light pen

The Da Vinci Code

A black-light (or black light) pen is used to write messages or make marks that are invisible in normal light but glow brightly under ultraviolet black light. These pens are used by law enforcement agencies and museums to identify forgeries and recover stolen merchandise. Saunière uses one in the novel before he dies to leave coded messages for his granddaughter.

Blind drop services

The Da Vinci Code

A blind drop service is one in which clients can deposit and withdraw valuable items anonymously. Saunière used this service at the fictional Depository Bank of Zurich (see Depository Bank of Zurich) to store the rosewood box holding the cryptex (see cryptex) that Sophie and Langdon find there.

Boaz

The Da Vinci Code

Boaz (in strength), also called the Mason's Pillar, was the name of the northern of the two pillars that stood on the eastern portico in front of Solomon's Temple. The bronze pillars were crafted by Hiram, an expert worker of bronze, from Tyre. Each was eighteen cubits high and twelve cubits around (about twenty seven feet high and eighteen feet around). The other pillar was named Jachin, but the purpose of the pillars is unknown. Duplicates of these pillars reside in many Masonic temples.

Bois de Boulogne

The Da Vinci Code

The Bois de Boulogne is a park in Paris bordering on the western suburb of Neuilly-sur-Seine. It was named after Notre-Dame de Boulogne le Petit during the reign of Philippe IV. In 1848, it became the property of the state and, in 1852, was made into a park by Napoleon III.

Today, this 2,090-acre park contains the race courses of Auteuil and Longchamps, and is infamous for the presence of prostitutes and transvestites at night, which makes Sophie and Langdon's drive through it rather memorable.

Bolling Air Force Base

Deception Point

The District of Columbia's Bolling Air Force Base is named for Colonel Raynal Cawthorne Bolling, who laid the foundation for the United States Military Aviation Service and was the first high-ranking United States officer to be killed in combat in World War I (in 1918). The base was opened near the Anacostia River, in the same year, and was then the only military airfield near the US capital. It moved to its present location in southwest Washington, D.C., in the 1930s.

Home to the eleventh Wing, the United States Air Force Band, and the United States Air Force Honor Guard, Bolling provides ceremonial support to the White House, chairman of the joint chiefs of staff, secretary of the Air Force, and the Air Force chief of staff.

This is where Rachel and Michael intended to land, before they diverted to Atlantic City and the *Goya*.

Boniface IV

Angels & Demons

Pope St. Boniface IV (circa 550–615) was the son of John, a physician, from Valeria, Abruzzi, Italy, and served as a Benedictine monk in Rome, where he distributed alms. He was elected pope in 608. In 609, he obtained permission from Emperor Phocas to convert the Pantheon into a Christian Church and consecrated it to the Virgin Mary and all the saints. It was the first time Rome had converted a pagan temple to Christian worship. It is said that twenty-eight cartloads of sacred bones were transferred from the catacombs to the newly consecrated Pantheon. Boniface IV was later commemorated as a saint.

Boniface VIII

Angels & Demons

Boniface VIII, born Benedict Gaetano (or Cajetan) (circa 1235–1303) was Pope of the Roman Catholic Church from 1294 to 1303. His predecessor, Celestine V, had abdicated on Boniface's urging, and one of Boniface's first acts in the office of pontiff was to imprison Celestine (see Celestine V) to prevent a schism in the church.

However, there is little evidence to support Dan Brown's contention that Boniface VIII assisted in Celestine V's death, since Celestine died at the age of 91 in his narrow prison in Fumone, attended by two monks of his order.

Boniface VIII proclaimed that it "is necessary for salvation that every living creature be under submission to the Roman pontiff." His asser-

tion of papal supremacy over temporal matters and constant intervention in politics and foreign affairs led to many arguments with King
Albert I of Habsburg, the Colonnas family, and King Philip IV (Philip
the Fair) of France.

In feuding with the Colonnas, Boniface destroyed the city of Palest-
rina, killing six thousand people, then he excommunicated Philip in
1303. Philip and the Colonnas captured Boniface and demanded
he resign. Boniface refused, but he died a month later. He was
buried in St. Peter's Basilica, in an ostentatious tomb that he himself designed.

Book of Matthew

The Da Vinci Code

One of the four gospels of the New Testament, the Gospel of Matthew
is traditionally printed as the first book. Though it is usually considered the earliest gospel, most now believe that it postdates the Gospel
of Mark, from which it took much of its material, and some scholars
question that Saint Matthew actually wrote it.

The book consists of four sections, the first containing the genealogy
and infancy of Jesus, the second on John the Baptist, the third on Jesus
in Galilee, and the fourth on his death and resurrection. The primary
aim of the book is to show that Jesus was the Messiah. It also portrays
him as a descendant of the House of David.

Boolean search

The Da Vinci Code

Boolean logic, originally developed by George Boole in the mid-1800s,
is used extensively on the Internet for searches, and uses the operators
"AND," "OR," and "NOT" to look for specific data (normally hidden
from the user). For example, if you were searching for either Galileo or
Milton, a Boolean search would say, "Galileo *or* Milton," and would
give you a list of all Web pages where either name appeared.

If you wanted Web pages where Galileo was spoken of in connection with Milton, the Boolean search would say, "Milton *and* Galileo," and give you a list in which both names appeared. If, however, you didn't want to see pages where the famous painting *Galileo and Milton*, by Annibale Gatti, was mentioned, the search would say, "Galileo *and* Milton *not* Gatti."

Bordeaux

The Da Vinci Code

Bordeaux is a port city in the southwest of France, on the Garonne River, and is the capital of the Aquitaine region. The area is home to many vineyards, and the city serves as a trading center for its principal source of income, the wine trade. The wine produced there is also called by the generic name of Bordeaux.

Borgia Apartments

Angels & Demons

The Borgia Apartments in the Vatican are a suite of six rooms designed for Pope Alexander VI, the infamous Borgia pope from Spain. The apartments are notable for the Pinturicchio frescoes and also boast paintings by Giovanni da Udine and Pierin del Vaga.

Bosch, Hieronymus

The Da Vinci Code

Hieronymus (or Jeroen) Bosch (circa 1450–1516) was born with the surname van Aeken. He signed his paintings with the name Bosch, referring to his home town of 's-Hertogenbosch. A prolific Flemish painter, he created mostly religious works characterized by grotesque, macabre creatures and bizarre plants and animals mingling with human figures. He used brilliant colors and masterful detail as well as an original use of symbols to depict sin and human moral failings making him the forerunner of the surrealists. His most famous painting, mentioned in Dan Brown's novel, is the *Garden of Earthly Delights*.

Boston Harbor

Angels & Demons

Boston Harbor is a major estuary and port in the northeastern United States, near Boston, Massachusetts, formed by the mouths of the Mystic River, the Charles River, and the Chelsea River. This western extremity of Massachusetts Bay is split into the Inner and Outer Harbors by East Boston and Logan International Airport. It was also the location of the Boston Tea Party during the British colonial period.

Boston Magazine

The Da Vinci Code

Boston Magazine, which embarrassed Langdon by listing him as one of the city's top ten most intriguing people, covers activities in and around Boston, Massachusetts. The magazine includes politics, business, finance, leisure, arts and entertainment, and profiles of prominent Bostonians.

Botticelli, Sandro

Angels & Demons and *The Da Vinci Code*

Sandro Botticelli (originally Alessandro di Mariano dei Filipepi) (circa 1444–1510) was an Italian painter of the Florentine school in the early part of the Renaissance. The Medicis commissioned him to do many of their portraits, and Pope Sixtus IV asked him to help decorate the Sistine Chapel, where he painted three biblical frescoes. Extremely religious, Botticelli burned his own paintings with pagan themes in the notorious "Bonfire of the Vanities." He is best known for the *Birth of Venus*.

Though Botticelli is listed in *Les Dossiers Secrets* as a member of the Priory of Sion, the *dossiers* are believed to be a hoax (see *Dossiers Secrets, Les*).

Boucher, François

The Da Vinci Code

François Boucher (1703–1770) was a French artist who was the most fashionable painter of his day and a favorite of Madame de Pompadour. His rococo paintings and tapestries are representative of the frivolous and elegant spirit of his time.

Bowie, David

Deception Point

Born David Robert Jones in 1947, David Bowie is a rock star whose first big hit was 1969's "Space Oddity." In 1972, he recorded *The Rise and Fall of Ziggy Stardust and the Spiders from Mars.* A song from that album is what Rachel remembers in *Deception Point.*

Brahe, Tycho

Angels & Demons

Danish nobleman Tycho (or Tyge) Brahe (1546–1601) was raised by his paternal uncle. Though he studied law at his uncle's request, he soon became interested in astronomy when in 1560 he viewed an eclipse that had been predicted at a precise moment in time. Noting that none of the available charts of the planets and stars matched the others, he took on the project of mapping the heavens over a period of years, starting when he was seventeen.

Brahe's contributions to astronomy were enormous. Not only did his meticulous observation methods change the way astronomers viewed the heavens, but he radically changed the way instruments were constructed and calibrated, vastly improving their accuracy.

In 1566 he engaged in a drunken duel with another student and lost part of his nose. He wore a metal insert over the missing part of his nose for the rest of his life, which also gave him an interest in medicine and alchemy.

Though Brahe didn't subscribe to Copernicus's belief that the earth revolved around the sun, his accurate measurements led him to find anomalies in the orbits of the planets. These eventually led to the discovery by his assistant, Johannes Kepler, that planets move in elliptical orbits.

BrainStorm

Digital Fortress

BrainStorm is a software program that helps organize a series of related thoughts and ideas into a logical structure or plan, then publishes them to the Web for others to see. In the novel, Strathmore uses the program to run what-if scenarios.

Bramante, Donato

Angels & Demons

Donato Bramante (1444-1514) was an Italian Renaissance architect and painter. In 1503, Pope Julius II gave him the grand task of rebuilding St. Peter's Basilica. Bramante's design, a centralized Greek cross plan with four domed chapels filling the corner spaces between the transepts, was altered by subsequent architects, but he is responsible for the essential proportions of the east end.

Brandenburg Concerto number 4

Digital Fortress

One of six *Brandenburg Concerti* by Johann Sebastian Bach. The instrumental works in this collection have little in common with each other except that each uses several instruments. *Brandenburg Concerto number 4* is a concerto for violin and two recorders (or flutes) accompanied by two violins, a viola, and a basso continuo.

Brazel, William

Deception Point

In July 1947, William "Mac" Brazel, a rancher near Roswell Army Air Field in New Mexico, heard a tremendous explosion in the night sky and drove out on his property the next day to learn what might have happened (see Roswell incident). He discovered a large debris field scattered over an area a mile long and several hundred feet wide. The debris contained a light metallic cloth and strong lightweight metal with strange hieroglyphic markings on them.

As a result, many believe Brazel found the remains of a crashed alien craft—an unidentified flying object. Other explanations that have been put forth are that the crash was actually that of a lost Mogul spy balloon (Dan Brown's theory); or that the incident was the result of a "broken arrow" or lost, stolen, or accidentally destroyed nuclear weapon, and the intelligence office released a story about a flying disk rather than admit to an accident with a nuclear weapon.

Bridge of Angels

Angels & Demons

The Bridge of Angels (Ponte Sant'Angelo) crosses the Tiber River in Rome and was built by Hadrian in 134 as an approach to his mausoleum, now the Castel Sant'Angelo. The three center arches of the bridge survive from that time, and the other two date from the seventeenth century when Clement IX commissioned Bernini to design the ten angel statues that line the bridge today.

British Tatler

Angels & Demons

The original *Tatler* (not *Tattler*) was a British magazine founded in 1709 by Richard Steele to publish the gossip and news around London (hence the title). It was only published for two years.

The current glossy magazine, which started in 1901, may or may not be related to the original *Tatler*. It is Britain's most sophisticated social magazine, or high society's hottest gossip column—depending on whom you listen to.

Brown's Palace

Digital Fortress

The French Canadian critic in *Digital Fortress* implied he reviewed Brown's Palace unfavorably. He probably meant the Brown Palace Hotel, the oldest hotel in Denver, Colorado.

Henry Cordes Brown, a real-estate entrepreneur from Ohio, came to Denver in 1860. With so many people heading west to search for gold and stopping in Denver on the way, he decided that what Denver really needed was a grand hotel. So he hired architect Frank E. Edbrooke to design the building in the Italian Renaissance style, no expense spared.

The elegant Brown Palace Hotel opened in 1892 and hasn't closed for business one minute since. It is known for some unique features: it draws all of its water from its own original artesian wells on site, the Brown Palace bakery still uses a huge carousel oven daily (one of three known to be in existence), the building has an unusual triangular shape in which all rooms face the street, and the eight-story atrium lobby is stunningly elegant. No wonder its guest list includes so many politicians and celebrities.

Brunelleschi

The Da Vinci Code

Located in the middle of the historical downtown area of Florence, overlooking Filippo Brunelleschi's splendid cupola and Palazzo Vecchio, the Hotel Brunelleschi is a luxury four-star hotel in the heart of Renaissance Florence.

The hotel was reconstructed from the historic structures of the semicircular sixth-century Byzantine Torre Della Pagliazza and the Medieval Church of San Michele in Palchetto. Leaving the architectural characteristics of the era intact, the builders still managed to provide the hotel with completely modern services.

Buckingham Palace

The Da Vinci Code

Buckingham Palace, originally known as Buckingham House, was a town house built in London for the Duke of Buckingham in 1703. Acquired by King George III in 1762 for use as a private residence for the British royal family, it was enlarged over the next seventy-five years and refaced. Queen Victoria made Buckingham Palace the official residence of British sovereigns in 1837.

Buckingham Palace is the largest "working" royal palace in the world today. It is situated adjacent to St. James's Park, and in addition to being the London home of the queen, is used for state occasions and entertaining visiting heads of state. It is also a major tourist attraction.

Buddha

Angels & Demons

The title Buddha (meaning "the awakened," or "the enlightened") is given to anyone who experiences enlightenment, though it is commonly used to refer to The Buddha, Siddhārtha Gautama, the son of a Nepalese rajah. Estimates of his birth and death dates vary, but are generally regarded as being somewhere between four to six hundred years BC.

According to legend, Gautama left a life of luxury at age thirty and devoted himself to years of contemplation and self-denial. When he finally reached enlightenment, he became known as Buddha. He did not claim divine status or godly inspiration. Instead, he chose to spend his life teaching disciples about his beliefs and the goal of achieving the enlightened state of Nirvana.

Buddhism

Digital Fortress, The Da Vinci Code, and Angels & Demons

Buddhism is one of the major world religions, with over 300 million followers. Originating in India, its philosophy is based on the teachings of The Buddha, Siddhārtha Gautama (see above). Using moral discipline, meditative concentration and wisdom, Buddhism teaches followers the "four noble truths": existence is suffering, suffering has a cause, suffering can stop (to achieve Nirvana), and there is a path to Nirvana. Followers are enjoined to perform good actions and avoid harmful ones to end the suffering of cyclic existence.

Bug

Digital Fortress

As a computer term, a bug is an error or flaw in a computer software program that prevents it from working correctly or causes it to lock up. The term has been used as far back as 1878 to mean a mechanical malfunction, as shown in one of Thomas A. Edison's letters. In addition, an 1896 electrical handbook references the term bug to mean a fault or trouble in electric apparatus, and bug was used in World War II to refer to problems with radar electronics.

The story Dan Brown tells of a bug (a moth) found in the computer at Harvard is true (though our sources show it was the Mark II, not the Mark I). However, the operators who found it were no doubt already familiar with the term and amused by finding it displayed so graphically, claiming it was the first actual bug found in a machine.

Burgos

Digital Fortress

Burgos is a city in northern Spain on a mountainous plateau south-southwest of Bilbao, overlooking the Arlanzón River. Founded in the 800s, it was the capital of the kingdom of Castile in the eleventh century under Ferdinand I, and of Francisco Franco's regime during the Spanish Civil War (1936–39).

An important trade and tourist center, it boasts as one of its more notable points of interest the thirteenth-century gothic cathedral where El Cid is buried.

Bush, George

Angels & Demons

George Herbert Walker Bush (born 1924) was the forty-first president of the United States, from 1989 to1993. Before that, he served as United States congressman from Texas, ambassador to the United Nations, Republican National Committee chairman, director of the Central Intelligence Agency, and vice president of the United States under President Ronald Reagan.

Though Dan Brown states that George Bush was a well-documented "thirty third-degree" Freemason, the Masons themselves say they have no record of him or his son, President George W. Bush, belonging to any Masonic lodge. The assumption may have arisen from the senior Bush's use of the phrase "new world order" in a September 1990 televised address to a joint session of Congress, or from the fact that he was a member of the Skull and Bones fraternity (which has a superficial resemblance to Freemasonry) at Yale University.

Byelaya smert

Deception Point

In *Deception Point*, Delta-One uses what Dan Brown calls "byelaya smert" to kill Norah. This "white death" forces snow down a person's throat to suffocate him without leaving a trace. It was supposedly invented by the Russian mafia, but we were unable to find any reference to it. However, what an interesting literary device, even if it isn't true!

C

Digital Fortress

Mentioned in *Digital Fortress* as the programming language LIMBO borrows from, C was developed for the UNIX operating system in the early 1970s by Ken Thompson and Dennis Ritchie. Designed to make it easier to write large programs with fewer errors, it is now widely used on many other operating systems as well.

Caducei wands

The Da Vinci Code

A caduceus wand is a staff with two snakes twined around it, with wings at the top. It is modeled on the staff of the Greek god Hermes and was originally used as a Roman herald's wand to symbolize neutrality and truce. It was also used as a symbol of commerce, postal service, and ambassadorial positions.

Because it resembles the Rod of Aesculapius (the god of healing), which has only one snake winding about a staff, the two are often used interchangeably, especially in regard to the medical field. The caduceus has been the insignia of the medical branch of the United States Army since 1902.

Caen stone

The Da Vinci Code

Caen stone is a light creamy-yellow, finely grained Jurassic limestone and was a popular building material of the Normans in England, who imported it from France. The Temple Church mentioned in *The Da Vinci Code* is constructed of this material.

Caesar, Julius

The Da Vinci Code and Angels & Demons

Gaius Julius Caesar (101–44 BC) was a soldier, statesman, orator, and ruler who was instrumental in the establishment of the Roman empire. One of history's greatest generals, he was named dictator of Rome for life in 45 BC, but was stabbed to death in the Senate on March 15, 44 BC (the Ides of March), by a group of senators led by Marcus Junius Brutus. Caesar gave his name to the month of July and is said to be the first person in history to use a substitution cipher and other methods of coding messages.

Caesar Box

The Da Vinci Code and Digital Fortress

Julius Caesar devised a simple cipher to transport messages over long distances so that it was unreadable by anyone who intercepted it. To do this, he coded a message where the letters fit in a square that was four by four, five by five, six by six, etc., meaning the message was 16, 25, 36 characters long, respectively.

For example, the message, "Never give up, never surrender," has twenty-five characters, which means they would fit in a five-by-five box. Placing the letters in a five-by-five box, starting at the top left, and writing the letter down the first column, the Caesar box would look like this:

```
N  G  P  R  E
E  I  N  S  N
V  V  E  U  D
E  E  V  R  E
R  U  E  R  R
```

Now write the characters from left to right, which yields the cipher text NGPREEINSNVVEUDEEVRERUERR. This is the message Caesar would send out, which would be incomprehensible to anyone but the recipient who knew how to decipher the code. This is just one of the methods he devised for sending coded messages.

Caligula

Angels & Demons

Born Gaius Caesar Germanicus (12–41 AD), he was raised among Roman troops and received the nickname Caligula (meaning little boots) from his habit of wearing miniature versions of military garb as a child. He became the third Roman ruler of the Julio-Claudian dynasty in 37 AD, and his four years as emperor were marked by such erratic behavior, debauchery, and abuse of power that they are still remembered today.

Stories abound about Caligula's eccentricity, though whether these are fact or fiction is unknown. It is said he lavished his horse Incitatus with jewelry and planned to make him consul, committed incest with his sisters, had both enemies and friends killed indiscriminately, and generally ignored affairs of state.

Most historians agree that Caligula was mad, but speculations on the cause of his madness range from epilepsy to schizophrenia, encephalitis, antisocial personality disorder or a nervous breakdown from the pressures of being head of state. He was assassinated in 41 AD by soldiers from his own Praetorian Guard.

Callahan Tunnel

Angels & Demons

The Callahan Tunnel that Langdon drives through carries traffic from the North End of Boston, Massachusetts, to Logan International Airport in East Boston. The tunnel was opened in 1961 and named for the son of the Mass Pike's chairman at the time, Lieutenant William F. Callahan Jr., who was killed in Italy in World War II.

Cambridge

The Da Vinci Code

Cambridge, where Langdon lives, is a city in eastern Massachusetts across the Charles River from Boston. Originally settled in 1630 as New Towne, it was incorporated as a city in 1846 and is known for its research and educational facilities, including Harvard University, the Radcliff Institute for Higher Learning, Lesley University, Massachusetts Institute of Technology, and several theological seminaries.

Camerlengo

Angels & Demons

Camerlengo (chamberlain) is the title of several papal officials, and is used in several ways in the Catholic Church: for example, the Camerlengo of the Holy Roman Church, the Camerlengo of the Sacred College of Cardinals, and the Camerlengo of the Roman Clergy. Other chamberlains of the papal court, who may be clergymen or laymen, may have duties about the pope's quarters, though this title is usually given as an honorary award.

The term "Camerlengo" is most often used to refer to the chamberlain who manages the pope's secular affairs: the Camerlengo of the Holy Roman Church who administers the property and the revenues of the Holy See. Though usually a cardinal of the Catholic Church, the camerlengo may also be merely an ordained Catholic priest, though this is unlikely. The camerlengo's primary responsibilities are to formally verify the death of the reigning pope, take charge of the Sacred College of Cardinals until a new pope is elected, and direct the conclave (see conclave) that elects the new pope. Until a successor pope can be elected, the camerlengo serves as acting head of State of the Vatican City, though the College of Cardinals is responsible for limited government operations in the interim.

The Camerlengo of the Sacred College of Cardinals is the secretary-treasurer of that body, administers all fees and revenues belonging to the College, celebrates the requiem Mass for a deceased cardinal, and is charged with the registry of the *Acta Consistoralia*.

The Camerlengo of the Roman Clergy is elected by the canons and priests of Rome, has an honorary place in the great processions, presides over the conferences of the clergy in Rome, acts as arbiter in questions of precedence, and administers the "oath of free estate" to those who desire to marry.

Candied *amandes*

The Da Vinci Code

Candied *amandes*, or sweet caramelized almonds, are a popular snack in France and are often sold by street vendors in Paris, which is where Langdon sees them.

Canonization

Angels & Demons

Canonization is the process of declaring a person a saint in the Roman Catholic Church. It began in the 900s when the Church in Rome started keeping an official list of saints. Before that time, the process was much more informal and many early saints were never formally canonized. The first saint to be officially added to the official list was Saint Ulrich of Augsburg, canonized in 993.

Canonization involves a detailed study of the life of the proposed saint as well as the miracles attributed to that person after his or her death. Though bishops were originally given the power to canonize and beatify saints, abuses and carelessness in bestowing these honors led Pope Alexander III in the twelfth century to reserve this right for the pope. Many bishops didn't obey it, so Pope Urban VII issued a Papal Bull in 1634 reserving the right of beatification and canonization solely for the Holy See.

The procedure used to be more complicated, but the 1983 reform of the Roman Catholic Church's Code of Canon Law streamlined it considerably. The process of canonization involves several steps. First, the bishop at the diocesan level gives permission to investigate the life of the purported saint (after receiving permission from the Vatican) not sooner than five years after death. Once sufficient information has been obtained of an exemplary life, the person is dubbed a "Servant of God," and the Roman Curia gathers all information about his or her life. The Curia may then recommend to the pope that he make a proclamation of the nominees' heroic virtue, which bestows the title "Venerable."

If the Venerable is a martyr, the pope makes a declaration of martyrdom, which then yields beatification. If the Venerable is not a martyr, it must be proved that a miracle has taken place by his or her intercession. The beatified are then known as "Blessed." An additional miracle is needed to pass from Blessed to Saint, the final process of canonization.

Capella della Terra

Angels & Demons

Dan Brown states that the Chigi Chapel in the Santa Maria del Popolo used to be called *Capella della Terra*, which he translates as Chapel of the Earth. We were unable to confirm this, but Mr. Brown may have access to documentation we do not.

Capitol Hill

Deception Point

Capitol Hill is the hill in Washington, D.C., on which the United States Capitol building is located. It houses the legislative branch of the United States government: the Senate in the north wing and the House of Representatives in the south wing, connected by a central dome.

Caput mundi

Angels & Demons

A Latin phrase meaning "head of the world." Rome is often called *Roma caput mundi*: Rome, the capital of the world.

Carabiners

Deception Point

A carabiner resembles a link of chain and is used to link things together. Made of lightweight, strong alloys, it features a spring gate much like a giant safety pin that opens to clip onto a rope, harness, or other objects, then snaps closed.

Caravaggio

The Da Vinci Code

Painter Michelangelo Merisi da Carravaggio (circa 1571–1610) is one of the greatest artists who ever lived. Often called "the other Michelangelo," he's a pivotal figure in art history, one whose influence changed Western painting forever. Multiple spellings of the painter's name exist, including Caravaggio, which is the form used by Dan Brown in the opening passages of *The Da Vinci Code*. The painting hanging in the Grand Gallery of the Louvre is Caravaggio's *Death of the Virgin*, which was commissioned in 1601 for the Church of Santa Maria delia Scala del Trastevere in Rome. Caravaggio took his time filling the order—he didn't finish the painting until roughly four years later. Perhaps because of the gap in time between when the work was requested and its delivery, or perhaps because of the way the artist treated the iconic figures in the painting, the church's monks refused to accept the canvas.

The work shows the Virgin Mary on her deathbed, portrayed by the artist with an earthy reality and almost no sense of the mystery or majesty that was traditional for religious art of the day. The only concession Caravaggio gave to Mary's special place in the divine pantheon was a tiny sliver of halo above her head. The work derives its power and its purpose from its superb manipulation of light and dark, which gives the painting a sense of weight and majesty, and makes Mary's form so compelling that the viewer can't turn away. In the foreground of the painting, a figure that is most likely Mary Magdalene looks at the Virgin body sorrowfully. Given that the central mystery of *The Da Vinci Code* is the role of Mary Magdalene in the early church, Dan Brown's use of the painting is a superb device to bring the book's central issue into the prologue in a very subtle way.

Carrousel du Louvre

The Da Vinci Code

The Carrousel du Louvre is an underground shopping mall just west of the Louvre in Paris. Besides containing many shops and a food court, it hosts a live theater, an underground entrance to the Louvre, and an inverted glass pyramid—a smaller version of the large pyramid in front of the museum.

Cartier

Deception Point

Cartier manufactures fine jewelry and one of the most recognized brands of watches in the world. Louis-François Cartier founded the firm in Paris in 1847, and his son Alfred took it over in 1874. His sons—Louis, Pierre, and Jacques—established the now-famous worldwide brand name of Cartier.

The younger Louis is credited with creating the first men's wristwatch in 1904, when he designed one for Brazilian aviation pioneer Alberto Santos-Dumont, who needed a more suitable timepiece than the standard pocket watch for his daredevil flights. The Santos watch was born, and went on sale in 1911.

Today, Cartier is known for beauty, quality, and style, and many of its watches can be regarded as pieces of jewelry in their own right. Of course, this is the brand of watch that Senator Sexton wears in *Deception Point*.

Castel Gandolfo

The Da Vinci Code

The Castel Gandolfo is situated in central Italy in the Alban Hills, seventy-five miles southeast of Rome, on the edge of a crater now filled by Lake Albano. The castle, designed by Carlo Maderno for Pope Urban VIII in the seventeenth century, is the summer residence of the pope. It and the adjoining Villa Barberini enjoy extraterritorial rights granted by Mussolini in 1929.

Castel Gandolfo is believed to occupy the site of ancient Alba Longa, capital of the Sabine league, and is built on top of another, more ancient castle. Its name is derived from a fortification of the ducal Gandolfi family in the twelfth century. This is where Bishop Aringarosa visited the pope in Dan Brown's novel.

Castel Sant'Angelo

Angels & Demons and The Da Vinci Code

The Castel Sant'Angelo, a massive round building on the western bank of the Tiber River in Rome, was originally begun by Emperor Hadrian in

135 AD as a mausoleum for himself and his family. It took four years to finish and was later added to and fortified as a place of refuge for the popes, and connected to St. Peter's Basilica in the Vatican Palace by a secret passage called Passetto di Borgo (see Passetto, il). The Castel Sant'Angelo has served in the past as a fortress, military prison and barracks, and is now a museum.

It consists of five floors. The spiral ramp starts on the first floor, the second floor housed the prisons and storerooms, the third was the military floor, the fourth was the papal floor with the papal apartments, and the fifth and top floor has a large terrace dominated by a bronze archangel with a sword.

The characters in Dan Brown's novel speculate that Castel Sant'Angelo was the fifth and final point of the Path of Illumination, the infamous Church of Illumination.

Castilian Spanish

Digital Fortress

Castilian Spanish, which David speaks fluently in *Digital Fortress*, is an Iberian Romance language, and the third-most-widely spoken language in the world. Spaniards tend to call their language *español* (Spanish) when contrasting it with languages of other countries, but call it *castellano* (Castilian) when contrasting it with the languages of other regions of Spain.

Castilian Spanish is characterized by what many people, especially those accustomed to the pronunciation of Latin American Spanish, mistake for a lisp. According to legend, the "lisp" became common in medieval Castilian because one of the Spanish kings spoke with a lisp and his courtiers didn't want to embarrass him by speaking otherwise. It was all a sham to incur royal favor. If they did have a lisp, these spanish courtiers would have been unable to pronounce an "s," which they had no problem doing.

In reality, the Castilian form of Spanish evolved differently from other forms of the language. In Castilian Spanish, the letter *s* is always pronounced "s," but the letter *c* (when it comes before *e* and *i*) is pronounced like the "th" in think, which sounds like a lisp. This phenomenon, called *ceceo*, does not exist in other forms of Spanish.

Catholic Inquisition

The Da Vinci Code

The Inquisition was a former tribunal of the Roman Catholic Church charged with discovering and suppressing heresies. Heresies (beliefs at odds with established religious beliefs) have always been a problem for the Catholic Church, so it created a permanent structure to combat them. There were four Inquisitions: the Medieval Inquisition, the Spanish Inquisition, the Portuguese Inquisition, and the Roman Inquisition.

The Medieval Inquisition began in 1184 in response to the Catharist heresy and Albigensianism in southern France. In 1233, Pope Gregory IX sent Dominican friars there to conduct inquests. The accused were given a grace period to confess and recant their heresy. If they did, they were given a light penance. If they didn't, they were brought to a secretly conducted trial where torture became common to elicit confessions. Because of that, most trials resulted in a verdict of guilty, and those convicted were handed over to the secular authorities for punishment. In medieval times, the most common punishments were fines, imprisonment, and confiscation of property.

The Spanish Inquisition was established in 1478 by Spanish rulers Ferdinand and Isabella with the reluctant approval of Pope Sixtus IV. Its purpose was to deal with converted Muslims and Jews who were insincere. However, under Tomás de Torquemada, no Spaniard felt safe from it. The Spanish Inquisition was notorious for its use of torture, harsh judgments, and frequent autos-da-fé (burning at the stake). This inquisition was finally abolished in 1834.

The Portuguese Inquisition started in 1536 under King Joao III in Portugal and soon expanded into Portugal's colonies, including Brazil, Cape Verde and Goa. Much like the Spanish Inquisition, it tried cases of breaches of the tenets of orthodox Roman Catholicism until 1821.

The Roman Inquisition began in 1542 when Pope Paul III assigned the medieval Inquisition to the Congregation of the Inquisition, a permanent congregation staffed with cardinals and other officials. This institution, which became known as the Roman Inquisition, was intended to combat Protestantism, to maintain the integrity of the faith, and to proscribe errors and false doctrines, but it is perhaps best known historically for its condemnation of Galileo (see Galilei, Galileo).

Celestine V

Angels & Demons

After the death of Pope Nicholas IV, the conclave was in a two-year deadlock to choose a new pope. A humble hermit, Benedictine monk Pietro di Murrone (1215–1296), who founded the Celestine order in 1244, communicated to the conclave that God was displeased with them and would visit retribution upon them if they didn't choose a pope within four months. In response, they immediately elected him pope in August 1294.

The solitary ascetic tried to refuse the honor, but was persuaded otherwise and took the name Pope Celestine V. Unfortunately, he was an ineffectual pope and an easy prey to opportunists. Once in office, he issued a decree declaring the right of any pope to abdicate the papacy, then abdicated after five months in office.

His successor, Boniface VIII, canceled Celestine's official acts and, to ensure Celestine's followers didn't attempt to use him to create a schism, had him arrested and imprisoned in Castle Fumone, where he died ten months later. There is no proof that Boniface did anything to hasten the demise. Celestine was canonized in 1313.

Central Park

Angels & Demons

Central Park, one of the most famous parks in the world, is the largest in Manhattan, New York City, covering over 840 acres in a highly landscaped rectangular shape.

In 1853, influential New Yorkers expressed the need for a public park to have a stylish place for open-air driving, much like the Bois de

Boulogne in Paris, or London's Hyde Park. In 1856, the land was acquired by the city which announced a design competition in 1858.

Landscape architects Frederick Law Olmsted and Calvert Vaux won with their design called "Greensward," which took twenty years to implement. The park contains artificial lakes and ponds, walking tracks, bridle paths, park drives, ice-skating rinks, a wildlife sanctuary, playgrounds, and recreational areas, as well as housing the Metropolitan Museum of Art, a zoo, and a formal garden

An oasis of tranquility amid the skyscrapers, Central Park gained a reputation in the late 1900s as a dangerous place, especially at night. However, crime has declined in the park and in the rest of New York City, and Central Park is now one of the safest urban parks in the world.

CERN

Angels & Demons

Located partly in France, partly in Switzerland near Geneva, CERN is the world's largest particle physics laboratory, an international organization whose activities are sponsored by twenty European countries.

The origins of CERN lie in 1951, with the creation of a council called the *Conseil Européen pour la Recherche Nucléaire* (CERN). In 1953, the council decided to build a central laboratory near Geneva to concentrate on understanding the inside of the atom. Though the laboratory is officially called the *Organisation européenne pour la recherche nucléaire* (European Organization for Nuclear Research), most still use the name of the council to refer to the organization, which is why it is known as CERN.

The laboratory has since gone beyond the study of the atomic nucleus to look for effects between the forces of nature that become noticeable only at very high energies. Now a high-energy physics institute, CERN is the principal European center for research in particle physics.

To enhance collaboration on research documents pertaining to particle physics, Tim Berners-Lee (see Berners-Lee, Tim) invented the World

Wide Web, a system of internationally distributed, hypertext-linked materials on the Internet, at CERN in the early 1990s.

Chalice

The Da Vinci Code

A chalice is a cup or goblet and is the term used in the Christian religion for the communion cup holding the consecrated wine of the Eucharist. In Wiccan ritual, the chalice is a tool representing the west, water, and the feminine principle of creation (the womb). The Holy Grail is often thought to be a chalice.

Champs Élysées

The Da Vinci Code

The Champs Élysées is one of the most famous streets in the world. A beautiful tree-lined avenue in Paris, France, it runs for three kilometers from the Place de la Concorde to the Arc de Triomphe. The name refers to the Elysian Fields, the kingdom of the dead in Greek mythology.

The area currently occupied by the Champs-Élysées was originally fields and market gardens; plans for the avenue were begun by Louis XIV and completed by Louis XV. One of the principal tourist destinations in Paris, the avenue is known for its breadth, the elegance of its cafés, theaters, restaurants, and luxury specialty shops, and the fountain at its center. Over the years, the avenue has undergone numerous transitions, most recently in 1993, when the sidewalks were widened.

Chaos theory

Digital Fortress

Chaos theory (also called nonlinear dynamics) is a mathematical concept that deals with the underlying order of complex systems that seem to be without order, saying that small occurrences can significantly affect the outcomes of seemingly unrelated events.

Edward Lorenz was an early pioneer of the theory. He was using a computer in 1961 to predict weather and found that small changes in initial conditions produced large changes in the long-term outcome. Popularly known as the Butterfly Effect, this postulates that the beating of a butterfly's wings can have a slight but gradual effect on the weather until it results in a tornado or hurricane in another part of the world.

Chaos theory is used to predict such systems as the solar system, plate tectonics, turbulent fluids, economies, population growth, weather patterns, and the stock market.

Chapter House

The Da Vinci Code

A chapter house is a building in which the chapter of the clergy meets. The Chapter House in Westminster Abbey was built by the Royal Masons in 1250, used in the fourteenth century by the Benedictine monks, and housed the meetings of the House of Commons (the predecessor of today's Parliament) before the House found a permanent home in St. Stephen's Chapel after the death of Henry VIII in 1547. Octagonal in shape, the Westminster Abbey Chapter House has a vaulted ceiling and central column.

Charles de Gaulle Airport

The Da Vinci Code

Charles de Gaulle International Airport, also known as Roissy Airport, is located near Roissy, twenty-five kilometers northeast of Paris. Named after Charles de Gaulle, a French general and former French president, it serves Paris and is France's main international airport.

Charles II

The Da Vinci Code

Charles II (1630–1685), eldest surviving son of Charles I and Henrietta Maria of France, was king of England, Scotland, and Ireland. When his father, Charles I, was executed in 1649 following the English Civil War, the monarchy was abolished and the country became a republic under Oliver Cromwell. It wasn't until 1660, shortly after Cromwell's death, that the monarchy was restored to the House of Stuart under Charles II.

The Parliament of 1679 was vehemently opposed to the prospect of a Catholic monarch, so it introduced the Exclusion Bill, which sought to exclude the Duke of York, Charles II's brother, from the line of succession. Those who supported the bill became the Whig Party and those who opposed it became the Tory Party

The Exclusion Bill threatened to pass three times and each time, Charles dissolved Parliament, then finally ruled as absolute monarch until his death. Charles II left no legitimate children, though he did acknowledge fourteen illegitimate children by seven mistresses: Barbara Villiers, Countess of Castlemaine; Marguerite de Carteret; Nell Gwynne; Louise Renée de Penancoët de Kérouaille, Duchess of Portsmouth; Lucy Walter; Elizabeth Killigrew, Viscountess Shannon; and Catherine Pegge, Lady Greene. Charles II converted to Roman Catholicism on his deathbed, becoming the first Roman Catholic to reign over England since the death of Mary I in 1558 and over Scotland since Mary, Queen of Scots was deposed in 1567.

Charpak, Georges

Angels & Demons

Born in 1924, Georges Charpak is a Polish-born French physicist who served in the resistance in World War II. He was imprisoned in the Nazi concentration camp at Dachau in 1944, where he remained until the camp was liberated in 1945, then became a French citizen in 1946.

Charpak joined CERN in 1959, was made a member of the French Academy of Science in 1985, and won the Nobel Prize in Physics in 1992 for the invention of particle detectors, including the multi-wire proportional chamber.

Chartres Cathedral

The Da Vinci Code

The Cathedral of Chartres (Cathedral of Our Lady in Chartres), is located in Chartres, France, about fifty miles from Paris. It is one of the greatest of all French Gothic cathedrals. Construction began in 1145, but before its completion all but the west front of the cathedral was destroyed by fire. It was subsequently reconstructed over a twenty-six-year period with the help of donations from all over France. The local populace was so enthusiastic that they volunteered to haul the stone needed from local quarries five miles away. It was eventually dedicated in the presence of King Louis IX and his family in 1260.

The Chartres Cathedral is a mix of different styles, with two very different spires: a 349-foot plain pyramid dating from the 1140s, and a 377-foot early sixteenth-century flamboyant spire on top of an older tower. The roof is the pale green of aged copper, and flying buttresses surround the outside. The vast nave stands 121 feet high, the porches are adorned with sculptures from the middle of the twelfth century, and 152 of the original 186 magnificent stained-glass windows from the twelfth and thirteenth centuries have survived. The magnificent cathedral was added to UNESCO's list of World Heritage Sites in 1979.

Château Villette

The Da Vinci Code

The Château de Villette, where Sir Teabing lives in Dan Brown's novel, is located northwest of Paris in Burgundy near Versailles. Also known as La Petite Versailles, it was designed by architect François Mansart around 1668 for Jean Dyel, the Count d'Aufflay, Louis XIV's ambassador to Italy. Now a magnificent hotel renowned for its hospitality, tranquility, beauty, cuisine, and charm, this 17-room spread sits on 185 acres of beautifully landscaped grounds designed by Louis XIV's personal gardener, André Le Notre.

Chaucer, Geoffrey

Angels & Demons and *The Da Vinci Code*

Geoffrey Chaucer (circa 1340–1400) was an English author, poet, philosopher, courtier, and diplomat regarded as the greatest literary figure of medieval England. He is best known as the author of *The Canterbury Tales*, a collection of stories told by fictional pilgrims on the road to the cathedral at Canterbury.

Born in London to a family of well-to-do vintners, Chaucer served as a page for the Countess of Ulster and later in the royal court of Edward III as a valet to Edward's son Lionel of Antwerp. He was employed as a diplomat later in life, then held a number of official positions, among them comptroller of customs and clerk of the king's works. There is speculation that he was murdered by enemies of his patron Richard II. He was buried at Westminster Abbey in London, where his remains were transferred to a more ornate tomb in 1556, making Chaucer the first writer interred in the area now known as Poets' Corner.

Chemotropic cuttlefish

Deception Point

Chemotropic means movement toward a chemical stimulus. A cuttlefish is a squid-like cephalopod marine mollusk that has ten arms and a calcified internal shell. It swims by jet propulsion, though it isn't as fast as its cousin, the squid, and ejects a dark inky fluid when in danger. The ink is composed mostly of melanin and has been used as the artist's pigment sepia. In the novel, Michael Tolland did a video on chemotropic cuttlefish, which is what scored him the job at NBC.

Cherchi-Pardini

Angels & Demons

Dan Brown has the Swiss Guards at the Vatican armed with Cherchi-Pardini semiautomatics, but we were unable to find any reference to weapons with this name.

Chesapeake Bay

Deception Point

Chesapeake Bay is about two hundred miles long and three to thirty miles wide, separating the Delmarva Peninsula from mainland Maryland and Virginia. The largest estuary in the United States, it is an inlet that lies off the Atlantic Ocean.

Explored and charted by English colonist John Smith in 1608, the bay has more than 150 rivers and streams that drain into it, including the Potomac, Rappahannock, Pocomoke, and James. It is entered from the Atlantic Ocean through a twelve-mile-wide gap between Capes Henry and Charles, Virginia.

Chigi Chapel

Angels & Demons

The Chigi Chapel, which houses the first Altar of Science in Dan Brown's novel, is one of five chapels in the Church of Santa Maria del Popolo. Designed by Raphael in 1513 as a private chapel for the Sienese banker Agostino Chigi, it was finished by Bernini in 1520.

The chapel features a dome mosaic from a drawing by Raphael, figures of Jonah and Elijah by Lorenzetto, a winged skeleton with the Chigi coat of arms that covers the "demon's hole" and subterranean crypt, and Bernini's statues of *Habakkuk and the Angel* and *Daniel*.

Chigi, Agostino

Angels & Demons

A wealthy Sienese banker and entrepreneur, Agostino Chigi (1465–1520) came from a family of Roman bankers with a fortune in shipping and real estate. He was dubbed "The Magnificent" for his wealth, acumen, and the luxurious style of his domestic life. He often threw indulgent alfresco dinner parties at his villa on the Tiber river in Rome, where he encouraged his guests to toss their dishes into the river after each course.

Agostino Chigi also served as private financier for two popes and was a patron of the arts, setting up a Greek printing press and encouraging artists such as Raphael and Peruzzi. Chigi was commemorated in two monumental chapels, at Santa Maria della Pace and Santa Maria del Popolo, though both were completed after his death.

China Room

Deception Point

The China Room in the White House was once the quarters of a fireman hired by President Martin Van Buren to stoke the massive furnace, and was used as a cloakroom in 1902.

Caroline Harrison started the collection of White House china in 1890 and Edith Roosevelt continued it, but not until 1917 was it displayed by Edith Wilson in what was then called the Presidential Collection Room.

The room was redecorated in 1970, keeping the red color scheme designed to match the 1924 portrait of Grace Coolidge by Howard Chandler Christy. The red theme shows throughout, in the red-velvet-lined cabinets, silk taffeta draperies, and Indo-Ispahan rug. The paneling was made from old timbers removed from the White House during the Truman renovation of 1948–52.

Almost every president is represented, either by state or family china or glassware. The Presidents have always received government funds to purchase state china, but this caused problems in the Reagan administration in 1981, when Nancy Reagan wanted new china for the White House. Her red-rimmed Lenox pattern with a raised gold presidential seal in the center came to almost $210,000, raising cries of conspicuous consumption.

Chinese kissing fish

Deception Point

Chinese kissing fish, or Kissing Gourami (Helostoma Temmincki), are large tropical freshwater fish so named for their habit of puckering their lips. A highly important food fish that originated in Indonesia and is native to Southeast Asia and Africa, it has been introduced in China and South Asia, where it has become popular with hobbyists for its "kissing" behavior. It comes in two colors: olive green or the more prevalent pink (not orange as Dan Brown claims), and has become a unique and romantic gift for lovers . . . which is why Michael Tolland gives a pair to Rachel Sexton in the novel.

Chondrules

Deception Point

Chondrules are small (0.5 to 2 millimeters in diameter) silicate spherical objects of extraterrestrial origin found in a type of meteorite called chondrites. Up to 80 percent of the chondrite meteorite can be made up of chondrules in a fine-grained matrix. Most chondrules are composed of olivine, pyroxene, glass, and iron-nickel.

Chondrules are formed by rapid heating of solid material to incredible temperatures over 1,500 Celsius, then melting and cooling within a few hours. The oldest material within our solar system, they are believed to be the building blocks of the planetary system.

Christ's birthday

Angels & Demons

Though we celebrate the birth of Christ on December 25 each year, that is most likely not the date of his birth. The gospels do not indicate the day, month or year, but based on the appearance of the Star of Bethlehem in the night sky, the fact that shepherds watch their flocks by night only from spring through autumn, and the fact that Dionysis Exeguus (a Roman monk-mathematician-astronomer in the sixth century) miscalculated the year of Jesus's birth by at least five years, it is believed that Jesus was actually born in March, in 6 BC.

Christians did not celebrate Christ's birth for the first several hundred years. In 274 AD, the winter solstice fell on December 25 and Roman Emperor Aurelian proclaimed the date as *Natalis Solis Invicti*, the festival of the birth of the invincible sun. To coincide with the pagan festival, and perhaps to supplant it, in 320 AD Pope Julius I announced December 25 as the official date of the birth of Jesus Christ.

Christian Coalition

Angels & Demons

Based in Chesapeake, Virginia, the Christian Coalition of America is a United States political advocacy group founded to advance the agenda of political, social, and religious conservatives, and to preserve what it calls traditional American values. The coalition was established in 1989 by Reverend Pat Robertson after he failed to win the 1988 Republican presidential nomination.

The loudest voice in the conservative Christian movement in the 1990s, the coalition was very effective under the leadership of executive director Ralph Reed, but has made limited progress since then. In 1999, it lost its tax-exempt status and divided into two parts: the Christian Coalition International, which is its taxable political arm; and the Christian Coalition of America, the tax-exempt portion that focuses on voter education.

Chunnel

The Da Vinci Code

The Channel Tunnel, popularly called the "Chunnel" in English, is an underground rail that runs below the English Channel and connects Great Britain and France. It consists of two rail tunnels and a central maintenance tunnel, each 31 miles long and about 150 feet deep. Started in 1986, the Chunnel opened for passenger service in 1994 and is one of the longest rail tunnels in the world, second only to the Seikan Tunnel in Japan.

Church of Illumination

Angels & Demons

Dan Brown's fictional church, known as the secret headquarters of the Illuminati in Rome, at the Castel Sant'Angelo.

Church of Saint Ann

Angels & Demons

The Church of Saint Ann (or Anne, Anna, or Hannah), also known as the Church of Saint Anne of the Palafrieneri, is the parish church of the Vatican in Rome on the Via di Porta Angelica and is not open to the general public.

Dedicated to Saint Ann, the mother of the Virgin Mary, the church began construction in 1565 by Vignola, under Pope Pius IV. After Vignola's death, his son, Giacinto Barozzi, took over, in 1573.

According to the Gospel of James, Ann and her husband Joachim, after many years of childlessness, received a visit from an angel who told them that they would conceive a child. Ann promised to dedicate the child (Mary) to God's service. One of the most popular saints, Ann is the patron saint of Quebec and Brittany, and the patroness of miners and women in labor.

Churchill, Winston

Angels & Demons

Sir Winston Leonard Spenser Churchill (1874–1965) was a British soldier, writer, and politician who served as prime minister from 1940 to 1945 and from 1951 to 1955. Considered one of Britain's greatest twentieth-century heroes for leading his country to victory in World War II, he published several works, including *The Second World War* and *A History of the English-Speaking Peoples.* He won the Nobel Prize for literature in 1953, the same year he was knighted.

On February 8, 1920, Churchill published a piece in the *London*

Herald about the Illuminati that began, "From the days of Sparticus (Adam Weishaupt) to Karl Marx, to those of Trotsky, Bela-Kuhn, Rosa Luxembourg and Emma Goldman, this world-wide conspiracy has been steadily growing. This conspiracy has played a definitely recognizable role in the tragedy of the French Revolution. It has been the mainspring of every subversive movement in the nineteenth century; and now at last this band of extraordinary personalities from the underworld of the great cities of Europe and America have gripped the Russian people by the hair of their heads, and have become practically the undisputed masters of that enormous empire."

CIA

Digital Fortress, Deception Point, and *Angels & Demons*

The Central Intelligence Agency (CIA) is an independent executive bureau of the United States government, established by the National Security Act of 1947 that grew out of the wartime Office of Strategic Services. CIA operations are directed by the National Security Council (see National Security Council).

The CIA's major responsibility is to gather and coordinate strategic intelligence and counterintelligence outside the United States in the interest of national security. The extreme secrecy of many of the CIA's covert operations, as well as the statutes that provide it great leeway, have given the agency a lot of freedom that has generated criticism of its tactics.

Ciampino Charter Airport

The Da Vinci Code

Ciampino Charter Airport is a smaller airport about fifteen kilometers southeast of Rome, primarily used for discount airlines, budget flights, charter flights, express courier companies, and private aircraft.

THE UNAUTHORIZED DAN BROWN COMPANION

Ciccone, Madonna

Angels & Demons

Born in 1958, Madonna Louise Ciccone, known by the stage name Madonna, is one of the most famous recording artists of the twentieth century. Also an actress, author, activist, relentless self-promoter and pop culture icon, Madonna released her self-titled first album in 1983.

Cilice

The Da Vinci Code

The term cilice originally referred to the hair shirt or haircloth, a garment made of coarse cloth or animal hair. Goats were bred for the purpose of making this haircloth and most of it was made in Cilicia, a Roman province in southeast Asia Minor, which is where the Latin term for the cloth (cilicium) came from.

Saints, monks, and those who chose to do penance have worn them at various times in the history of the Christian faith for mortification of the flesh (disciplining the body and its appetites by self-denial or self-inflicted privation).

These days, the word cilice has come to refer to a spiked metal belt or chain worn tight around the upper thigh. This practice has existed in other parts of the Catholic Church, but has become associated with Opus Dei, which former members have stated requires its members to use the cilice for two hours a day. In Dan Brown's novel, Opus Dei member Silas wears one.

Cinderella

The Da Vinci Code

Cinderella is the heroine of one of the most famous fairy tales in the world. Though over five hundred versions of the story exist, the ones told by Charles Perrault and the Grimm brothers are the best known.

In the story, poor Cinderella is condemned to a life of drudgery among the cinders by her stepmother and stepsisters, but is rescued by her fairy godmother, who magically dresses her in finery and sends her to the prince's ball in style. The handsome prince falls in love with Cinderella and when she leaves nothing behind but a single glass slipper, he scours the kingdom until he finds the woman whose foot fits the shoe.

Cinquefoils

The Da Vinci Code

Cinquefoil can refer to a plant of the genus Potentilla in the rose family, many of which have leaves of five leaflets. The term is used in architecture to refer to an ornamental carving or design having five sides composed of converging arcs in a circle, resembling a rose.

Cipher-text

Digital Fortress

Cipher text (or cipher-text or ciphertext) is the result of using a key or algorithm to encrypt plain text (or clear text) so it is unreadable.

Citroën ZX

The Da Vinci Code

The Citroën ZX is the vehicle Lieutenant Collet uses to drive Langdon to the Louvre. Citroën launched this model early in 1991 as the French competitor in the Ford Escort class. Production ceased on the ZX in 1998.

Classic Wizard

Deception Point

The Classic Wizard network is the control system that integrates the Navy, Marines, Air Force, and Army to perform global ocean reconnaissance and surveillance. It is reputed to have ground stations in Guam;

Diego Garcia; Adak, Alaska; Winter Harbor, Maine; Maryland; Edzell, Scotland; and elsewhere, though all locations are cloaked in secrecy due to national security. It supports the White Cloud Naval Ocean Surveillance System (NOSS) satellite system. These three sets of satellites (each in a group of three) are used to track military ships at sea, as well as triangulate the position of radio and radar transmissions.

Claustrophobia

The Da Vinci Code

Calling it a phobia of enclosed spaces, Dan Brown gives this fear to his protagonist, Robert Langdon. As the character says, it is an anxiety disorder that involves the fear of narrow or small enclosed spaces. Claustrophobes who are placed in such environments as elevators, trains, or other confined spaces may suffer a panic attack.

Clavius, Christopher

Angels & Demons

Christopher Clavius (1538–1612), born Christoph Clau, was a German mathematician and one of the most respected astronomers in the world. In 1579, he was assigned to create a reformed calendar and developed the modern Gregorian calendar, which assigns a leap year every four years. By order of Pope Gregory XIII, this calendar was adopted in 1582 in Catholic countries, and is now used worldwide. A crater on the moon is named for Clavius.

Cleartext

Digital Fortress

Cleartext, also called clear text or plain text, is the original message of an encrypted code or cipher before it is encrypted, or the unencrypted form of an encrypted message.

Clement V

The Da Vinci Code

Born Bertrand de Goth (1264–1314), Clement V was elected pope though he was neither an Italian nor a cardinal, and served in that office from 1305 to 1314. As a Frenchman, he was befriended by King Philip IV of France, who convinced Clement to move the papal residence from Rome to Avignon, France, where Philip kept the pope firmly under his thumb. As a result, Clement supported Philip's financially motivated suppression of the Knights Templar, starting with the infamous arrest of all of the knights on October 13, 1307. Dante, in his *Divine Comedy*, wrote of a special place awaiting Clement in the eighth circle of hell.

Clinton, Bill

Angels & Demons

William Jefferson Clinton was born in Arkansas in 1946, as William Jefferson Blythe. Three months before he was born, his father, William Blythe, died in a car accident. So, after his mother remarried when he was four years old, the future forty second president of the United States took the last name of his stepfather, Roger Clinton.

Bill Clinton graduated from Georgetown University, won a Rhodes Scholarship to Oxford University in 1968, and received a law degree from Yale University in 1973. He served as a law professor, attorney general of Arkansas, and governor of Arkansas, then was elected president of the United States. He held the office from 1993 to 2001, with his first term characterized by a strong economic recovery and his second by scandal.

Cloisonné

The Da Vinci Code

Cloisonné is the process of decorating surfaces such as vases, boxes, and jewelry using metal filaments to outline a design, then filling in the design with colored enamel paste. The object is then heated to fuse the enamel to the metal and the surface, giving a smooth, even surface. The art of cloisonné has been highly perfected by the Chinese, the Japanese, and the French.

Club Embrujo

Digital Fortress

We were unable to find any reference to a Club Embrujo in Seville, but did find El Palacio del Embrujo. Since the latter is a flamenco bar and dance club in which regional music is played to a mostly middle-aged audience, it is highly unlikely that this is where David found a huge crowd of punks. So we suspect the Club Embrujo is fictional. In our dictionary, embrujo translates to "spell" or "charm," not "warlock."

CNN

Deception Point and Angels & Demons

A division of the Turner Broadcasting System owned by Time Warner, Cable News Network (CNN) is a cable television network founded in 1980 by Ted Turner and Reese Schonfeld. It broadcasts from its headquarters in Atlanta and from studios in New York City and Washington, D.C., and introduced the concept of twenty-four-hour news coverage.

Cocteau, Jean

The Da Vinci Code

Jean Cocteau (1889–1963) was a French writer, visual artist, and surrealistic filmmaker who was a leader of the French avant-garde movement in the 1920s. His first success was the novel *Les Enfants Terribles*, which he made into a film in 1950. Later in life, he redecorated churches. In *Les Dossiers Secrets*, he is listed as the last Grand Master of the Priory of Sion, from 1918 until his death.

Code

Digital Fortress and *Deception Point*

In cryptography, a code is a method for converting a piece of information or message into an obscured form so that those without authorization are prevented from understanding the message.

"Code" and "cipher" are often used interchangeably, but are in actuality two different things. A code is used to translate a word or phrase into another word or phrase (for example, President George Bush was given the code name Timberwolf); a cipher is used to translate individual letters. A simple cipher that uses the following letter of the alphabet to substitute for the previous one would turn "Bush" into "Cvti" and would, of course, be very easy to crack.

Though codes were considered more secure than ciphers for many years, a code book was often required to translate the code into something intelligible, rendering the code useless if the book fell into enemy hands. Codes also had a predictability that made them easy to break. With the advent of the computer, ciphers have come to dominate cryptography.

Codex Leicester

The Da Vinci Code

The Codex Leicester is a collection of writings by Leonardo Da Vinci, named after Thomas Coke (later the first Earl of Leicester) who purchased it in 1717. The only set of Da Vinci's writings in private hands, it was bought from the Leicester estate in 1980 by Armand Hammer and renamed the Codex Hammer. Subsequently, it was purchased by Bill Gates in 1994 for $30.8 million, and is once again known as the Codex Leicester.

The codex (meaning a book formed of bound leaves of paper or parchment) is a seventy-two-page manuscript written between 1506 and 1510. Penned in da Vinci's characteristic mirror writing, it also includes many sketches. The codex covers a wide range of his observations and theories on astronomy, the movement of water, hydraulics, geology, air, and celestial light.

College Garden

The Da Vinci Code

College Garden is a small private park in Westminster Abbey in London, named for the Westminster School when it was still part of the abbey. Established in the eleventh century as the infirmary garden of this great medieval monastery, it was used to grow medicinal herbs to care for the sick, as well as fruit and vegetables. The garden has been under continuous cultivation for more than nine hundred years, and the oldest living things there are five plane trees, planted in 1850. Some herbs are still grown in the garden today, but because of the high lead content of the soil, they cannot be used for medicinal purposes. College Garden is open to the public a limited number of days per week.

College of Cardinals

Angels & Demons

The Sacred College of Cardinals is composed of all cardinals of the Roman Catholic Church. A cardinal is an official of the second-highest rank of the Roman Catholic Church, inferior in rank only to the pope. This body elects the pope when that position becomes vacant (the *sede vacante* period), advises the pontiff about church matters when he summons them to a consistory (meeting), and administers the Holy See during the *sede vacante* period (though its powers are very limited).

In 1586, Pope Sixtus V fixed the number of cardinals in the Sacred College at seventy; it has since been increased several times and stands at 185 today.

Columbus, Christopher

Digital Fortress

Christopher Columbus (1451–1506) was a maritime explorer best known as the discoverer of the New World. Financed by King Ferdinand and Queen Isabella of Spain, Columbus sailed west across the Atlantic Ocean in search of a sea passage to India, intending to open new trade routes and bring Christianity and Western civilization to new lands.

He made four voyages, always believing he had reached Asia. In 1492, he first sailed with three ships (*Niña, Pinta,* and *Santa Maria*) and made landfall first in the Canary Islands, then on Watling Island in the Bahamas. Taking possession for Spain, he continued to explore and discovered other islands in the neighborhood, including Cuba and Hispaniola. The second expedition took colonists to the Lesser Antilles and Columbus discovered the Leeward Islands, Puerto Rico, and Jamaica.

The third expedition made landfall on Trinidad and sailed across the mouth of the Orinoco River in Venezuela; and the fourth, on which Columbus hoped to find Asia or Japan, made it to Honduras.

Though a character in Dan Brown's novel gleefully states that Christopher Columbus's relic—his scrotum—resides in a church in Seville, we have been unable to confirm this interesting tidbit. In fact, there is some dispute as to where he is actually buried—in Seville, or in the Dominican Republic.

Comédie-Française

The Da Vinci Code

The Comédie Française is the state theater of France and was founded by a decree of Louis XIV in 1680 to merge two French companies of actors in Paris: the troupes of the Hôtel Guénégaud and the Hôtel de Bourgogne. An annual grant was allotted from the royal treasury the next year to build a new theater for the company.

The Comédie-Française was closed briefly in 1793 during the French revolution, and the actors were imprisoned. The troupe was reformed in 1799 and was reorganized and reopened in 1803 under Napoleon I.

The Comédie Française has had several homes since its inception and is currently housed in a theater on the Rue de Richelieu. Its mission is to preserve the heritage of French drama and has a repertoire of three thousand works. The best-known playwright associated with the Comédie-Française is Molière, which is why the Comédie Française is often called La Maison de Molière.

COMINT

Digital Fortress

COMINT is an acronym for Communications Intelligence, which is National Security Agency's global reconnaissance division for the covert interception of foreign communications, including commercial satellites, long-distance communications from space, undersea cables, and the Internet. It is a subcategory of SIGINT (signals intelligence).

Compass rose

The Da Vinci Code

The compass rose first appeared on charts and maps in the 1300s. A graduated circle, usually marked in degrees, a compass rose is a figure displaying the cardinal directions north, south, east, and west on a map.

Originally, it was used to indicate the directions of the winds (and was called a wind rose), the thirty two points of the compass coming from the directions of the eight major winds, the eight half-winds and the sixteen quarter-winds. Apprentice seamen who were able to name all thirty two points were said to be "boxing the compass."

The arcs of the compass resemble the petals of a rose, so it is called a compass rose. A "T" was often used on the compass to indicate the direction north for the north wind, Tramontana. This evolved into a spearhead and later into the fleur-de-lis figure, around the time of Columbus.

Computer virus

Digital Fortress

A computer virus is software that is designed to replicate itself by copying itself into other programs stored in a computer. It is most often used to destroy data, disrupt program operation, or cause the system to malfunction.

Viruses are spread via floppy disks, networks, and e-mail messages with attachments. More than eighty thousand viruses have been identified, but most infections are variants of a few hundred originals.

Computerized triangulation

Deception Point

Triangulation is the process of finding the location of an unknown point by creating a triangle using that point and the location of two known points, traditionally used in surveying, navigation, and astrometry. Computerized triangulation uses satellite surveillance to perform the triangulation.

COMSEC

Digital Fortress

COMSEC (COMmunications SECurity) is an acronym used by the United States military to indicate controls for ensuring secure communications by denying information of value to unauthorized persons or by misleading them in the interpretation of such data. Communications security includes crypto security, transmission security, emission security, traffic-flow security, and physical security of communications security materials and information.

Conclave

Angels & Demons

The selection of a new pope was originally reserved to the emperors. Later, various secular authorities, including Holy Roman Emperors, were given the authority to confirm the election. However, in 1179, Pope Alexander III changed that so that the vote of two-thirds of the college of cardinals was necessary for the lawful election of a pope, and was no longer subject to approval by secular authority.

Over the years, the sovereigns of Spain, France, and Austria came to be given the right of veto for a single candidate, providing they notified the Sacred College before the election took place. However, Pope Pius X abolished this practice in 1904.

The longest vacancy the Pontifical See has ever known occurred after the death of Pope Clement IV, in 1268. The seventeen cardinals in conclave were unable to reach an agreement after over two years, so in 1271, the irritated populace confined them within the palace, walled up the exits, removed the roof of the building, and put the cardinals on a diet of bread and water, saying they would not be released until they came to an agreement. Almost immediately, the Sacred College elected Pope Gregory X. He was so impressed with the procedure that he instituted confining the electors to the palace and feeding them only bread and water as the stringent rules of conclave so that future elections would move more swiftly. It worked—his successor was elected in less than twenty-four hours.

Conclave has changed a little over the years (they soon did away with the bread and water diet), but the procedure today, refined most recently by Pope John Paul II, is very much the same.

The Sacred College of Cardinals used to be confined in the Sistine Chapel in the Vatican in conclave until the election was completed (though they were allowed other conclavists, such as the cardinals' secretaries and servants, physicians, a sacrist, masons, and carpenters). However, under Pope John Paul II's reforms in 1996, a hotel residence called Domus Sanctae Marthae (Saint Martha's House) was built adjacent to Saint Peter's Basilica to house the cardinals taking part in conclave, though they still vote in the Sistine Chapel.

The three kinds of election used to be by acclamation, by compromise (in which the college transfers its votes to a quorum), and by scrutiny (ballot). The third has traditionally been the most common, and Pope John Paul II's new rules did away with the first two. Votes are held twice a day, with two ballots each time, and a two-thirds plus one vote is required for the election to be valid. However, John Paul's change now allows for an absolute majority if no pope is elected after thirty three or thirty four votes. Cardinals less than eighty years of age are eligible to vote and must be present for their vote to count; absentee voting is not allowed.

If there is no majority or valid election, the votes are burned with chemicals to produce black smoke. Once the election of a new pope has been confirmed, the votes are burned to produce white smoke and a senior cardinal appears at a window of Saint Peter's to announce the election.

Any Roman Catholic male may be elected to the papal throne (Gregory XVI, who was only a priest, was elected in 1831), but the new pope has traditionally been a cardinal.

Confraternity of the Immaculate Conception

The Da Vinci Code

A confraternity is a group of people united in a common purpose or profession. The confraternities were established in medieval times when laypersons wished to take part in the religious orders, and the Confraternity of the Immaculate Conception celebrated the Virgin Mary.

The specific Confraternity of the Immaculate Conception that Dan Brown refers to is the one in Milan that hired Leonardo Da Vinci and the de Predis brothers in 1483 to do a series of paintings for their church (see *The Madonna of the Rocks*).

Congenital heart defect

Digital Fortress

A congenital heart defect (what Tankado has) is a defect in the structure of the heart and blood vessels of a newborn child. Less than one percent of all newborns have congenital heart disease.

Constantine the Great

The Da Vinci Code

Constantine I or Constantine the Great (circa 272–337) was born Flavius Valerius Constantinus and served as emperor of Rome from 306 to 337. He is best known for rebuilding Constantinople (now Istanbul) as the new Rome in 330 and stopping the persecution of Christians.

It is said that Constantine saw a great flaming cross in the sky on the eve of a battle in 312, inscribed with the words, "In this sign thou shalt conquer." He adopted the sign of the cross as his own and was victorious. In 313, he and fellow emperor Licinius issued the Edict of Milan, which declared that Christianity would be tolerated throughout the empire, thereby ending the persecution of Christians.

This made Christianity lawful, though Constantine continued to tolerate pagan beliefs. In 325, he headed the First Ecumenical Council of Christianity in Nicaea to deal with the Arian heresy, thereby establishing the first ecumenical council and unofficially sponsoring Christianity, a major factor in allowing the religion to spread.

However, historians can't agree on the depth of Constantine's conversion to Christianity. Some portray him as a devout convert, others as using his conversion as a political tool to unify his empire. He was baptized on his deathbed in 337.

Content editor

Deception Point

In the context used in the novel, a content editor is a person who edits written material for content prior to publication, as opposed to merely editing for grammar, punctuation, etc., which is a copy editor's job.

Copernicus, Nicholas

Angels & Demons and The Da Vinci Code

Nicolas Copernicus (1473–1543), born Niclas Kopernik, was a Polish mathematician, astronomer, and economist who published the heliocentric theory of the solar system that proved that the sun is the center of our solar system.

The Catholic Church, however, still held that Ptolemy's geocentric version, whereby the entire universe revolved around the earth, was true. Hesitant to go against the church's 1,500 years of tradition and be charged with heresy, Copernicus summarized his work in 1530 and distributed it to scholars, but it wasn't published in full until 1543, a few weeks before he died. It was banned by the church and not taken off the Vatican's list of banned books until 1835.

Today, Copernicus theory is considered an important discovery—the start of the scientific revolution, and the basis of modern astronomy.

Coptic Scrolls

The Da Vinci Code

The Coptic Scrolls were discovered in 1945 in a sealed jar buried at Nag Hammadi in Upper Egypt. These gospels begin where the Dead Sea Scrolls end. Originally written in Greek, they were translated into Coptic in the second or third century and date from the fourth century. They include fifty-three works in all, including the gospel of Thomas, the secret book of James, and many others.

They speak of Christ's ministry in very human terms, and there is controversy over whether they are mere spiritual allegories or historical accounts that were purposefully left out of the Bible by those who had a specific political agenda.

Core sample

Deception Point

A cylindrical sample of soil, rock, or ice, obtained by driving a hollow tube into the material and withdrawing it in the form of a tubular sample or core for the purpose of further study.

An ice core, removed from an ice sheet, contains ice formed over many years and can be used to reconstruct a detailed climatic record over the age range of the core, up to hundreds of thousands of years. It provides information on a wide variety of climatic aspects for each time period, including such things as the amount of precipitation, volcanic eruptions, forest fires, and atmospheric chemical composition.

Cornell University

Deception Point

Cornell University, an Ivy League private university located primarily in Ithaca, New York, was chartered in 1865 and opened in 1868. It was founded by Ezra Cornell and Andrew Dickson White and named for Cornell, who donated money and land for its construction. Cornell University has thirteen colleges and schools throughout the state.

Corpo di Vigilanza barracks

Angels & Demons

Meaning Body of Vigilance or Vigilance brigade, this is the barracks of the Swiss Guard in the Vatican.

Côte D'Azur

The Da Vinci Code

The Côte d'Azur (or the Azure Coast) is the Mediterranean coast of southeast France, the French Riviera. Lying between La Spezia, Italy, and Cannes, France, the area is known for its year-round mild climate and fashionable, popular resorts.

Council of Nicaea

The Da Vinci Code

The First Council of Nicaea (or Nicea) took place during the reign of Emperor Constantine I, in 325, and was the first ecumenical conference of bishops of the Christian Church. The council (also called a synod) met to resolve differences of faith and to define the tenets of the orthodox Christian religion to which Christians would adhere.

The purpose of the council was to discuss the Arian heresy (which stated that Jesus was a supernatural creature but denied his divinity), the Meletian schism—a clash between Arianism and orthodoxy in the Antioch Church, the validity of baptism of heretics, the status of lapsed Christians, and to agree on a date when all the churches would celebrate Easter. The statement of beliefs that the council generated is known as the Nicene Creed (see Nicene Creed).

Courtyard of the Belvedere

Angels & Demons

The Courtyard of the Belvedere (meaning "fair view" in Italian) was created in 1503 when Pope Julius II commissioned Donato Bramante to connect the Palace of the Belvedere with Vatican City and placed a statue of Apollo (the famous antique sculpture *Apollo Belvedere*) in the courtyard. Additional statues and artifacts were subsequently added to the collection over the next two centuries, and the resulting collections were eventually reorganized to found the Vatican museums.

The Palace of the Belvedere, a small garden casino originally built for Pope Innocent VIII by Antonio Pollaiolo on the hillside above the Vatican Palace, is now a museum hosting many of those sculptures. When the museum was enlarged in 1775, the courtyard was made into an octagon by forming recesses in the four corners.

Cousteau, Jacques

Deception Point

Jacques-Yves Cousteau (1910–1997) was a French naval officer, filmmaker, researcher, oceanographer, and the most famous undersea explorer in the world.

In 1943, after two accidents with rebreathers in World War II, he and Emile Gagnan invented the Aqua-Lung, an underwater breathing apparatus that was the first type of scuba equipment made. He also developed techniques for minesweeping harbors and pioneered techniques in underwater photography.

In 1950 Cousteau purchased his famous vessel, *Calypso*, and undertook to study the oceans of the world (as well as some rivers) and all forms of life in water. During these trips, he produced many books and films, winning Oscars for "The Silent World," "The Golden Fish" and "World Without Sun," as well as many other top awards.

In his later years, Cousteau devoted himself to educating the public on environmental issues, and founded the Cousteau Society in 1973 to raise funds for research around the globe and influence environmental politics to "improve the quality of life on the Water Planet."

Cray supercomputer

Deception Point

Seymour Cray was an architect and designer of large-scale computers who founded Cray Research in 1972 and whose name is synonymous with fast supercomputers. Now named Cray Inc., the company is located in Seattle, Washington, and still manufactures and supports the fast, high-performance computer systems known as supercomputers.

Cray/Josephson II Computer

Digital Fortress

This appears to be a fictional computer since we can't find any reference to it. However, we speculate that Dan Brown's use of this name means that the NSA's fictional computer was built by marrying the Cray supercomputer with Josephson junctions.

A Josephson junction, originally conceived by Brian Josephson, is an ultra-fast switching technology (allowing switching in mere picoseconds—one trillionth of a second) that uses superconductor materials at cryogenic temperatures. The Josephson junction was once thought to be the answer to computers' silicon limitations, but no one has been able to make the Josephson junction work.

Creationist theory

Angels & Demons

Creationist theory, or creationism, is the literal belief in the account of creation of the universe and all living things in six calendar days as recounted in the Bible's Book of Genesis. Advocates of creationism, often fundamentalist Christians, have campaigned to have it taught in United States public schools along with evolution, which they reject.

Crestliner Phantom 2100

Deception Point

The Crestliner Phantom 2100 is a twenty-one foot speedboat or power-boat. With a 250 horsepower Mercury engine on a lightweight aluminum hull, the Phantom comes with many standard features and is fast and maneuverable. This is what Corky uses in the novel to escape from the Delta Force on the *Goya*.

Creully

The Da Vinci Code

A village in Normandy, France, Cruelly is located between Caen and Bayeaux, not far from the beaches of Normandy where the Allies landed in World War II in 1944. In fact, Château de Creully was the BBC's communication center during the invasion.

Cromolyn

Angels & Demons

Cromolyn, or cromoglicate, is one of the drugs Maximilian Kohler uses in the novel to assist his breathing. It is a synthetic compound that is used to prevent the production of chemicals such as histamine in mast cells and prevent some allergic reactions. The oral inhaler form is used to prevent asthma episodes caused by allergies by preventing spasm and opening up the breathing tubes of the lungs. Apparently, this is what Kohler used it for.

Crown of Thorns

The Da Vinci Code

The Crown of Thorns was a mock crown made of thorn branches that Roman soldiers placed on Jesus's head before his crucifixion. The relic was purported to have been venerated at Jerusalem from the fifth century on.

Saint Louis, King of France, acquired the crown in 1238 from Baldwin II, the Emperor of Constantinople, who was eager to gain France's support. Saint Louis built the Sainte-Chapelle in Paris for it, where it remained until the French Revolution, when it was restored to the Church and deposited in the Cathedral of Notre Dame.

However, the relic that is still displayed once a year on Good Friday is a twisted band of rushes, devoid of thorns, which the Catholic Church says was used to hold the thorns together. The sixty or seventy thorns from the crown were removed by Saint Louis and his successors and distributed to various secular and religious personages throughout the world. Though over 700 thorns are claimed to be from the original crown, it appears some thorns only touched those in the original, which leaves the claims of most of them doubtful.

Both tradition and existing remains confirm that the thorns came from the jujube tree, which grows in abundance around Jerusalem.

Crucifix

The Da Vinci Code

The crucifix, a Christian cross with the figure of Jesus nailed to it, is a primary symbol of the Christian religion, representing Jesus's crucifixion by the Romans and his sacrifice. It is used primarily in Roman Catholic, Eastern Orthodox, and Anglican circles; most Protestant denominations prefer to depict the cross alone, to emphasize Christ's resurrection.

Cruise, Tom

The Da Vinci Code

Tom Cruise, born Thomas Cruise Mapother IV in 1962, in Syracuse, New York, is a popular American movie actor and producer. A string of successful top-grossing movies has propelled him onto the A-list of movie stars, and he is best known for his roles in *Top Gun, Rain Man, Jerry Maguire, A Few Good Men, Mission: Impossible,* and *War of the Worlds.*

As Dan Brown mentions in the novel, Tom Cruise's character gets an up-close-and-personal view of Hieros Gamos sex rites in the film *Eyes Wide Shut.*

Crusades

Angels & Demons and *The Da Vinci Code*

The Crusades were a series of military campaigns, usually sanctioned by the Pope, undertaken by European Christians in the late-eleventh through the thirteenth centuries to recover the Holy Land, where Jesus had lived, from the Muslims.

The First Crusade (1095–99) took place when Byzantine Emperor Alexius I, threatened by the Seljuk Turks, appealed to the West for assistance. Pope Urban II, needing to strengthen the weakened papacy, exaggerated the anti-Christian acts of the Muslims and called upon Christendom to go to war.

The word spread widely throughout Europe, causing sixty-eighty thousand men to heed the call and take up arms to defend the cross. The campaign was completed in 1099 when they took Jerusalem and massacred the city's Muslims and Jews.

It was the only crusade to achieve Christian victory. The later crusades were primarily expeditions to assist those who already were in the Holy Land and defend the lands they had captured. The Ninth (and final) Crusade ended in 1271 when the Crusaders were driven out.

Crustaceans

Deception Point

Crustaceans are aquatic arthropods that include lobsters, crabs, shrimps, and barnacles, characteristically having a segmented body with three distinct body parts (head, thorax, and abdomen), a chitinous exoskeleton, two pairs of antennae, compound eyes, three pairs of mouthparts, and paired, jointed limbs.

Crux gemmata

The Da Vinci Code

The crux gemmata is a cross set with thirteen precious stones representing Jesus and his twelve apostles. It is also said that the wood of the cross symbolizes Jesus's suffering and death, and the gemstones his resurrection. During the first centuries, this cross is what Jesus's followers used instead of a crucifix.

Cryptex

The Da Vinci Code

Cryptex, a combination of cryptography and codex, which Dan Brown says Leonardo Da Vinci outlined in one of his secret diaries, is a physical, portable security device that requires a password to open. Any attempt to break it results in the destruction of the contents.

This appears to be a literary invention by Dan Brown, and there is no proof that Leonardo Da Vinci made such blueprints, but what a fascinating concept! It fact, it has inspired several inventors to create cryptices as described in the novel.

Cubist movement

The Da Vinci Code

The cubist movement, or cubism, was started in 1907 by Pablo Picasso and Georges Braque, who were influenced by Cezanne's landscapes. Creating a new way of seeing the world, the cubists rendered fragments of an object into multiple facets of geometric shapes so the viewer could see several surfaces or faces of the object simultaneously, resulting in a distorted, abstract painting. The elements of the composition were compiled for aesthetic reasons rather than reality and were intended to show them not as the eye perceives them, but as the mind does—from all sides at once. Though it began as an intellectual revolt against the artistic expression of previous eras, this break from visual realism became a turning point in modern art.

Curiazi and Orazi clans

The Da Vinci Code

According to a tale by Titus Livius, the Curiazi and Orazi clans (or Curiatii and Horatii) were two sets of male triplets who fought on the sides of Alba Longa and Rome, respectively, during the reign of Tullus Hostilius (circa 672–642 BC).

To avoid bloodshed, Alba and Rome decided that the outcome of the war would be determined by one battle between the Horatii and the Curiatii. During the battle, two of the Horatians were killed and the Curiatians were injured. The remaining Horatian triplet pretended to run away and was pursued by the Curiatians. Their variety of injuries spread them out such that he was able to kill all three one by one, giving the Romans the victory.

When the victorious Horatian returned, his sister realized the Curiatian she had been engaged to was dead and grieved for him. Her brother killed her for mourning the enemy and was in turn condemned to death. However, he was saved when he appealed to the people. Historians speculate that this legend, which Dan Brown treats as fact, was probably created to explain the practice of why the condemned in Rome were allowed to appeal to the populace.

Cyclone fence

Digital Fortress

A chain-link fence made of galvanized steel designed to stay intact even under the force of a cyclone.

Dagobert

The Da Vinci Code

When Dan Brown refers to King Dagobert in his novel, he is referring to King Dagobert II, not King Dagobert I. However, it is interesting to take a look at both. King Dagobert I (circa 603–639), was the king of the Franks from 629 to 639. Son and successor to King Clotaire II, Dagobert I became king of Austrasia when his father was forced to appoint him as such by Pepin of Landen (or Pepin the Elder or Pepin I), mayor of the palace and de facto leader of the great nobles.

The last of the Merovingians to exercise any real royal power, Dagobert I was the most powerful of the Merovingian kings and made himself independent of the nobles. However, the nobles of Austrasia revolted under Pepin I in 632, and Dagobert was forced to appease them by putting his three-year-old son Sigisbert III on the Austrasian throne in 634.

Sigisbert III fathered Dagobert II (650–679) and after Sigisbert died in 656, the nobles ordered Dagobert II's death. He was spirited out of the country, then restored to the throne in 676 where he reigned only three years until he was murdered on orders from Pepin the Fat.

This pattern, where the king was only a figurehead and the real power remained in control of the mayor of the palace and the noble families, continued until Pepin III finally deposed the last Merovingian king in 751, establishing the Carolingian dynasty.

Daniel and the Lion

Angels & Demons

Daniel and the Lion (or *Daniel in the Lions' Den*) is a marble sculpture from the baroque period which was done by Bernini in 1650 and commissioned by Fabio Chigi, the future Pope Alexander VII. It resides in the Chigi Chapel in the Church of Santa Maria del Popolo in Rome. Another version, in terracotta from 1655, resides in the Vatican museums.

The sculpture depicts the story of Daniel, who was beloved of King Darius. Other subjects, jealous of Daniel's popularity, prevailed on the king to make praying to God illegal. Daniel refused to obey this law and was thrown to the lions. In return for his loyalty and belief, God protected him from the beasts.

Darwinian system of terrestrial taxonomy and classification

Deception Point

Taxonomy is the scientific classification of biological organisms in an ordered system that indicates natural relationships. Carolus Linnaeus (1707–1778), in his Systema Naturae, created the method of modern classification (kingdom, phylum, species, etc.) which grouped species according to shared physical characteristics by placing each organism into a layered hierarchy of groups. His system made it easy to unambiguously identify any given species of plant or animal.

Though Linnaeus's system has remained in standard practice for at least two centuries, it has been revised since to improve consistency with the Darwinian principle of common descent, with descendants of a single ancestor being grouped together.

David

The Da Vinci Code

According to the bible, David (circa 1010–970 BC), meaning "beloved," was an ordinary shepherd who slew the Philistine giant Goliath with a stone flung from a sling. Though he gave David command of his army, King Saul became jealous of him and David spent many years fleeing from him. David finally succeeded Saul as king, making David the second king of Israel.

When Jerusalem was captured, David moved his capital there and planned a temple, but God told him his successor would build it, and promised David that his line would endure forever in the Israelite and Jewish monarchies. That is why the Jews believe that the Jewish Messiah will be a direct descendant of King David. The Christian Gospels say also that Jesus was descended from him.

David's reign was a popular one but began to decline when he committed adultery with Bathsheba and murdered her husband in order to marry her. Later, anarchy prevailed among David's children, leading to his son Absalom's attempt to usurp the throne. He failed, and David's second son by Bathsheba, Solomon, became David's successor. (Their first son died.) Immortalized in marble by Michelangelo, David is the reputed author of many of the Psalms.

Davide

Deception Point

Davide is an Italian restaurant located in the historic North End of Boston, Massachusetts. It first opened in 1982 and has been serving outstanding regional Italian cuisine for more than two decades, earning a Five-Diamond award from AAA, a rating of Excellent from *Zagat Survey*, the *Wine Spectator's* Award of Excellence, the Best Grappa Award, and recognition as one of the United States's top fifty Italian restaurants.

Dawn of the Dead

Digital Fortress

The 2004 *Dawn of the Dead* movie is a remake of George Romero's 1978 film of the same name. Directed by Zack Snyder and written by James Gunn, *Dawn of the Dead* is a story about a worldwide plague that produces flesh-eating zombies who attack the living, and the survivors who take refuge in a mega-shopping mall.

de Bouillon, Godefroi

The Da Vinci Code

Godefroi de Bouillon (Godfrey of Bouillon) (circa 1058–1100) fought for Holy Roman Emperor Henry IV against Pope Gregory VII and Rudolf of Swabia, and was rewarded with the duchy of Lower Lorraine in France. Later, he commanded the First Crusade, in which he captured Jerusalem. Given his alleged Davidic inheritance through the Merovingians (see Merovingians), he was offered the title of king but refused on religious grounds and was proclaimed Defender of the Holy Sepulchre instead. Godefroi was distinguished for his piety and simplicity, and founded the Order of Sion to be the Knight protectors of the Holy Sepulchre. The order shared the same Grand Master with the Knights Templar until 1188 when a legendary episode known as "The Splitting of the Elm" at Gisors, France, divided the organizations.

DEA

Digital Fortress and Deception Point

The Drug Enforcement Administration (DEA) was formed in 1973 from the Bureau of Narcotics and Dangerous Drugs of the United States Department of the Treasury, and the Bureau of Drug Abuse Control of the United States Department of Health, Education, and Welfare. Established in the Department of Justice, the DEA enforces federal laws and regulations (including the Controlled Substances Act of 1970) dealing with narcotics and other dangerous recreational drugs. It shares jurisdiction with the Federal Bureau of Investigations and cooperates with local law enforcement agencies.

Located in Arlington, Virginia, the DEA has a presence in over 350 locations around the world and jointly runs the El Paso Intelligence Center to enforce drug and immigration laws along the United States borders with Mexico.

Dead room

Deception Point

A dead room, also called an anechoic (literally, "without echo") chamber or soundproof room, is a room that is isolated from external sound or electromagnetic radiation sources and is constructed such that its walls, ceiling, and floor are covered by sound-absorbing material that eliminates reverberation. Such rooms are often used for testing microphones and loudspeakers, measuring the properties of acoustic instruments, and in the aerospace industry for radar cross-section measurement, among other things.

Dead Sea Scrolls

The Da Vinci Code

A collection of about 850 documents in ancient leather and papyrus scrolls and scroll fragments, the Dead Sea Scrolls were discovered between 1947 and 1960, in eleven caves on the northwest shore of the Dead Sea. They dated mostly from the mid-second century BC to the first century AD.

Written in Hebrew, Aramaic, and Greek, three types of documents comprise the Dead Sea Scrolls: copies of books of the Hebrew Bible, copies of books now collected in the Old Testament Apocrypha and Pseudepigrapha, and documents composed by an ascetic community believed to be the Essenes.

The Dead Sea Scrolls are important for reconstructing the compilation of the Hebrew Scriptures because they are practically the only Jewish biblical documents from that period, and for understanding Jewish culture and the political and religious context in the era immediately preceding the birth of Jesus.

Dead zones

Deception Point

Dead zones, first discovered in the 1970s, are low-oxygen areas in the world's oceans where marine life cannot be supported. The United Nations Environment Programme reported 146 dead zones throughout the world in 2003. The areas range in size from one kilometer to seventy thousand square kilometers, and most are caused by agricultural runoff or municipal and industrial waste that generate excessive amounts of nitrogen and phosphorus. These then trigger algae blooms, which use up available oxygen, killing marine life.

Death Valley sun scorpion

Deception Point

The sun scorpion, also called a sun spider or wind scorpion, because they run as fast as the wind, is not really a scorpion but comes from the same class as spiders. Non-venomous, sun scorpions live in sandy, dry areas like the desert, hiding under rocks or in shallow burrows during the day, then coming out at night to hunt insects and small vertebrates. There are almost 120 species in North America out of 800 to 900 world-wide and they are classified as an endangered species.

Debussy, Claude

The Da Vinci Code

Claude Achille Debussy (1862–1918) was a French composer who is considered the inventor of musical impressionism. He studied for eleven years at the Paris Conservatory, receiving its Grand Prix de Rome in 1884 for his cantata *L'Enfant Prodigue.*

He used the whole-tone scale instead of the traditional scale of Western music and explored unusual harmonic relationships and dissonances to achieve new nuances of mood and expression. As Dan Brown mentions, Debussy consciously used phi, or the golden ratio, in his music.

Delphi

The Da Vinci Code

An ancient town in Phocis, Greece, near the foot of the south slope of Mount Parnassus, Delphi dates back to at least the seventh century BC, and was the seat of the famous oracle of Delphi.

The oracle, who originated in an earth goddess's worship, was later passed to Apollo and housed in a temple dedicated to him in the sixth century BC. A priestess known as a pythia (or sybil) entered a trance when she inhaled the vapors beneath the temple's floor, and uttered oracular messages which were interpreted by a priest.

The oracle was consulted by the Greeks prior to all major undertakings, and was presented with sumptuous gifts by those seeking her help. Because of this, the city of Delphi grew very wealthy and became an important social and political center of ancient Greece for several centuries.

Delta Force

Deception Point

The United States Army's first Special Forces Operational Detachment-Delta (SFOD-D), known as Delta Force, is a special operations force of the United States Army Special Operations Command and is one of two US government principal units tasked with counterterrorist operations outside the United States. (The other is Naval Special Warfare Development Group.) Though the purpose of Delta Force is counterterrorism, it is extremely versatile.

The federal government denied the detachment's existence for years, but by the 1990s that existence was obvious, as the Army began to recruit new members. To fill its ranks, Delta Force draws primarily on the US Army Special Forces (Green Berets) and the elite Ranger battalions, though it will consider personnel recommended by those it trusts, or may seek out a person who has needed skills.

Created by US Army colonel Charles Beckwith in 1977 in response to terrorist incidents that occurred in the 1970s, Delta Force is headquartered at Fort Bragg, North Carolina, and is organized into three operating squadrons. These are further subdivided into small groups known as troops, which specialize in specific skill groups. It is rumored that the Delta Force also hosts a platoon composed solely of women, who are deployed alone in situations where women would arouse less suspicion than men.

As the Army's elite counterterrorist unit, Delta Force troopers are provided with the best training and equipped with the most advanced weaponry and equipment available, having it customized to fit their needs when necessary.

Delta Force has participated in a number of operations, including response to the hijacking of a Kuwaiti Airlines plane in 1984, response to the hijacking of a TWA plane in Cyprus in 1985, rescue of an imprisoned United States citizen in Panama, location and destruction of Iraqi SCUD launchers in 1991, apprehension of warlord Mohamad Farah Aidid in Mogadishu in 1993, the offensive against the Taliban in Afghanistan in 2002, and the invasion of Iraq in 2003.

Denon Wing

The Da Vinci Code

The Denon Wing is a section of the Louvre Museum in Paris that houses such art as Greek, Etruscan, and Roman Antiquities, and the Italian painters. It includes paintings by Leonardo Da Vinci such as the *Mona Lisa*, *St. John the Baptist*, and *The Virgin of the Rocks*, plus masterpieces by Raphael and Giuseppe Arcimboldo.

Depository Bank of Zurich

The Da Vinci Code

This is a fictional secure depository bank, created for the novel. However, it is amusing to note that Dan Brown's publisher created a fake Web site for the bank in which the customer login is a solution to a contest used to promote the book.

Desrochers, Edouard

The Da Vinci Code

Edouard Desrochers is listed as a senior archivist at the Mitterand library, among the people who are being eavesdropped on at the listening post at Sir Teabing's estate. Interestingly enough, in real life, Edouard Desrochers is an archivist at Phillips Exeter Academy from which Dan Brown graduated, and his appearance in the book is a cameo.

Devil's Advocate

Angels & Demons

The Devil's Advocate position in the Roman Catholic Church does not have to do with the election of the new pope in conclave as Dan Brown suggests. Instead, the Devil's Advocate was a canon lawyer official appointed to present arguments against a proposed canonization or beatification of saints, to take a skeptical view of the proceedings and look for holes in the evidence to ensure the candidate is thoroughly researched and worthy.

The term has passed into general use to indicate any person who is designated to argue against a position.

Devonshire

The Da Vinci Code

Devon is a county in Southwest England, bordering on Cornwall, Dorset, Somerset, and the Bristol and English Channels. The name Devonshire was once common as a name for the area but is now rarely used, although it does still feature in some titles on signs in the county.

A land of rolling hills, forests and rugged stone, Devon is used primarily for farming, cattle, and some fishing and is a popular vacation area.

Diagramma della Verita

Angels & Demons

Dan Brown mentions the *Diagramma della Verita* (or *Diagram of Truth*) as a secret document produced by Galileo (see Galilei, Galileo). This is a fictional publication, designed to allow the author to insert clues needed for his plot without having to force them to fit an existing publication.

Dialogo

Angels & Demons

Dialogo (Dialogue) or *The Dialogue Concerning Two Chief World Systems*, published in 1632, was written by Galileo as a discussion among three men, defending the Copernican heliocentric theory against the traditional Ptolemaic geocentric system. Though Galileo's manuscript was originally titled *Dialogue on the Tides*, the Inquisition made him remove all mention of tides from the title so that his inquisitioners would not appear to be granting approval to his theory, which used the tides to prove that the Earth did not remain motionless.

Though Galileo adhered to the Inquisition's instructions, the book was placed on the *Index of Prohibited Books* and he stood trial before the Inquisition, which convicted him of heresy in 1633. His book was not removed from the *Index* until 1822.

Dionysus

The Da Vinci Code

The Greek god of wine, fertility, and creativity, Dionysus's Roman counterpart was Bacchus. Some legends say he is the son of Zeus and Persephone, others that he was born of Zeus and Semele. Dionysus is known as the patron deity of agriculture and the theater.

Direction Centrale Police Judiciaire (DCPJ)

The Da Vinci Code

The Direction Centrale Police Judiciaire (DCPJ), or Judicial Police, is the French internal security service under the National Police, which is tasked with repressing organized crime by searching for infractions of the law, observing suspects, gathering evidence, and identifying criminals and apprehending them.

Discorsi

Angels & Demons

Discorsi (Discourses), also called *Discourses on the Tides* or *The Discourses and Mathematical Demonstrations Relating to Two New Sciences* was Galileo's final book, published in 1638. Using the same method of discussion among three friends as did *Dialogo*, it covered much of his work in physics over his lifetime.

Since the Roman Inquisition had banned publication of any work by Galileo after his trial in 1633, *Discorsi* wasn't published with a license from the Inquisition like his earlier books. After failing to publish it in

France, Germany, and Poland, Galileo finally managed to do so in the Netherlands, where the Inquisition held little sway:

Discovery Channel

Deception Point

An American cable television network, based in Silver Spring, Maryland, The Discovery Channel was launched in 1984. It has a variety of programming, primarily scientific, in the area of documentaries and nature.

Disney, Walt

The Da Vinci Code

Walt Disney (1901-1966) began as a cartoonist in 1920, creating Mickey Mouse, then moving into short and full-length animated features, live-action films, and television, thereby founding an animation and entertainment empire that still bears his name. He produced the first animated film with sound, "Steamboat Willie," in 1928, and the first full-length animated feature, *Snow White*, in 1938. He holds the record for career Academy Award nominations, with sixty-four, and his studios won forty-eight Academy Awards during his lifetime.

In 1955, Disney opened Disneyland, a theme park, in Anaheim, California, which was an immediate hit. Other Disney theme parks have followed around the world. Characters animated by Disney include Mickey Mouse, Donald Duck, Winnie the Pooh, Ariel the mermaid, Pinocchio the wooden boy, and Princess Jasmine.

Though Dan Brown's book mentions Walt Disney as a thirty-third-degree Freemason, there is no proof that he was ever a Freemason. However, he was a member of the Order of DeMolay in Kansas City, Missouri.

Divine proportion

The Da Vinci Code

(see Phi)

Doric column

Angels & Demons

A Doric column is the earlier and simplest of the three main styles of columns of classical Greek architecture, and the one Greek architects employed most. It has no base, and the column is heavily fluted with plain, saucer-shaped capitals.

Doshisha University

Digital Fortress

Doshisha University is a private university in Kyoto, Japan, founded by an ex-samurai named Niijima Jou. Having studied in Boston, Massachusetts, at Phillips Academy, Amherst College, and Andover Theological Seminary under the name Joseph Hardy Neeshima, Jou returned to Japan in 1875 to found Doshisha University.

A full-fledged university by the 1920s, Doshisha has a long-standing faculty and student exchange program with Amherst College and hosts the annual Associated Kyoto Program, offering American students the opportunity to study abroad for eight months. Doshisha has undergraduate students on three campuses studying theology, letters, law, commerce, economics, policy, and engineering, and graduate students in the areas of American studies and policy and management.

Dossiers Secrets, Les

The Da Vinci Code

Les Dossiers Secrets (the secret files), deposited in the Bibliothèque Nationale in Paris in the 1960s, is a loose collection of papers that, among other things, details the story of Rennes-le-Château, has pages of genealogy showing the Merovingian bloodline, and lists the Grand Masters of the Priory of Sion. The documents point to the Merovingians as joining with the descendants of Jesus and Mary Magdalene, the Priory of Sion as the protectors of the secret, and Pierre Plantard (who also adopted the name St. Clair in 1975) as a direct descendant of the Merovingians.

These documents have been attributed to Henri Lobineau, which the *dossiers* purport to be a pseudonym for an Austrian historian named Leo Schidlof. However, Schidlof's daughter vehemently denies this charge and it is generally believed that Plantard planted the documents himself. And since Plantard was previously convicted for fraud in 1953, most believe *Les Dossiers Secrets* to be a forgery.

Draco

The Da Vinci Code

Draco was a politician of ancient Athens, Greece, who was the first to codify the laws of Athens (circa 621 BC). Contrary to popular belief, he did not create the laws; he merely transcribed them. The laws were noted for their harshness, assessing the death penalty for even trivial offenses or forcing debtors into slavery. The severity of the laws he codified gave rise to expressions such as draconian punishment and draconian measures. Draco's transcription was replaced by Solon's rule of law about twenty years later.

Dulles International Airport

Digital Fortress

Dulles International Airport, located twenty-six miles west of downtown Washington, D.C., serves the greater Washington, D.C., metropolitan area and is named for John Foster Dulles, United States secretary of state under President Dwight D. Eisenhower. It serves as a hub for United Airlines and Independence Air and is a major station for Jet Blue.

Dürer, Albrecht

The Da Vinci Code

Albrecht Dürer (1471–1528) was a German painter, engraver, and mathematician who was the most influential artist of the German school.

He was best known for his woodcuts and used phi, or the golden section, in his work.

Earl of Leicester

The Da Vinci Code

Thomas Coke, first Earl of Leicester (1697–1759) was a wealthy English landowner and patron of the arts who, on his six-year "Grand Tour" in Europe, purchased many works of art, including Leonardo Da Vinci's work known as the Codex Leicester. Coke is also noted for building Holkham Hall in north Norfolk, which was intended to house his artwork, but he died before its renovation was completed.

Earth Observation System (EOS)

Deception Point

The Earth Observation System (EOS) is a NASA program composed of a series of satellites and scientific instruments in Earth orbit. These are designed for long-term observations of the interactions of Earth's environment, including land surface, biosphere, atmosphere, and oceans. The program is the centerpiece of NASA's Earth Science Enterprise (ESE).

East Room

Deception Point

The East Room of the White House was intended by the original architect to be the Public Audience Room, but remained unfinished for twenty-nine years, which is why First Lady Abigail Adams wrote of hanging her laundry there in 1800. It has subsequently been used as the office and living quarters for President Jefferson's secretary, for wrestling and boxing matches during President Theodore Roosevelt's tenure, as a court for the Harlem Globetrotters, a playroom where Caroline Kennedy rode her tricycle, and the site of Susan Ford's senior prom. It is now the largest room on the State Floor, used for official duties and entertaining guests.

The only original White House possession that still survives today hangs in the East Room—the 1797 portrait of George Washington by Gilbert Stuart, which First Lady Dolley Madison saved from the British troops who set fire to the White House in 1814.

Ecstasy of St. Teresa, The

Angels & Demons

The Ecstasy of St. Teresa (or Theresa) is a marble statue sculpted by Bernini that resides in the Cornaro Chapel, Santa Maria della Vittoria, Rome. It depicts a moment in the life of Saint Teresa, as recounted in her writings, when an angel pierced her heart with a dart and withdrew it, causing both great pain and joy. The sculpture was intended to represent the ecstasy of divine love, not the passion of sexual union.

Saint Teresa (1515–1582), known as Teresa of Avila, was a Spanish nun born Teresa Sanchez Cepeda Davila y Ahumada, who reformed the order of the Carmelite nuns. An ascetic who experienced mystical visions from God, she was beatified in 1614, canonized in 1622, and made a Doctor of the Church in 1970.

Edelweiss

Angels & Demons

Edelweiss, from the German edel (noble) and weiss (white), is an alpine plant native to Europe, having leaves covered with whitish down and small white flowers. It prefers rocky, inaccessible places at high altitudes and is a protected plant in many countries.

Edward the Confessor

The Da Vinci Code

Edward the Confessor (circa 1003–1066) became king of the English in 1042. His reign was marked by political conflict between Norman and English groups, and though he was an able ruler, he was unable to assert his authority over his earls. This resulted in his becoming more absorbed in his religion, his piety giving him the title of Edward the Confessor. He was canonized as a saint in 1161.

Edwards Air Force Base

Deception Point

Established in 1933, Edwards Air Force Base is a United States military installation located in Southern California in the Antelope Valley and is one of the largest air bases in the US, with the world's longest runway. Named in 1950 for test pilot Glen Edwards who died in the line of duty, it has long been used for flight research, testing, and as a proving ground for military aircraft. It's no wonder many sight "UFOs" in the area.

Eglise de Saint-Sulpice

The Da Vinci Code

The Eglise de Saint-Sulpice (Church of Saint-Sulpice) is situated in the south of Saint-Germain des Près and was started in 1646 by architect Louis Le Vau but wasn't finished until 134 years later, with six different architects working on it.

The church is known for the Delacroix frescoes that adorn its walls, and for having the largest organ in Europe, dating from the nineteenth century. Baudelaire and the Marquis de Sade were baptized here, and Victor Hugo was married here.

According to church signage, it was never a pagan church and the brass gnomon (see gnomon) that Dan Brown notes in the church is not part of the original zero-longitude line (which is several hundred meters east). Instead, the gnomon was used to determine the exact dates of Easter and the winter and summer equinoxes. It's interesting that the Priory of Sion should make this site significant, since Saint Sulpicius, for whom the church is named, was a bishop noted not only for his piety, but also for his resistance to the Merovingian kings of France.

Eiffel Tower

Deception Point and The Da Vinci Code

The Eiffel Tower, named after its designer, engineer Gustave Eiffel, was built for the Paris Exposition of 1889. This metallic tower on the Champ de Mars in Paris, France, rises 984 feet and was the tallest building in the world until 1930. Today, it is a famous landmark and symbol of Paris, and a popular tourist destination.

Einstein, Albert

Angels & Demons

The most famous scientist in the world, Albert Einstein (1879–1955) was a German physicist best known for creating the theory of relativity (including his famous equation $E = Mc^2$). This groundbreaking theory laid the foundation for much of modern physics, and he made major contributions to the development of quantum mechanics, statistical mechanics, and cosmology as well. Einstein won the Nobel Prize for Physics in 1921 for his 1905 work on the photoelectric effect, and was named the leading figure of the twentieth century by *Time* magazine in 2000.

Electromagnets

Angels & Demons

An electromagnet is a magnet energized by electricity. A coil of insulated wire is wrapped around an iron core and generates a magnetic field only when current flows through the wire.

Electronic Frontier Foundation (EFF)

Digital Fortress

The Electronic Frontier Foundation is a nonprofit civil liberties organization founded in 1990 by Mitchell Kapor and John Perry Barlow in

Cambridge, Massachusetts. Now located in San Francisco, California, the EFF works to protect First Amendment rights in today's digital age, to ensure privacy and freedom of expression in the arenas of computers and the Internet, and to educate the public on these matters. Foundation members consider themselves modern freedom fighters, much like our founding fathers, only with cyberspace as their battlefield.

Elements

Angels & Demons

According to Empedocles, a Greek philosopher, scientist, and healer who lived in Sicily in the fifth century BC, all matter comprises four primary substances, or elements: earth, air, fire, and water. Different mixtures of these elements produced the different natures of things. Astrology assigns these same four elements to three each of the twelve zodiacal signs.

Ellesmere Island

Deception Point

An island of northern Nunavut, Canada, Ellesmere was discovered by English explorer William Baffin in 1616, explored in the latter half of the nineteenth century, and named in 1852 after Francis Egerton, first Earl of Ellesmere. The world's tenth-largest island, it is separated from Greenland by a narrow passage.

Ellesmere Island consists of parks, fjords, glaciers, mountains, and ice shelves, and has a small population of scientific stations and some Inuit (Eskimo) settlements.

Emergency transponder

The Da Vinci Code

In the sense Dan Brown uses it in his novel, a transponder is an automatic device that transmits a message in response to a specific, predetermined signal. Used in the event of an emergency such as the hijacking of an armored car, the transponder can send a signal giving the exact location of the stolen vehicle.

Encryption algorithm

Digital Fortress

In cryptography, an encryption algorithm is a formula used to turn cleartext into coded ciphertext. Each algorithm uses a key to perform the calculations to scramble and unscramble the cipher. The need for strong encryption started with government agencies and moved into the public sector. It is now widely used to protect systems such as banks' automatic teller machines, mobile telephone networks, and Internet e-commerce.

English Channel

The Da Vinci Code

An arm of the Atlantic Ocean between southern England and western France, the English Channel has as its principal islands the Isle of Wight and the Channel Islands. The Strait of Dover connects the Channel with the North Sea.

A train-ferry service was opened in 1936 to connect London and Paris, and the Channel is traversed by means of a ferry service or the "Chunnel" rail tunnel beneath the channel, which opened in 1994.

The Channel has been the scene of many battles and invasions, and has presented an irresistible challenge to those who have attempted to cross it by a variety of means. J.P. Blanchard and Dr. John Jeffries were the first to cross the Channel in a balloon, in 1785; Matthew Webb was the first person to swim across, in 1875; and Louis Blériot was the first to cross by airplane, in 1909.

Enigma machine

Digital Fortress

The Enigma machine was a portable cipher machine invented and used by the Germans, about the size of a typewriter, that was used to encrypt and decrypt messages. There were different types of Enigma machines, but all of them used an electro-mechanical system, rotors, and a plug board to randomly change cleartext into ciphertext, and back again.

The Enigma machine was in use from the 1920s on, most famously in World War II by the Nazis, who thought the Enigma's code to be unbreakable since the ways in which a message could be ciphered were between two and three billion. However, Allied cryptologists from Poland and England exploited weaknesses in the use of the machine and were able to decrypt the messages, increasing their ability to avoid U-boats and anticipate attacks.

The ability of the Allies to decrypt German messages was so vital to the war effort that when Prime Minister Churchill learned the Germans planned to bomb Coventry in 1940, he deliberately did not evacuate the populace or bolster the defenses there for fear of alerting the Germans that their secret communications were decodable by the Allies. The machines the British built to decrypt messages from Enigma were the precursors of the first computer.

Escher, M.C.

Angels & Demons

Maurits Cornelis Escher (1898–1972) was a Dutch artist known for his mind-bending woodcuts, lithographs, and mezzotints, which featured impossible constructions and explorations of infinity by playing with perspective, perception, and space. For example, *Ascending and Descending* features staircases which seem to move in impossible directions, defying gravity in an infinite loop, and *Drawing Hands* features two hands which are drawing each other.

Escrivá, Father Josemaría

The Da Vinci Code

Josemaría Escrivá (1902–1975) was born in Barbastro, Spain, into a very religious family. As a boy, he saw "footprints in the snow" left by a monk walking barefoot in winter. This made him believe he had been chosen for something and he prayed for many years to find out what it was. After attending several seminaries, he was ordained as a priest in 1925 and in 1928, he finally had a revelation as to what he should do with his life: open up a new vocational path in the church, aimed at seeking holiness in daily life, through the use of prayer and penance. From that moment onward, he devoted all his energies to the fulfillment of his mission, founding Opus Dei with the central message, "Joy comes from knowing we are children of God" (see Opus Dei).

He amassed a huge international following for Opus Dei and at the time of his death, in 1975, the congregation had spread to all five continents, with over 60,000 members. In 1982, Pope John Paul II approved Opus Dei as a Personal Prelature. Father Escrivá was beatified in 1992 and canonized as a saint in 2002.

Euhemerus

Angels & Demons

Euhemerus (circa 316 BC) was a philosopher and mythographer in Macedonia who theorized that the gods and mythological accounts originated from the actual historical events of heroes and conquerors whose stories were shaped over the years by exaggeration and retelling.

In Dan Brown's novel, Langdon says that Christian canonization is taken from the god-making ritual of Euhemerus. We couldn't find any reference to such a ritual, and it seems to be at odds with Euhemerus's actual teachings, that godhood evolved over a number of years based on the retelling of stories. It is interesting to note that after Euhemerus propounded his theory, only two new gods were created in Greco-European culture—Apollonius and Christ—and early Christians actually used Euhemerus's argument to support their position that pagan gods merely came from stories of human invention.

Expander cycle engine

Deception Point

The expander cycle engine, which Dan Brown's characters used to create a fusion crust on the meteorite, is a bipropellant rocket engine that uses waste heat from the combustion chamber to vaporize the liquid hydrogen that drives the turbine. The Vinci re-ignitable expander cycle engine is planned to be used on the future cryogenic upper stage of Ariane 5, the European Space Agency's launch rocket.

Extremadura

Digital Fortress

The Extremadura, the Spanish landscape where David Becker lands, is an area in west central Spain on the border with Portugal, encompassing the provinces of Badajoz and Cáceres. Much of it is poverty ridden, a rugged landscape used primarily for farming, sheep grazing, and wildlife reserves.

F-14 Tomcat

Deception Point

The F-14 Tomcat that Rachel Sexton takes to the Arctic is a supersonic, twin-engine, variable sweep wing, two-seat strike jet fighter manufactured by Grumman Aircraft Corporation and used by the United States Navy. The Tomcat's primary missions are fleet air defense, air superiority, and precision strike against ground targets. It was developed to take the place of the cancelled F-111B and entered the fleet in 1973 to replace the F-4 Phantom II.

Fast ice

Deception Point

Fast ice is sea ice (frozen salt water from the ocean) that has frozen along coasts and extends out from land, usually smooth and level. It remains attached to land—unlike icebergs, which are chunks of ice shelves or glaciers that calve into the ocean.

Fatima, third prophecy

Angels & Demons

In 1917, three young shepherds, Lucia Abobora dos Santos and her cousins Jacinta and Francisco Marto, claimed to have had a vision of the Virgin Mary in the village of Fatima, Portugal, in which Mary entrusted them with three secrets in the form of prophecies.

The first two prophecies were revealed in 1941, and Lucia asked that the third not be revealed until 1960, saying, "by that time it will be more clearly understood." The first prophecy correctly predicted the end of World War I and the coming of World War II. The second foresaw the fall of the Soviet Union and was an appeal to pray for the conversion of its inhabitants to Christianity.

The Vatican did not reveal the third prophecy until 2000, on the eighty-third anniversary of the vision. It described the vision as showing a bishop in white (the pope) crossing a sea of corpses to make his way to the Cross, but suddenly cut down by a burst of gunfire. Vatican officials released the prophecy because they believed it was fulfilled by the attempted assassination of Pope John Paul II in Saint Peter's Square, in 1981. Not only did the assassin say his attempt was connected to the third secret of Fatima (which he had no way of knowing), but it occurred exactly sixty-four years after the vision first appeared to the girls.

However, some believe that is only part of the third secret, since 1) if the secret had referred only to the assassination attempt of 1981, there was no reason to keep it hidden for another nineteen years, 2) the pope was not murdered and did not have to walk across the corpses of martyrs to reach the cross, and 3) Father Joseph Schweigl, who interrogated Sister Lucia at the pope's request, said there were two parts to the secret, one about the pope, the other the words: "In Portugal, the dogma of the Faith will always be preserved," implying that the Christian faith would not be preserved elsewhere.

FBI

Digital Fortress and *Deception Point*

The Federal Bureau of Investigation (FBI) is the principal investigative arm of the United States Department of Justice, charged with investigating violations of federal laws in over 200 investigative matters, giving it the broadest range of investigative authority of any federal law enforcement agency.

Created in 1908 as the Bureau of Investigation, it originally conducted investigations only for the Justice Department. After J. Edgar Hoover became director in 1924, Congress gradually added more duties until the agency was reorganized in 1933; it wasn't designated the Federal Bureau of Investigation until 1935.

The stated mission of the FBI is "to protect and defend the United States against terrorist and foreign intelligence threats and to enforce the criminal laws of the United States." As of 2002, its primary task is counterterrorism, but it also investigates in areas such as subversive activities, kidnapping, extortion, bank robbery, interstate transportation of stolen property, civil rights matters, interstate gambling violations, narcotics smuggling, and fraud against the government.

FDR Memorial

Deception Point

In Dan Brown's novel, Pickering and Tench arrange to meet next to the FDR Memorial, referring to the open-air memorial for United States President Franklin Delano Roosevelt, on the Tidal Basin near the National Mall, in Washington, D.C. In four outdoor rooms, the memorial traces the history of each of FDR's terms of office over twelve years.

A simpler memorial of a plain block of stone, crafted to Roosevelt's wishes, was placed on the northwest corner of the National Archives grounds on Pennsylvania Avenue. The larger memorial took almost fifty years to complete, with a heated debate about how (or whether) to portray Roosevelt in the wheelchair he used after polio left him unable to walk, since few people in his own lifetime knew that he used one. The memorial was finally dedicated in 1997 and does portray him in a wheelchair much like the one he used.

Ferragamo

Digital Fortress

Salvatore Ferragamo (1898–1960) was an Italian footwear designer, one of the most influential designers of the twentieth century. He started his career in Hollywood (most notably making the ruby slippers for Dorothy in the 1939 film *The Wizard of Oz*), and opened a shop for repair and unique made-to-order shoes, which fast became popular with celebrities. His designs, ranging from the classically elegant to the strikingly bizarre, resulted in the creation of an international company that now produces shoes and other luxury consumer goods such as bags, eyewear, silk accessories, watches, perfumes and a ready-to-wear clothing line.

Fibonacci sequence

The Da Vinci Code

The Fibonacci sequence is a sequence of numbers, 1, 1, 2, 3, 5, 8, 13, 21, etc., in which each succeeding number is equal to the sum of the two preceding numbers.

Though referred to by Indian mathematicians as early as 500 BC, it was first studied in the West by Leonardo of Pisa, a.k.a. Fibonacci (circa 1200), to describe the growth of an idealized rabbit population.

Flamel, Nicholas

The Da Vinci Code

Nicholas (or Nicolas) Flamel was a fifteenth-century French alchemist whom legend says achieved the alchemist's ultimate goal: creation of the Philosopher's Stone that turns lead into gold and confers immortality upon the bearer.

The story says that Flamel, a bookseller, received a mysterious ancient book, written by Abraham the Jew, and made translating it his life's work. The knowledge he gained over twenty-one years made him a master of alchemy. Did he really achieve immortality? Well, the tomb that is supposed to bear his remains is empty. Some say it was robbed by those who wanted to learn his secrets; others say there is another explanation. . . .

In Dan Brown's novel, Flamel is listed as a grand master of the Priory of Sion. You may also remember Nicholas Flamel appearing offstage in another popular work, J.K. Rowling's *Harry Potter and the Sorcerer's Stone*, in which Flamel, still alive, creates the Philosopher's Stone (or Sorcerer's Stone) that Harry finds.

Flash-bang

Deception Point

A flash-bang (or flashbang) is a nonlethal concussion grenade or stun grenade used to confuse or disorient people for five or six seconds without causing lasting injury. It produces a blinding flash and loud blast without fragmentation.

Fleet Street

The Da Vinci Code

Fleet Street is a road in London, England, that used to be the center of English journalism. As such, "Fleet Street" is often used to refer to British journalists, and to journalism in general.

Fleur-de-lis

The Da Vinci Code

The fleur-de-lis (also spelled fleur-de-lys) is a stylized iris or lily heraldic symbol associated with the French monarchy. Legends say that the lily appeared at Merovingian King Clovis I's baptism as a gift from the Virgin Mary, and the symbol is also supposed to represent her as well as the Holy Trinity. Subsequent kings, such as King Philip I, Louis VII,

Charles V and Edward II, used different versions of the golden fleurs-de-lis on a blue background as their armorial emblem.

Because of its association with the Virgin Mary and the French Merovingian kings, some also see the fleur-de-lis as a symbol of the holy grail theory stating that the line of Merovingian kings contained the bloodline of Christ.

For-hire launch platform

Deception Point

Commercial launch services have been for hire from the United States and European Ariane consortium for quite a while, but today's market also has providers in other nations, with more on the way. The problem, as Dan Brown alludes to in his novel, is that any nation now has access to space through these providers and could launch disguised military payloads detrimental to United States interests.

In addition, some countries, like China and India, are not party to the Missile Technology Control Regime (MTCR), an informal and voluntary association of countries that seeks to limit the spread of unmanned delivery systems capable of delivering weapons of mass destruction, and to restrict exports of missiles and technologies supporting such systems. The fear is that countries not party to the MTCR may use the launch platform or technologies for hostile purposes.

Fountain of the Four Rivers

Angels & Demons

The Fountain of the Four Rivers in the Piazza Navona in Rome is the fourth Altar of Science in Dan Brown's novel, and represents water. Designed by Bernini for Pope Innocent X in 1651, the rustic fountain symbolizes the four quarters of the world: the Danube for Europe, the Ganges for Asia, the Rio de la Plata for America, and the Nile for Africa (whose veiled head indicates the source of the river was unknown at the time). The fountain is topped by an Egyptian obelisk recovered from the Circus Maxentius.

The story is that Pope Innocent X wanted to steal a march on Pope Urban VIII, his predecessor and nemesis, so Innocent diverted the flow of water from Triton Fountain, which Bernini had completed for the Barberini family (of which Urban was a member) to supply the Fountain of the Four Rivers. Because he had designed the Barberini fountain, Bernini was out of favor with Innocent, but the wily sculptor tricked the pope into choosing his design by making him believe it was by Borromini.

On his Web site, Dan Brown notes that the dove atop the obelisk that points the way to the next stop on the Path of Illumination is taken down and cleaned every three years, so it sometimes points in the opposite direction.

Fragonard

The Da Vinci Code

Jean Honoré Fragonard (1732–1806) was a French artist best known for his rococo style of paintings of exotic landscapes and delicately erotic love scenes that typified the frivolity and charm of life in the royal court of Louis XV in France in the eighteenth century. Some of his best-known works are *Love's Vow*, *The Swing*, and *The Music Lesson*.

Franklin, Benjamin

Angels & Demons

Benjamin Franklin (1706–1790) was a statesman, writer, scientist and inventor, and printer. A man of many talents, and accomplishments, he was a signer of the Declaration of Independence (which he helped to draft); published the famous *Poor Richard's Almanac*, coining many popular sayings still in use today; served as postmaster of Philadelphia; founded the first American fire insurance company; was American ambassador to France; made major contributions to the theory of electricity; had the Gulf Stream mapped for the first time; and invented useful objects like the lightning rod, the Franklin stove, and bifocal glasses.

Franklin became a Freemason in 1731 and Provincial Grand Master of Pennsylvania in 1734, printing the first Freemasonry book to be published in America.

Free fall tube

Angels & Demons

The free fall tube, or vertical wind tunnel, that Langdon sees in the novel may not exist at CERN, but models can be found in Switzerland, France, England, New Zealand, Tennessee, and Nevada, among other sites. Used for the sport called bodyflying or indoor skydiving, the motorized vertical wind tunnel produces a strong air stream that pushes your body upward, simulating the same movements a skydiver experiences. It gives the feeling of freefall without the hazard of jumping out of a plane. Sounds like fun!

Freemasonry

Angels & Demons and The Da Vinci Code

Freemasonry (sometimes referred to simply as Masonry) is a worldwide fraternal organization in which men join together in shared ideals. In most parts of the world, freemasonry is not a secret society, though some aspects of its internal workings are intended to remain hidden from the public. Freemasonry upholds the principles of "Brotherly Love, Relief and Truth," and besides providing a social environment for its members, is often involved in public service and charity work.

The precise origins of Freemasonry are unknown. Some say it rose from the English and Scottish stonemasons in the early Middle Ages or even further back in antiquity, which is why the organization relies heavily on the symbolism of the medieval masons who worked in stone (for example, the square and compasses). Others say Freemasonry dates back to only the late seventeenth century and has no connection to earlier guilds.

The oldest jurisdiction in the Anglo branch of Freemasonry is the Grand Lodge of England, founded in 1717, which later became the

United Grand Lodge of England (UGLE) when it joined with another (the Antients) in 1813.

Today, there are about five million members worldwide. While many important public and political figures have freely admitted their affiliation, membership claimed for historical figures can be difficult to verify since individual lodges keep their own records, which may have been inadvertently lost or destroyed over the years. To be a member, the applicant must be a man (in most jurisdictions); believe in a Supreme Being; be of sound mind and body, and of good morals; and be free (meaning not a slave or bondsman).

Through study, Freemasons rise through the ranks in three primary degrees: Entered Apprentice, Fellow Craft, and Master Mason. Once a Mason achieves the degree of Master Mason, he has the option of going on through one of many different rites awarding different degrees. For example, the Scottish Rite awards thirty higher degrees (which is why you hear of "thirty-third degree" masons), and the York Rite awards ten degrees.

The Masons also sponsor subsidiary groups for their relatives, including the Order of the Eastern Star (for Master Masons and their female relatives); DeMolay, an organization for boys aged 12 to 21; Job's Daughters, for girls aged 10 to 20; and the International Order of the Rainbow for girls who are aged 11 to 20.

Co-Masonry, which allows female membership, began in 1882 but has not been very prevalent. Membership of African Americans, the Prince Hall form of Freemasonry, began in 1775 when African Americans formed their own lodge. They separated themselves from UGLE-recognized Masonry in 1883 but are slowly making their way back into the fold. Not all jurisdictions recognize the validity of Co-Masonry or the Prince Hall lodges.

This emphasis on male-only membership has led to some criticism of the Freemasons, but there has always been controversy surrounding the society, partially because of its secretive nature. The Freemasons' ecumenical, tolerant stance toward religious choice, and its often anti-clerical attitude, have led the Catholic Church and others to discourage their members from joining. Critics of freemasonry say that Masons practice influence peddling or worship Satan, and conspiracy theorists insist they are bent on world domination and involved in covert polit-

THE UNAUTHORIZED DAN BROWN COMPANION

ical activities. The Freemasons deny these allegations, saying the charges assume that if one person in a group is bad, the whole group is bad . . . which could be applied to Christians as well.

Friday the thirteenth

The Da Vinci Code

There are many theories of the origin of the superstition that Friday the thirteenth is an unlucky day. Among other speculations, it is said by some to be linked to the thirteen people at the Last Supper of Jesus, or to the ancient Egyptian belief that the thirteenth stage of life is death, or to a Norse myth about an uninvited thirteenth guest at a feast of the gods who arranged for one of them to strike another leading to the downfall of all the gods. But the version that Dan Brown refers to in his novel makes more sense.

The Knights Templar (see Knights Templar) became very wealthy and powerful in the early fourteenth century, so much so that King Philip IV of France (who owed the Templars a large amount of money) and Pope Clement V feared them. Monarch and pontiff plotted secretly to get rid of the Templars, and on Friday, October 13, 1307, coordinated a mass arrest of Jacques DeMolay, Grand Master of the Knights Templar, and his senior knights all over France. The knights were subsequently charged with heresy and other crimes, then tortured. They "confessed," and were burnt at the stake. Their order was suppressed and their considerable properties were confiscated. Many escaped to Portugal and Scotland, where they refused to take part in the persecution of other Templars. From then on, the Templars considered Friday the Thirteenth a very unlucky day . . . and so did the rest of the world.

FTP

Digital Fortress

FTP, or file transfer protocol, is a software protocol used to transfer files over a network. This is how many users upload HTML pages of text and images from their local computers to their Web sites.

Fusion crust

Deception Point

A fusion crust is the thin melted glassy exterior of a meteorite, which forms during the atmospheric passage of a meteor. When a meteor enters the atmosphere at many miles per second, friction causes the exterior to melt. The melted portion sloughs off and the process repeats, causing the meteor to lose most of its mass on its descent through the atmosphere. The last melt cools to form the fusion crust, usually no more than one or two millimeters thick.

Galilei, Galileo

Angels & Demons and The Da Vinci Code

Galileo Galilei (1564–1642) was an Italian astronomer and physicist, considered the first scientist of the Scientific Revolution. His many achievements include demonstrating that all bodies fall at the same speed in a vacuum regardless of their weights; showing that the path of a projectile is a parabola; building the first astronomical telescope to study the stars; confirming the Copernican theory of the solar system; discovering the moons of Jupiter and phases of Venus (among other astronomical discoveries); inventing the thermometer; and contributing to the study of mathematical infinity.

Galileo was denounced for heresy by the church in Rome because of his outspoken advocacy of Copernicus's heliocentric theory that the sun forms the center of the universe, and was forced to renounce his belief for fear of torture. In 1968, the Vatican finally reconsidered Galileo's case, 326 years after his death, and officially recognized the validity of his work in 1993. The Galileo Affair, as it came to be called, was the longest and most expensive legal proceeding in Vatican history.

Galileo and Milton

Angels & Demons

This nineteenth-century oil painting by Annibale Gatti shows the presumed meeting of Galileo and English poet John Milton. Milton is peering through Galileo's telescope at villa Il Gioiello, Galileo's farm in Arcetri, where he spent the last years of his life after his condemnation by the Inquisition in 1633.

GAO Directory

Digital Fortress

This is the telephone directory of the United States Government Accountability Office (formerly the General Accounting Office). Founded in 1921, The GAO is a non-partisan audit, evaluation, and investigative agency designed to support the United States Congress in meeting its constitutional responsibilities and to help improve the performance and ensure the accountability of the federal government on behalf of the American people.

Garden of Earthly Delights

The Da Vinci Code

The Garden of Earthly Delights is a triptych oil painting on wood panels by Dutch painter Hieronymus Bosch. When the panels are closed like shutters, they reveal the biblical account of the third day of creation of Earth. When open, the three panels depict the Garden of Eden and original sin, the descent of mankind into sin, and hell. The title refers to the lush garden in the center, which represents a world wholly engaged in sinful pleasures. Painted circa 1504, it is currently housed in the Museo del Prado, in Madrid, Spain.

Geisha

Angels & Demons

Professional female artist-entertainers in Japan, geisha are trained in traditional Japanese arts such as tea ceremony, flower arranging, poetry, dancing, singing, and conversation, in order to entertain professional or social gatherings of men. Contrary to how they have been depicted in some media, they are not prostitutes.

The geisha (meaning "artisan") evolved from a position similar to that of the court jester, and the first were male. Now exclusively female, geisha were very common in the eighteenth and nineteenth centuries, when their training began at a very early age in a wide range of arts. They still exist today, though in much-reduced numbers. Today, becoming a geisha is wholly voluntary, so they begin their training at an older age.

Gershwin

The Da Vinci Code

The Gershwin referred to in the novel is probably George Gershwin (1898–1937). Born Jacob Gershwin, he was an American composer who wrote popular songs as well as the scores for many musical comedies produced in the United States, like *Funny Face*, and the folk opera *Porgy and Bess*. His brother, Ira Gershwin (1896–1983), wrote many of the lyrics for his compositions. George Gershwin was an acknowledged Freemason.

Giralda, La

Digital Fortress

The Giralda is a tower in Seville, Spain, originally built as a minaret for a Moorish Mosque. The Cathedral of Seville, the largest Gothic building in the world, now stands where the mosque used to be. Yousouf Yacoub al-Mansour, the Almohad ruler, started construction on the tower about 1184 and it took twelve years to finish.

Four bright copper spheres were added to the top of the tower in 1198, but were destroyed by an earthquake in 1356. In 1400, the Christian cross and bell were added in their place. The Giralda was converted to a bell tower in 1568, adding 123 feet to its 197 feet height. A spiral ramp inside allows visitors to climb to the top. La Giralda is where David confronts Hulohot for the last time.

Glaciologist

Deception Point

A glaciologist studies glaciers and their effects on the climate, the land, and the life forms that live there, integrating the disciplines of geology, climatology, meteorology, hydrology, biology, and ecology.

Glastonbury

The Da Vinci Code

A municipal borough of southwest England in Somerset, near Bristol, with a history rich in legend. Glastonbury is where Joseph of Arimathea is supposed to have planted his staff to found the first Christian church in England, and is also said to be the fabled site of King Arthur's Isle of Avalon. There are extensive remains of an Iron Age lake village nearby and the area is said to be the center of several ley lines, or convergences of energy in the earth.

Global Hawks

Deception Point

The Northrop Grumman-produced Global Hawk is a high-altitude unmanned reconnaissance aircraft used by the United States Air Force for surveillance and intelligence collection. It provides high-resolution radar that can penetrate most kinds of weather, and electro-optical/infrared imagery at long range over target areas to allow precise targeting of weapons and improved protection of military forces. The RQ-4 Global Hawk is the first unmanned aerial vehicle given a national certificate of authorization by the Federal Aviation Administration to file its own flight plans and fly in national airspace.

Global Positioning System (GPS)

Deception Point, Angels & Demons, and The Da Vinci Code

A system of satellites, computers, and receivers operated by the United States Department of Defense that is used to provide extremely accurate time references and determine exact locations almost anywhere on Earth. The intermediate circular orbit satellite system, consisting of at least twenty-four satellites, is free to anyone and uses the time difference in the signals from different satellites to the receiver to determine location, velocity, and time navigation information.

Gnomon

The Da Vinci Code

The stationary arm of a sundial that casts a shadow used to indicate the time of day on the dial.

Goddess iconographer

The Da Vinci Code

A goddess iconographer, such as the fictional Saunière, studies the symbolic meanings in works of art and other objects, used to convey ideas important to goddess worship. In iconography, the physical appearance of the goddess in a portrait or sculpture is less important than the symbols that reveal her spiritual aspects.

Goddess worship

The Da Vinci Code

Goddess worship is the veneration of a female deity or deities. Many believe goddess worship started in prehistoric times in gathering societies where the importance of fertility and domestication was stressed, as opposed to in hunting societies, which stressed more male-oriented pursuits.

For example, some historians and archaeologists believe the female figurines from old European culture represent goddesses and a matrilineal society, and that the suppression of goddess worship began a few thousand years BC, when the Indo-Europeans invaded and brought with them a more male-oriented society. As Judaism and Christianity evolved, the Pagan religions were suppressed and the female principle was gradually reduced in importance until women were treated as inferior to men.

The twentieth century brought a resurgence in Paganism, with its worship of goddesses and gods, though not all goddess worship is pagan. Most pagan traditions worship the Goddess and God in balance, but some feminist groups have seen the role of the Goddess grow in importance.

Gospel of Mary Magdalene

The Da Vinci Code

The Papyrus Berolinensis (PB) 8502 codex was acquired by a German scholar—Dr. Carl Rheinhardt—in Cairo, in 1896, and is known as the Berlin Gnostic Codex or the Akhmim Codex. Not published until 1955, it contains three important Gnostic texts written in Coptic: the Apocryphon of John, the Sophia of Jesus Christ, and the Gospel of Mary, purported to be that of Mary Magdalene. The first two also appear in Nag Hammadi texts, though the Gospel of Mary does not. Two other small fragments of the Gospel of Mary, from separate Greek editions, were later found in Northern Egypt, but ten or eleven pages are still missing from the text.

The Gospel of Mary reveals some of the gender conflicts and spiritual divisions of the early Christian movement by relating the confrontation of Mary Magdalene and Peter, an encounter which is also described in The Gospel of Thomas, Pistis Sophia, and The Gospel of the Egyptians. In it, Peter rejects Mary's authority to teach as if she were one of the apostles, and denies the validity of Gnostic esoteric revelation.

Gospel of Philip

The Da Vinci Code

The Gospel of Philip was one of the Gnostic texts written in Coptic (see Coptic Scrolls) found at Nag Hammadi. The text isn't actually from Philip but is so named because he is the only apostle mentioned in the texts. It is a collection of aphorisms, parables, and other wise sayings, purportedly from Jesus. Its primary theme is the value of five sacraments, including the sacrament of the bridal chamber, which some say suggests that Jesus himself practiced this sacrament.

Grand Gallery

The Da Vinci Code

The Grand Gallery is a gallery in the Denon Wing of the Louvre, more than 1,300 feet long, that displays paintings of Old Masters, including the *Mona Lisa* at one time. It has a beautiful parquet wooden floor done in a geometric, herringbone-type design.

Grave rubbings

The Da Vinci Code

Grave rubbing is the practice of laying a sheet of paper on a gravestone or bas-relief and rubbing the paper with graphite, wax, or chalk to obtain the impression of the design. Often used as decorative art, rubbings also create a useful record for gravestones that may deteriorate or be vandalized. Westminster Abbey, where Langdon saw the technique in practice, is a popular spot for making grave rubbings.

Great Elector

Angels & Demons

Dan Brown states that the Great Elector is the papal conclave's master of ceremonies. However, this isn't an official title. Instead, the term is used to refer to any cardinal who actively supports another cardinal in conclave and is successful in getting him elected.

Great Fire of London

The Da Vinci Code

This is one of two major fires that devastated the city of London, England. The first fire, in 1212, was known by that name until it was superseded by the fire of 1666. This broke out on September 2, 1666, in Pudding Lane, at the house of a baker to King Charles II who forgot to extinguish his oven for the night. Most buildings at that time were constructed of highly combustible materials like wood and straw, covered with pitch, and built very close together. Sparks emanating from the baker's shop fell onto the Star Inn, then engulfed St. Margaret's church and moved onto Thames Street where there were warehouses and wharves packed with flammable materials.

Fanned by a strong wind, the fire spread swiftly, its fierceness and the primitive nature of firefighting equipment making it impossible to stop. Though the conflagration could have been halted by pulling down some houses to create a fire break, the Lord Mayor refused to do so without the consent of the owners.

When the fire finally came to an end five days later, it had consumed almost five-sixths of London, destroying 13,200 houses and many other structures, including churches, prisons, a palace, bridges, and city gates. The fire made a full one-sixth of the city's population homeless, though, amazingly, only six to sixteen people are known to have died in it.

Great Seal of the United States
Angels & Demons

The principal seal of the United States government, this is used to authenticate official documents. It took six years, three committees, and the combined efforts of fourteen men to accomplish the adoption of the Great Seal of the United States by the Continental Congress, in 1782. The seal is still in use today, with minor changes in its design.

According to a publication from the US Department of State, the following is the origin and meaning of the symbols on the obverse and reverse sides of the seal—which show no reference to the freemasonry origins mentioned by Dan Brown.

The obverse side of the seal is an American bald eagle holding in its beak a scroll inscribed "*E pluribus unum*" (out of many, one). The eagle holds an olive branch in one talon and a bundle of thirteen arrows in the other, representing the power of peace and of war. The eagle's breast is covered by a shield with thirteen alternate red and white stripes, and a blue top that unites the shield and represents Congress. Over the eagle's head, a cloud of thirteen stars represents the new nation taking its place among other sovereign powers. The repeated number thirteen references the original thirteen states.

The reverse side has an unfinished thirteen-step pyramid that signifies strength and duration. The Eye of Providence above it and the motto, *Annuit Coeptis* (He has favored our undertakings), refer to the many interventions of Providence in favor of the American cause. The date underneath is that of the Declaration of Independence, and the words under it, *Novus Ordo Seclorum* (a new order of the ages), herald the beginning of the new American era in 1776.

Ground-penetrating radar (GPR)
Deception Point

Ground-penetrating radar uses pulses of electromagnetic radiation to detect underground structures and objects. GPR is used in archaeological exploration; in construction to locate subsurface objects such as buried lines, pipes, and storage tanks; by law enforcement and rescue services; and by other commercial and scientific organizations.

Guerenets of France
Angels & Demons

The Guerenets (usually spelled Guerinets) of France were a mystical sect in France from 1623 to 1635. Similar to the Alumbrados of Spain, the Guerenets, also known as the Illuminés of France, originated as an off-shoot of the sixteenth-century Afghani secret society called the Roshaniya—the illuminated ones—also known as an earlier version of the Illuminati.

Guerre d'Algérie
The Da Vinci Code

The Algerian War raged from 1954 to 1962. In many ways, it was to France what Vietnam was to America. And it ran concurrently with the final stages of France's own difficulties in Indochina. The Algerian War was a multiparty war—pitting Algerian nationalists, the French government, and French colonists in Algeria against each other—and ultimately all of them against Charles de Gaulle.

The horror of the Algerian War eventually brought down the French government, brought Charles de Gaulle back into power, and almost brought the French army to its knees and to the point of total rebellion.

Hostilities between Muslim nationalists and French colonists had been building for decades when, on November 1, 1954, the war erupted. Activist Muslims staged coordinated attacks on multiple targets throughout Algeria, including army barracks, mines, utility plants, government offices, police stations, and national media stations, among many others. The nationalists—the FLN or National Liberation Front—weren't successful in most of their attacks, despite the fact that the French army's peacetime rules included instructions to keep all troops' weapons unloaded at all times, and the ammunition for those weapons sewn shut into the soldiers' pouches.

The French authorities, heartily embarrassed at being caught so unprepared, cracked down hard on the rebellious Algerians. The French army razed whole villages to eliminate anyone it suspected was involved in a raid. In addition, the French were not afraid to stoop to torture in their quest for information about the enemy. More than 8,000 of the prisoners taken by the French by 1957 were never released—substantiated accounts of brutality by the soldiers indicated that those Algerians were most likely tortured to death.

Advances in aircraft, particularly in the development of helicopters, and such modern weapons as napalm and helicopter-mounted missiles, gave the French army powerful tools and great mobility in its fight against the nationalists, and the French used that technology to the fullest.

The FLN began a widespread campaign of bombing popular French-colonial gathering spots, with many of the bombs planted by young women—deemed by the rebels to be the least likely to be caught and searched. The nationalists also instituted a policy of attacking any Muslim who cooperated with the French colonial powers.

Large-scale carnage among civilians resulted from actions on both sides of the conflict.

The war escalated when neighboring Morocco and Tunisia gained their independence from the French. The governments of both of these countries eventually supported the rebels with weapons, funds, and sites for safe bases outside of Algeria. The French responded by turning Algeria into a fortress state, with minefields and patrolled electric fences surrounding the land borders, and a naval blockade keeping the colony isolated from support arriving by sea.

But the fighting in Algeria was having a devastating effect on the political front back in France. The French government fell, and it was felt by all that a strong hand was needed to deal with the situation. So Charles de Gaulle, in political exile since 1946, was in 1958 once again given the chance to lead France.

The French army had essentially ground the nationalists, now known as the ALN, to a military halt in Algeria, but the political war was much more problematic. The ALN was threatening to institute attacks on French soil. The casualties in Algeria were high—some estimates ran as high as a million deaths of Algerian civilians and rebels, and as many as twenty-five-thousand French soldiers. De Gaulle began to pursue a policy of "self-determination" for Algeria. French troops, who had fought hard to keep Algeria French, felt betrayed, and the French army was significantly destabilized by their torn loyalties. It almost rebelled against the government itself.

But despite the threatened mutiny of the army, Algeria was declared an independent nation in July 1962.

Gulf of St. Lawrence

Deception Point

The world's largest estuary, the Gulf of St. Lawrence is an arm of the northwest Atlantic Ocean off southeast Canada, extending from the mouth of the Saint Lawrence River to Newfoundland and bordered by New Brunswick, Nova Scotia, Newfoundland, and Quebec. Islands in the gulf include Anticosti Island, Prince Edward Island, the Magdalen Islands, and numerous other small islands near the north shore.

Habakkuk and the Angel

Angels & Demons

Dan Brown's first Altar of Science, representing the element earth, is the angel from the Habakkuk and the *Angel* sculpture by Bernini in the Chigi Chapel of the Santa Maria del Popolo. The seventeenth century marble sculpture represents the scene when the angel is getting ready to lift Habakkuk by his hair to take his food to Daniel's cave. A smaller version of the statue, in terracotta, resides in the Vatican museums.

Hack sack

Deception Point

This doesn't refer to the small bag filled with beans or sand used to play footbag, but to the air motion–sickness container Rachel needed on the F-14 Tomcat, also popularly known as a "barf bag."

Hadrian

Angels & Demons

Publius Aelius Traianus Hadrianus (76–138) (Hadrian, in English) followed his uncle Trajan as emperor of Rome, ruling from 117 to 138. Known as one of the five good emperors, he distinguished himself as a military commander and an administrator, and was generous to the poor.

He traveled extensively in his empire and ordered the construction of Hadrian's Wall, seventy-three miles long, five meters high, and three meters wide. The wall, near the modern border of England and Scotland, marked the northern edge of the Roman empire at the time. Hadrian also dedicated a temple to Jupiter Capitolinus in Jerusalem, built the Arch of Hadrian in Athens, rebuilt the Pantheon, added to the Roman Forum, and erected for his family a mausoleum that became Castel Sant'Angelo.

Haiku

Digital Fortress

A haiku is an unrhymed Japanese poem, a lyric verse form having three lines of five, seven, and five syllables. Haikus traditionally record a keen insight or the essence of a moment, using an aspect of nature or the seasons with a feeling of elegant simplicity.

The numbers associated with haiku are all prime numbers: three lines, five and seven syllables, for a total of seventeen syllables in the poem.

Haleite

Digital Fortress

The characters in the novel nickname Greg Hale "Haleite." The mineral "halite" is the sodium chloride (salt) residue left behind when an enclosed lake, playa, or sea dries up. Deposits can be found in western New York, Michigan, Ohio, Kansas and New Mexico in the United States; and in Ontario, Nova Scotia, and Saskatchewan in Canada.

Hanssen, Robert

The Da Vinci Code

Robert Philip Hanssen (born 1944) was an FBI agent who was convicted of spying for the Soviet Union. He was convicted in 2003 of selling American secrets to Moscow for over a million dollars in cash and diamonds over a fifteen-year period. He was sentenced to life imprisonment without parole.

While working as an FBI agent and selling secrets to the Russians, Hanssen called himself a devout member of the Catholic church and a member of Opus Dei, yet also allegedly posted sex stories and pornographic photographs of his wife on the Internet.

Harvard

The Da Vinci Code

Harvard is a private university in Cambridge, Massachusetts, a member of the Ivy League, and the oldest institution of higher education in the United States. Founded in 1636 with a grant from the General Court of the Massachusetts Bay Colony, it was later named for its first benefactor, John Harvard. Though it was originally intended to educate Puritan ministers, it grew to be an institution of general education.

Hassassin

Angels & Demons

Members of a mystic secret society founded by a militant group of the Nizari branch of Ismaeli Muslims in Persia and Syria, hassassins were thought to be active in the eighth through the fourteenth centuries. They gained a terrifying reputation for fearlessly executing assassinations of political leaders. They often slayed their victims in public—usually with a dagger—and would not commit suicide, preferring to be killed by their captors. They are still in existence today, in the Bombay area of India as well as in Syria and Iran, and are known as Khojas or Mawlas.

The origin of the word hassassin, or assassin, is in some dispute. Given to society members by their Muslim enemies, it is commonly believed to derive from the Arabic "hashish-eaters," from hassassins' use of hashish to either aid them in battle or create celestial visions. Others believe it simply means "followers of Al-Hassan" (or Hasan-i Sabbah, the Sheikh of Alamut).

Haz-Mat

Angels & Demons

Haz-Mat (or HAZMAT) is an abbreviation for hazardous material, meaning any solid, liquid, or gas that can cause harm to humans, animals, and the environment due to flammability, explosivity, radioactivity, toxicity, or other negative properties. Because of their nature, hazardous materials are handled with great care, especially regarding their storage, transport, or disposal

Heathrow

The Da Vinci Code

London Heathrow Airport, often referred to simply as Heathrow, is located in the London Borough of Hillingdon. Named after the hamlet Heath Row, which was demolished to make way for it, the airport was opened in the 1930s and is the United Kingdom's busiest airport.

Heckler and Koch USP 40

The Da Vinci Code

The Heckler and Koch USP (*Universale Selbstladepistole*, German for Universal Self-loading Pistol) that Silas uses in the novel is a semi-automatic pistol from the German arms manufacturer Heckler and Koch. Designed especially for American shooters, it provides features favored by United States law enforcement and military users. Using a Browning linkless locked breech action, developed by John Browning, it can be safely carried "cocked and locked."

heliocentricity

Angels & Demons

In astronomy, heliocentricity (helios meaning sun and kentron meaning center) means that the sun is the center of the solar system. The theory became the focus of a major dispute in the sixteenth and seventeenth centuries when Copernicus, Galileo, and Kepler advanced it in opposition to the Catholic church's belief in geocentrism, which placed the earth at the center.

Henry V

The Da Vinci Code

England's Henry V (1387–1422) was the son of King Henry IV, and succeeded him to the throne in 1413, ruling until dying in 1422. As king, Henry V dismissed the incumbent ministers, resulting in a rebellion by the Lollards, led by Sir John Oldcastle, until Oldcastle's execution in 1417. Believing France was his by right, Henry reopened the Hundred Years' War, defeating the French at Agincourt in 1415, and capturing all of Normandy by 1419. In 1420, he married Catherine of Valois, daughter of France's Charles IV, under the Treaty of Troyes, and agreed to rule France in Charles's name. However, Henry continued his conquests to amass lands and embarked on his third invasion of France, but died in September 1422 without achieving his aims.

Heparin

Angels & Demons

This medicine, taken by the pope in Dan Brown's novel to treat thrombosis, is an injectable anticoagulant. A complex organic acid that is found especially in lung and liver tissue, it is now made synthetically.

Heraclius, Patriarch of Jerusalem

The Da Vinci Code

Heraclius of Caesarea was archbishop of Caesarea and Latin Patriarch of Jerusalem. The Crusaders captured Jerusalem in 1099, creating the Kingdom of Jerusalem, and a Roman Catholic hierarchy was established in the kingdom under a Latin Patriarch. Heraclius assumed the position in 1180, and in 1184, traveled to Europe with the grand masters of the Knights Templar and Knights Hospitaller to solve the upcoming succession crisis in the kingdom. He offered the crown to both Philip II of France and Henry II of England but was refused. While in England, Heraclius consecrated the Knights Templar Temple Church in London.

Hermaphrodite

The Da Vinci Code

A hermaphrodite is an animal (or plant) that possesses both male and female reproductive organs, producing both eggs and sperm. While the condition is rare among humans, many plants and lower animals are naturally hermaphroditic.

Herod's Temple

The Da Vinci Code

The Temple Mount in Jerusalem, on Mount Moriah, is where the Jews believe Abraham almost sacrificed his son Isaac at the command of God. Solomon's Temple, also known as the First Temple , was built on this spot to replace the Tabernacle, the portable holy place of the Hebrews that housed the Ark of the Covenant. The temple was destroyed in 586 BC when the Jews were exiled.

The Jews started construction on the Second Temple over the remains of the first after their return from the Babylonian Captivity (circa 536 BC) and completed it in 515 BC. This second temple was missing some of the holy items from the First Temple: the Ark of the Covenant, the Ten Commandments, Aaron's rod, and others.

Herod the Great (circa 73–4 BC), King of Judea, tried to mollify the Jews in 19 BC by renovating the Temple Mount and greatly expanding the Second Temple. The resulting work is known as Herod's Temple and was later destroyed by Roman troops under Titus, circa 70 AD.

The last vestiges of the temple were removed when an Islamic shrine was built between 687 and 691. The Dome of the Rock was built by the ninth Caliph, Abd al-Malik, and the rock in the center of the dome is believed to be the spot from which Muhammad ascended to God.

HH-65 Dolphin helicopter

Deception Point

This is the Coast Guard helicopter Dan Brown's characters take to the
Goya. A mEDEVAC-capable short-range recovery helicopter operated by
the United States Coast Guard, the HH-65A twin-engine Dolphin helicopters can operate up to 150 miles offshore and fly at 120 knots for
three hours. Used ashore or on Coast Guard Cutters, the Dolphins assist
in search and rescue, cargo shipment, drug interdiction, ice breaking,
pollution control, military readiness, and airlift supplies.

Hibakusha

Digital Fortress

The word *hibakusha* means bomb-affected people and refers to those
who were radiated by and survived the atomic bombs dropped by the
United States military on Nagasaki (on August 6, 1945) or Hiroshima
(August 9, 1945) in Japan during World War II.

Hieros Gamos

The Da Vinci Code

Hieros Gamos (from the Greek, meaning holy coupling) is a sacred ritual
dating back more than 5,500 years. In this ancient marriage ritual, the
high priestess performed as an avatar for the goddess and had sex with
the king. Through this sacred coupling, the king symbolically married the
land and encouraged the fertility of the land and his people.

Hoban, James

Deception Point

James Hoban (1762–1831) was an Irish-born architect who won the
competition to design a residence for the United States President in
Washington, D.C., in 1792. His neoclassical plan was very similar to a

project in James Gibbs's *Book of Architecture*. In 1800, President John Adams moved in, though the building wasn't fully complete.

Benjamin Henry Latrobe, the principal architect of the United States Capitol, later added to the residence porticos on both fronts and additional pavilions at either end (added in 1800 in collaboration with Thomas Jefferson). After the building was burned by the British in 1814, Hoban supervised its reconstruction. There have been many changes to the White House since then, but James Hoban's original vision still stands.

Holy Blood, Holy Grail

The Da Vinci Code

Holy Blood, Holy Grail is a 1982 *New York Times* bestseller written by Michael Baigent, Richard Leigh, and Henry Lincoln, which Dan Brown appears to have drawn upon heavily in writing *The Da Vinci Code*.

The book starts with its authors' quest to understand the mysterious parchments found in the village church of Rennes-le-Château in southern France, in 1891. Their subsequent decade of research led them to hypothesize that the Priory of Sion secret society has existed since the First Crusades; that it is dedicated to returning the Merovingian dynasty to the thrones of Europe and Jerusalem; that the descendants of the Merovingians may be the literal descendants of Jesus and his wife, Mary Magdalene; and that the Roman Catholic Church tried to suppress knowledge of Jesus's marriage and children since this view of a more human savior conflicted with the Church's view of his divinity.

These theories have created great controversy and outrage among some historians and religious communities, but the authors have said they cannot prove it, only that it is a plausible hypothesis that might be true.

Holy Grail

The Da Vinci Code

Many believe the Holy Grail to be a chalice or dish used by Jesus at the Last Supper. There have been many stories about the Grail and miracles associated with it, including its ability to provide endless food and drink, and to heal all wounds.

The first Grail romance appeared in the twelfth century, written by Chrétien de Troyes, who claimed to be working from an earlier document, but the Grail didn't take on its holy nature until Robert de Boron's account of 1202. In that story, Joseph of Arimathea used the chalice from the Last Supper to catch Jesus's blood when he was on the cross, then took it to England and founded a line of protective Grail keepers.

Today's ownership of the legendary Grail is attributed to various groups, and a number of cups are claimed to be the Grail. Other stories assert that the Holy Grail is the secret bloodline of Jesus and his wife, Mary Magdalene (see Mary Magdalene), who took the Grail (the bloodline embodied in their child) to France, and that their bloodline still persists in the Merovingian bloodline today.

In some stories, the Grail is buried beneath Rosslyn Chapel or in the spring beneath Glastonbury Tor. In Dan Brown's novel, he invents a new, modern location for the grail: the Inverted Pyramid in front of the Louvre museum, a synchronicity which has the happy result of bringing his novel full circle back to where it began. Strangely enough, so many people believed this fictional account that the museum had to rope off the location to deter Grail seekers who wanted to access the alleged hidden chamber.

Holy Land

The Da Vinci Code

Holy Land usually refers to the biblical Palestine or the Land of Israel on the east coast of the Mediterranean, which has been under dispute for hundreds, if not thousands, of years. The holiness derives from those areas (such as the Church of the Holy Sepulcher, Bethlehem, the Western Wall, and the Dome of the Rock on the Temple Mount) that hold significant religious importance to three different religions: Judaism, Christianity, and Islam.

Holy See

Angels & Demons and The Da Vinci Code

The word "see" is the Latin word for "seat," so the Holy See is the holy seat of government for the Roman Catholic Church. This is the official name for the jurisdiction of the pope and includes the authority, jurisdiction, administration, and governmental functions associated with the papacy in the state of the Vatican City, which gained independence from Italy in 1929.

Hotel Bernini

Angels & Demons

Built in 1870 in a palace in the Piazza Barberini in Rome next to the famous Triton fountain, the Hotel Bernini Bristol has served many royalty, artists, and celebrities over the years. Recently renovated, it creates an Old World ambiance of luxury and refinement, while offering the most modern conveniences and amenities.

Hôtel de Crillon

The Da Vinci Code

The Hôtel de Crillon, located on the foot of the Champs-Élysées on the north end of Place de la Concorde in Paris is one of the oldest and most prestigious five-star luxury hotels in the world.

In 1758, King Louis XV commissioned two identical buildings to be used as government offices, built by architect Louis François Trouard, on both sides of the Rue Royale. One became the Hôtel de Crillon and the other still serves as the French Naval Ministry.

The last French-owned palace hotel in Paris, the opulent accommodation has served many statesmen and celebrities over the years. It also hosts an annual Debutante Ball for twenty-four young women of the international social set, which benefits the Pierre and Marie Curie Foundation.

Hôtel Ritz Paris

The Da Vinci Code

The Hôtel Ritz on Place Vendôme in Paris was designed by Jules Hardouin Mansart and constructed in the early part of the eighteenth century as a private dwelling. Converted to a luxury hotel by César Ritz, it opened in 1898 and quickly gained a reputation for opulence, service, and fine dining.

The Ritz family sold the hotel to Mohamed Al-Fayed in 1979, who renovated it. This is from where the owner's son, Dodi Al-Fayed, and his companion, Diana, Princess of Wales, departed on the night of their fatal crash in the Pont de l'Alma tunnel.

HOTOL

Angels & Demons

In 1982, British engineers Alan Bond and Robert Parkinson created a design for HOTOL (Horizontal Take-Off and Landing), a revolutionary new single-stage-to-orbit reusable winged launch vehicle. HOTOL was designed to extract oxygen from the air to burn with its fuel, which allowed it to be extremely efficient. It was intended to take off from a normal runway like any standard aircraft, then after reaching orbit, to re-enter the atmosphere and glide down to land on a conventional runway.

Development began with government funding in 1986, but problems with the design and funding caused this project to be abandoned in 1989.

House of David

The Da Vinci Code

Though the Bible sometimes specifies the House of David as a physical place or structure, the House of David is usually taken to mean the lineage of biblical King David, denoting the kingly line of Judah—those who had David as their forefather and were in line to occupy the Throne of David.

King David's reign over the united Kingdom of Israel lasted from about 1005 to 965 BC, and the Bible says that, in reward for David's piety, God promised that the Davidic line would endure forever. Jesus was of the House of David, and Judaism believes that the Jewish Messiah will be a direct descendant of King David.

Though some believe David never existed and that the stories told about his life were made up much later, others consider him a real historical figure whose deeds have come to belong more to the realm of myth than reality.

Hubble, Edwin

Angels & Demons

Edwin Powell Hubble (1889–1953) was an American astronomer who was the first to discover the galaxies beyond the Milky Way. His discovery, known as Hubble's Law, that galaxies' redshift increases in direct ratio to their distance, helped to substantiate the Big Bang Theory and the expansion of the universe. Hubble also worked with Milton Humason to develop the method still used for classifying the different types of galaxies: three types of spirals, barred spiral, elliptical, irregular, etc. The Hubble Space Telescope is named for him, in honor of his discoveries.

Hugo, Victor

The Da Vinci Code

Victor Marie Hugo (1802–1885) was one of France's most distinguished writers and poets. His most famous novels are *Les Misérables* and *The Hunchback of Notre Dame*, both of which have been adapted many times for stage and screen. Hugo went into exile after Napoleon III seized power in 1851, but returned to France in 1870, where he enjoyed great success. He is also cited as the alleged Grand Master of the Priory of Sion from 1844 to 1885.

Hydrophobia

Deception Point

Hydrophobia refers to either (1) an abnormal fear of being in deep water, or (2) to symptoms of rabies, a disease in which the victim has difficulty swallowing, has an aversion to swallowing liquids, and cannot quench his or her thirst. Hydrophobia has also been used to mean rabies itself.

Rachel Sexton, in the novel, suffers from hydrophobia in the first sense; being afraid of deep water.

Hypothermia

Deception Point

Hypothermia is a medical condition in which the victim's core body temperature drops abnormally low, below 95 degrees Fahrenheit. If body temperature falls below 90 Fahrenheit, the condition can become critical or fatal.

There are several types of hypothermia: acute, subacute, and chronic. In acute hypothermia, the body temperature goes down very swiftly, often in a matter of seconds or minutes, usually as a result of immersion in icy water. Subacute hypothermia takes a matter of hours and results from cold air, while chronic hypothermia occurs when the body temperature goes down over a period of days with prolonged exposure to the cold.

Symptoms of hypothermia include shivering, goose bumps, muscle incoordination, and confusion. The confusion may get progressively worse until the person has difficulty moving and exhibits amnesia, difficulty speaking, and signs of depression, then loses consciousness.

Iambic pentameter

Angels & Demons and The Da Vinci Code

Iambic pentameter is the building block of medieval and Renaissance English verse and is the most common meter in English verse. It is a rhythmic pattern of syllables that goes from an unstressed syllable to a stressed one, which is the meaning of iambic. So, on a line ten syllables long, every other syllable is accented, for a total of five (where the pentameter comes from). Geoffrey Chaucer, William Shakespeare, John Milton, and Christopher Marlowe, among others, wrote in iambic pentameter.

An example by John Milton from his sonnet "Methought I Saw My Late Espousèd Saint":

"I waked, she fled, and day brought back my night."

Iberia Airlines

Digital Fortress

Iberia Airlines of Spain, often shortened to Iberia, is the name of the national airline of Spain. In operation since 1927, it is one of the oldest airlines in the world.

Ice calving

Deception Point

The process by which huge chunks of ice break off the terminus of a tidewater glacier into a body of water, often accompanied by a loud cracking or booming sound. These broken pieces of ice become icebergs.

Icebergs

Deception Point

A massive floating body of ice that has become detached, or calved, from the edge of a glacier or ice sheet and is floating on the ocean. Because ice is not as dense as water, only about nine to ten percent of its mass projects above the surface of the water.

Most of the icebergs in the North Atlantic come from Greenland and are usually peaked and irregular in shape, the shape usually associated with an iceberg. Antarctic icebergs have flat tops and steep sides.

IceRover

Deception Point

An all-terrain highly mobile people carrier that uses the shock-system design of the Mars Pathfinder from NASA.

Illuminati

Angels & Demons

Illuminati (Latin for enlightened ones) has been the name of many groups, both real and fictitious, but it most commonly refers to the Bavarian Illuminati, a rationalistic society of republican freethinkers founded in Ingolstadt, Bavaria (now Germany), in 1776, by ex-Jesuit Adam Weishaupt and Baron Adolph von Knigge. Because Weishaupt's rationalistic tendencies exerted a growing influence on his students, he came into conflict with the Church and government officials. Using many of the tenets of Freemasonry, he founded the Illuminati with utmost secrecy and required the blind obedience of subordinates. He called it "Illuminated Freemasonry," bringing a number of prominent Masons into the fold.

For Weishaupt, enlightenment meant men were to be liberated from their prejudices and outgrow the religious and political tutelage of Church and State through secret schools of wisdom. Naturally, Church and State didn't care for this new society. The Catholic Church condemned it and the Bavarian government banned all secret societies, including the Illuminati and the Freemasons, in 1785, then later banned them from recruiting for the order under penalty of death. This put an end to the order in Bavaria, though Weishaupt later reconciled with the Catholic Church before his death.

Other organizations that have been called Illuminati are the Alumbrados of Spain, the Guerenets of France, the Brethren of the Free Spirit, the Rosicrucians, the French Martinists, and other, more modern, organizations that wish to trade upon the Illuminati's infamy.

The Illuminati have had a far greater impact on modern history than would be supposed from their brief life span, thanks to conspiracy theorists throughout history who have suggested that the Illuminati conspired to establish a New World Order. This new world government is supposed to occur through assassination, bribery, blackmail, and the control of financial institutions and governments. Some have even blamed the Illuminati for the French Revolution in 1789, as well as for the Russian Revolution of 1917.

Infrared binoculars

Deception Point

Infrared (meaning below red) radiation is electromagnetic radiation using a wavelength longer than visible light. It is used in night-vision equipment, when there is insufficient visible light. Using infrared binoculars, the Delta Force in the novel can detect hotter objects, such as human beings and operational vehicles.

Innocent II

The Da Vinci Code

Roman Gregorio Papareschi (died 1143) was elected Pope Innocent II in 1130. However, a rival faction elected Cardinal Pietro Pierleoni as Anacletus II, and Innocent had to leave Rome. He gathered support in France, Germany, Spain, and England, and tried repeatedly to reclaim the papacy from antipope Anacletus. The struggle between the opposing pontiffs wasn't resolved until Anacletus died in 1138. Another antipope, Victor IV, was elected, but he soon resigned.

In 1138, Innocent II signed the original charter for the Knights Templar (see Knights Templar), granting them extraordinary privileges and authority.

International Space Station (ISS)

Deception Point

The International Space Station (ISS), located in low orbit around the Earth, is a joint project of the United States, Russia, Japan, Canada, Brazil, and eleven European countries. The first section of the construction was put in orbit in 1998 and the first crew arrived on November 2, 2000: United States astronaut William Shepherd and Russian cosmonauts Yuri Gidzenko and Sergei Krikalev. It has been manned by a crew of at least two ever since.

Presently, the station can house three crew members, but is still under construction and is planned to have a crew of six. Since it's more expensive than NASA originally projected, and given the problems plaguing the space shuttle program since the Space Shuttle Columbia explosion, the future of the space station is in question.

Critics view the project as a waste of resources that could be used to fund unmanned scientific missions or spent on fixing problems on Earth. However, its proponents point out that manned space research and exploration have produced billions of dollars of tangible benefits to people on Earth, and that technologies developed during manned space exploration has returned from three to seven times the initial investment to the economy.

The ISS has hosted a couple of firsts: the first space tourist, Dennis Tito, who spent $20 million to fly aboard a Russian supply mission, and the first space wedding, between Yuri Malenchenko (orbiting the Earth) and Ekaterina Dmitriev (who was in Texas at the time).

Internet

Digital Fortress

The Internet, a publicly accessible system of networks that connects computers around the world, transmits data by packet switching using standardized Internet protocols. The largest network in the world, it carries electronic mail and online chat and web pages on the Worldwide Web; and is made up of more than 100 million commercial, academic, domestic, and government networks and computers in more than 100 countries.

The Internet began under the auspices of the United States Department of Defense Advanced Research Projects Agency (ARPA), in 1969. On January 1, 1983, ARPANET's core networking protocol was changed to TCP/IP, making the exchange of information among the networked users possible and marking the start of the Internet as we know it today.

In 1991, Tim Berners-Lee (see Berners-Lee, Tim) publicized his new World wide Web project, which allowed users to build and view Web pages using HTML and HTTP. In the mid-1990s, when the major online e-mail services began to exchange e-mail with each other and graphics-based Web browsers became available, Internet usage surged, increasing a hundredfold in 1995 and 1996 alone. With the proliferation of Internet service providers (ISPs) which offered access to individuals, the Internet grew exponentially. Today, this worldwide information highway provides information on every subject on Earth.

Interpol

Angels & Demons and The Da Vinci Code

Interpol is a worldwide clearinghouse for police information that was conceived in 1914 and created in 1923 to facilitate international criminal police cooperation. Originally known as the International Criminal Police Commission (ICPC), it was changed to the International Criminal Police Organization in 1956, but became known as Interpol for the organization's telegraphic address.

Interpol's first headquarters in 1923 was in Vienna, Austria, but when Hitler annexed Austria in 1938 and moved the ICPC to Berlin in 1942, many countries withdrew from the organization in protest and it was essentially disbanded. After World War II, the agency was reconstituted in 1946 with headquarters in Paris, France, then moved to Lyons, France, in 1989.

Interpol is one of the world's largest international organizations, second only to the United Nations. Its constitution forbids any involvement in crimes that do not involve several member countries, or in any political, military, religious, or racial crimes. It is designed to provide more than 140 member nations with information on international criminals, to organize seminars on scientific crime detection, and to facilitate the apprehension of criminals in the areas of public safety, terrorism, organized crime, counterfeiting, forgery, child pornography, financial and high-tech crime, smuggling, and the narcotics trade.

Ionic column

Angels & Demons

One of the early orders of architecture, with a base, slender fluted column, and spiral scroll-shaped capital. The Ionic order originated in the fifth century BC in Greece, but is primarily a product of Ionia on the southwestern shores of Asia Minor in the sixth century BC, which was settled by Ionian Greeks.

IRS

Digital Fortress and *Deception Point*

The Internal Revenue Service (IRS) is a federal agency, part of the United States Treasury Department, responsible for the enforcement of tax laws and the assessment and collection of most federal taxes, primarily income and Social Security taxes.

The agency was established in 1862 during the Civil War, when President Lincoln and Congress levied an income tax to pay war expenses. Repealed ten years later, it was revived again in 1894 by Congress, but the Supreme Court ruled it unconstitutional in 1895. However, the Sixteenth Amendment to the Constitution gave Congress the authority to levy an income tax, and that amendment was ratified by the states in 1913. The highest the tax has been was in 1918, when the top rate rose to a height of 77 percent to fund World War I.

Isis

The Da Vinci Code

Isis is an ancient Egyptian goddess of magic, motherhood, and fertility. No other Egyptian deity has been as widely accepted and worshiped as she. Her worship grew throughout the Mediterranean world and was embraced by the Greeks and Romans up through the sixth century, when it was banned by Christians; temples to Isis have been found throughout Europe, Africa, and Asia. She is still venerated today in some neopagan groups.

In Egyptian myth, Isis was the daughter of Nut, goddess of the sky, and Seb, god of earth. She married her brother Osiris, and when he was murdered by Set, she reassembled his body to bring him back to life, then bore him a son, Horus.

Isis had many names, and was considered the goddess of the underworld and the beneficent mother goddess, as well as patron goddess of royalty, seafarers, magicians, mothers, and wives. In art, there is a strong resemblance between the image of the seated Isis holding her son and the seated Virgin Mary holding hers. For this and other reasons, some scholars believe that the relationship between Isis and her son Horus influenced the way Christians regarded the Virgin Mary and the baby Jesus.

Islam

The Da Vinci Code

Islam, meaning submission to God, refers to the Muslim world that practices the religion of Islam, or to the religion itself. Founded in the seventh century by the Prophet Muhammad, Islam is a monotheistic religion characterized by the acceptance of the doctrine of submission to God, or Allah. Muslims submit to Him, praise Him as the only god, and seek knowledge of Him. Besides Muhammed, they also recognize prophets from the Old Testament and New Testament, as well as a number of non-biblical prophets.

Muslims' faith is built on the five Pillars of Islam: (1) that "there is no god but God, and Muhammad is the Messenger of God"; (2) ritual prayer, performed five times a day (dawn, noon, mid-afternoon, sunset, and nightfall), using verses from the Quran (or Qur'an or Koran); (3) charity, the giving of alms; (4) fasting, abstaining from food, drink, and sexual relations during the lunar month of Ramadan from first light until sundown for self-purification; and (5) pilgrimage to Mecca.

There are more than a billion Muslims worldwide, and Islam is the principal religion of much of Asia, though it can be found in other parts of the world as well.

Isle of Avalon

The Da Vinci Code

In Arthurian and Celtic legend, the Isle of Avalon was the legendary island in the British Isles where Morgan le Fay took King Arthur after his death and from which he is expected to return some day. Since the beginning of the eleventh century, tradition has it that the Isle of Avalon is in present-day Glastonbury, where Joseph of Arimathea is said to have brought the Holy Grail.

Isopod

Deception Point

Isopod refers to numerous crustaceans of the order Isopoda, characterized by a flattened body, lack of a carapace, gills on the abdominal appendages, and seven pairs of legs. In the same subclass as lobsters and crayfish, most isopods are aquatic, though some live under rocks or surface litter on land. Most isopods are small, but they can be over a foot long, such as the deep-sea bathynomous giganteus the characters find in Dan Brown's novel.

J23

Digital Fortress

The J23 stun gun that hits David Becker in the novel is an electroshock gun used to temporarily incapacitate a person by administering a high-voltage, low-current electrical shock. Intended to be nonlethal and avoid severe injury, the stun gun confuses the central nervous system, causing the recipient to experience great pain, paralysis, and/or muscle spasms. A half-second charge will cause intense pain and muscle contractions, two to three seconds will cause confusion and incapacitate the person, and over three seconds can completely disorient a person putting him out of action for up to fifteen minutes.

Jachin

The Da Vinci Code

Jachin or Jakin ("He shall establish"), also called the Apprentice Pillar, was the name of the southern of the two pillars that stood on the eastern portico in front of Solomon's Temple. The bronze pillars were crafted by Hiram, an expert worker of bronze, from Tyre. The other pillar is called Boaz, but the purpose of the pillars is unknown. Duplicates of these pillars reside in many Masonic temples.

Janus

Angels & Demons

Janus, the name Dan Brown gives to his villain, is not only a moon of Saturn, but in Roman mythology, he is the god of gates, doorways, beginnings, and endings. He was usually depicted with two bearded faces looking in opposite directions so that he could watch both ways at once.

The god of change and transition from one state, condition, or time to another, Janus was worshipped at beginnings such as harvest and planting times, marriages, and births. The first hour of the day, the first day of the month, and the first month of the year (January was named for him) were sacred to him. Historically, he was one of the few Roman gods who had no Greek counterpart.

Jardin de los Naranjos

Digital Fortress

The Jardin de los Naranjos (Garden of the Oranges) or Patio de los Naranjos (courtyard of the orange trees) is the oldest extant garden in Seville, Spain. It is a cloister of Seville's cathedral, the largest in Spain, built on the remains of an old mosque that uses the twelfth-century minaret La Giralda as its belfry.

As the story goes, English marmalade was first made from the bitter Seville oranges when Janet Keiller from Dundee, Scotland, tried to find a use for them. It is certainly true that her family built the first marmalade factory in 1797, and that is probably where the present-day version of the bittersweet preserve originated.

However, the word marmalade derives from the Portuguese word *marmelada*, which was a solid paste made from cooked-down quinces and sugar. First mentioned at the end of the fifteenth century, it was used by Mary, Queen of Scots.

Today under European law, "marmalade" can only be applied to fruit preserves made from citrus fruits. Those made with other fruits must be called jam.

J-Frame Medusa

The Da Vinci Code

Teabing's J-Frame Medusa revolver is the world's only patented multi-caliber revolver, having the capability to use cartridges in the 9 millimeters, .357, or .38 caliber ranges.

John Paul I

Angels & Demons

Italian Albino Luciani (1912–1978) was elected pope in 1978. He was the first to take a double name (to honor his two immediate predecessors) and the first pope to use "the first" in his name. He served for only thirty-three days before dying of a heart attack.

In 1984, David A. Yallop wrote *In God's Name: An Investigation into the Murder of Pope John Paul I*, a controversial book in which he cited irregularities in the Vatican's report of John Paul's death and alleged that he was murdered by Vatican officials in conspiracy with the mafia and the Freemasons. According to Yallop, they feared the pope would uncover alleged corruption in the Institute of Religious Works, known as the Vatican Bank. However, John Cornwall's book *A Thief in the Night* examines the evidence and refutes each of Yallop's accusations.

Johns Hopkins

Digital Fortress

Johns Hopkins University is a prestigious private institution of higher learning located in Baltimore, Maryland, with additional campuses in greater Maryland, Washington, D.C., Italy, and China.

It began in 1867 when Johns Hopkins incorporated a university and hospital, endowing them with three and a half million dollars each. The university opened in 1876, Johns Hopkins Hospital in 1889, and the famous medical school in 1893. It covers academic fields ranging from social sciences and humanities to natural sciences and engineering.

Joseph of Arimathea

The Da Vinci Code

The Bible portrays Joseph of Arimathea (a legendary city of Judea) as a wealthy man who donated his own tomb for Jesus's burial after his Crucifixion. Legend says that Joseph was the Virgin Mary's paternal uncle, Jesus's great-uncle, who caught Christ's blood in the Holy Grail.

After the Crucifixion, Joseph and a group of apostles fled to France. Later, in either 37 or 63 AD (sources vary), St. Philip sent Joseph to establish Christianity in England. As the story goes, when Joseph planted his staff grown from Christ's Holy Crown of Thorns, it miraculously took root and bloomed as the "Glastonbury thorn," which flowers each Christmas Day. He is supposed to have secreted the Holy Grail somewhere near Glastonbury Tor, where he established Glastonbury Abbey, the first church in the British Isles.

Some Christians have always honored Joseph of Arimathea, but since there is little historical substance for his legend, it has never received the approval of the Catholic Church.

Judaism

The Da Vinci Code

Judaism consists of the religious beliefs, practices, and culture of the Jews, based on the teachings of the Torah. The Torah, the part of the Hebrew Bible that contains the divinely revealed teachings of Jewish law and belief, specifies a number of laws, known as the 613 *mitzvot*, that must be followed.

One of the first recorded monotheistic faiths, Judaism believes that there is only one God and that the Jews are His Chosen People. Judaism prohibits worship of other deities or iconic representations of God.

Judaism's origins lie circa 2000 BC when, according to the Bible, God established a divine covenant with Abraham. Later, Moses led his people out of captivity in Egypt, and received the Ten Commandments, the laws of the Israelites, from God. After years of wandering through the wilderness, Joshua led the tribes into the promised land of Palestine, still under dispute today.

Throughout Judaism's 4,000-year history, Jews have been enslaved, conquered, exiled, and persecuted, the most infamous example being the attempted genocide by Nazi Germany during World War II. There are currently about eighteen million Jews throughout the world, primarily in North America and Israel.

Jungersol Fall

Deception Point

We were unable to find any reference to this, which Dan Brown calls a "famous" meteorite fall in 1716. It appears to be a literary invention.

Kabbala

The Da Vinci Code

There are two dozen or so different spellings of this word, which refers to the religious mystical system of Judaism and esoteric system of interpretation of the Hebrew Scriptures claiming an insight into divine nature.

Based upon oral monologues said to have been handed down from Abraham, kabbalistic interpretation of Scripture holds that every letter, word, number, and accent in the Hebrew Bible contains hidden meanings, and teaches how to ascertain those meanings. Kabbalists believe all of the names for God hold miraculous power, even that each letter of the name is very powerful.

In kabbalistic teaching, God has two attributes. One stresses strength, discipline, and justice (the female side), and the other (the male side) stands for love and mercy. The contrast between the two is a fundamental doctrine of the kabbala. It also teaches that God is the creator of the universe but that God, neither matter nor spirit, does not dwell in the universe. He has two aspects: God himself who is unknowable, and the revealed aspect of God who created the universe and interacts with humans.

From this second aspect of God came the ten emanations, the doctrine of the sefirot, which are the powers emanating from God through which he created the world and which allow for interaction between the unknowable God and the universe. The ten *sefirot* are wisdom, insight, cognition, strength, power, inexorableness, justice, right, love, and mercy.

Christian versions of the kabbala began to develop by the early eighteenth century and a recent modern (and controversial) revival has attracted many non-Jewish adherents, including a number of celebrities.

Karma

Angels & Demons

A Sanskrit word dating back to 1500 BC that denotes a concept common to Hinduism, Buddhism, and Jainism. Karma means that your state in this life is the result of the total effect of your actions and conduct in past lives, and that your actions in this life will determine your states of existence in future incarnations. Karma is solely the impersonal result of cause and effect and does not recognize deities that might judge you for your sins.

Katabatic wind

Deception Point

A katabatic wind (from the Greek meaning "going downhill"), is a cold-air-current wind that blows down a slope such as a hill, mountain, or glacier. These winds are usually found when cooling begins after nightfall.

Kepler

Angels & Demons and The Da Vinci Code

Johannes Kepler (1571–1630) was a German mathematician, astronomer, and astrologer who developed the three laws of planetary motion that shaped our current understanding of the solar system. These three laws describe a planet's elliptical orbit, the speed at which it travels, and the time it needs to complete one revolution around the sun.

A student of Tycho Brahe's, Kepler built on Brahe's work to support Copernicus's heliocentric theory. Kepler also helped found the modern science of optics by explaining how the eye works, how eyeglasses work, and how telescopes work.

King Arthur and the Knights of the Round Table

The Da Vinci Code

King Arthur, known in legend as the ruler of Camelot, is one of the great mythic figures of English literature, the ideal of kingship. However, historians disagree on whether he was a real person living around the sixth century or if his legendary deeds were loosely based on a real historical figure.

The stories vary, but most have similar elements. King Arthur asserted his right to kingship by either pulling the sword Excalibur from a stone when others tried and failed or having it handed to him by a sorceress from a lake. He established a court at Camelot, where he gathered the greatest warriors in Europe, the Knights of the Round Table, including Sir Lancelot, Sir Galahad, Sir Percival, and Sir Gawain. The Knights of the Round Table engaged in chivalrous quests, including a quest for the Holy Grail.

Advised by the wizard Merlin, King Arthur was married to Queen Guinevere (who fell in love with his champion, Sir Lancelot) and fathered a son by his half-sister, the sorceress Morgan le Fay. Their son, Mordred, went on to become Arthur's enemy and caused his downfall. After a battle with Mordred's armies, Arthur received a mortal wound and sailed to Avalon (which some identify as Glastonbury). Some say he will one day return from there, which is why he is often called "the once and future king." Arthur is sometimes depicted as the leader of the Wild Hunt, a ghostly group of huntsmen who ride in mad pursuit across the skies.

Kistler Aerospace

Deception Point

Dan Brown's novel mentions Kistler Aerospace as one of the private aerospace companies that offered bribes to Senator Sexton to put space exploration in the hands of the private sector. Kistler Aerospace Corporation, a privately funded United States company headquartered in Kirkland, Washington, developed the K-1 reusable launch vehicle, designed to deliver commercial and government payloads to low Earth orbit from the Woomera Spaceport in Australia, and later the Nevada Test Site.

In 2003, faced with over $600 million in debt and insufficient market for the K-1, Kistler Aerospace Corporation filed bankruptcy under Chapter 11 of the United States code, to restructure the company.

Knights Templar

Angels & Demons and The Da Vinci Code

An order of knights founded in 1118 during the Second Crusade when Hughes de Payens and eight other French knights received permission from King Baldwin II in Jerusalem to form a monastic order. Taking vows of poverty, chastity and obedience, they swore to protect the new Kingdom of Jerusalem and the Holy Sepulcher, and to guard pilgrims in the Holy Land. Founded as the "Poor Knights of Christ and of the Temple of Solomon," they were known as the Knights Templar and identified by their white surcoats with a distinctive red cross emblazoned on the chest.

The Templars were showered with gifts of estates and money, but were responsible only to the pope, who permitted them to levy taxes and accept tithes in the areas under their control, giving them a great deal of power. In 1135, the order started lending money to Spanish pilgrims traveling to the Holy Land and became increasingly involved in banking activities and international politics. By 1291, after the Crusades had failed, the Templars ceased to be a primarily fighting organization and became the leading money handlers of Europe.

Because of their special privileges, their freedom from secular control, and their great military and financial strength, they aroused opposition from secular leaders and clergy. As the Templars grew more successful, powerful, and decadent, they attracted the concern of the nobility and royalty of Europe as well.

On October 13, 1307 (see Friday the Thirteenth), King Philip IV of France, who wanted to acquire the Templars' wealth and power for himself, obtained the support of Pope Clement V and arrested knights of the order all over France, then tortured them to extract confessions of sacrilegious practices and heresy. Philip seized the Templars' treasury and broke up their banking system, then much of their property in France was acquired by secular rulers and the pope transferred property outside France to the Knights Hospitaller.

Several leaders of the Knights Templar were tried and sentenced to life imprisonment but in 1314 denied their confession and were burned at the stake. As Jacques DeMolay, Grand Master of the Knights Templar, died in the fire, he laid a curse on King Philip and Pope Clement that they meet justice within the year. The curse was apparently successful—Clement died one month later and Philip seven months after that. In addition, some attribute the rapid succession and death of Philip's sons to the curse as well, which ended the Capetian Dynasty.

Clement dissolved the order of the Templars by papal bull in 1312 and they were completely destroyed by 1314. Many surviving Templars were accepted into the Knights Hospitaller, and Robert the Bruce, the King of Scots, who had already been excommunicated, welcomed them in his lands.

The Catholic Church's position is that Pope Clement V was manipulated into suppressing them, and in 2001, the Chinon Parchment was found in the Secret Vatican Archives to support this, showing that Clement had secretly pardoned the Knights Templar in 1314.

Legends concerning the Knights Templar say that because of their long occupation of the Temple Mount in Jerusalem, they recovered holy artifacts such as the Holy Grail and the Ark of the Covenant, and acquired Masonic mysteries. Among other mystical or secret organizations they have been linked to are the Rosicrucians, the Priory of Sion, the Cathars, the Hermetics, the Gnostics, and the Essenes. Though some have tried to link the Freemasons to the Knights Templar, no direct link has been claimed by the Freemasons or proven.

Koyaanisqatsi

Angels & Demons and *The Da Vinci Code*

This Hopi Native American term translates to "life out of balance," "life of moral corruption and turmoil," "crazy life," "life in turmoil," or "life disintegrating," etc. According to Hopi cosmology, seven worlds were created at the beginning. The first three were destroyed because of humans' greed, corruption, and disrespect for religion and life on Mother Earth. We now live in the Fourth World, in koyaanisqatsi, and if we don't change our ways, we may destroy this world as well.

Labrador Sea

Deception Point

The Labrador Sea is an arm of the North Atlantic Ocean between Labrador, in northeastern Canada and southwest Greenland.

Labrys axe

The Da Vinci Code

The labrys or double-headed axe has been found in many mythologies, including Minoan Crete, the Neolithic period, Europe, India, Egypt,

Asia, and Africa. It is used primarily in matriarchal societies as a weapon and a harvesting tool, and represents female power, community, and self-sufficiency. As such, the labrys is often used as a lesbian and feminist symbol.

Large Hadron Collider

Angels & Demons

The Large Hadron Collider (LHC) is a particle accelerator and collider at CERN (see CERN) that is in a circular tunnel about 100 meters underground and 27 kilometers in circumference. The purpose of the LHC is to produce enormously high concentrations of energy in a minute space to resemble the state of the universe close to the Big Bang. It is intended to answer questions in physics such as what mass is, why elementary particles have different masses, what dark matter is, if there are extra dimensions, etc.

Last Judgment

Angels & Demons

At Pope Clement VIII's request, Michelangelo started painting the *Last Judgment* fresco at the rear of the Sistine Chapel in 1534 and finished in 1541. The painting depicts the Day of Judgment, showing the resurrection of the dead with the saved rising to heaven and the sinners being conveyed to hell by Charon, the mythological ferryman who rowed the dead across the River Styx into the underworld. Strangely enough, Michelangelo included his self-portrait in the fresco as the flayed skin of one of the condemned.

The Last Judgment was Michelangelo's most controversial work. Though art lovers considered it a masterpiece for its artistry, conservative churchmen denounced it as obscene for its nudity. A censorship campaign was mounted to have the fresco destroyed, but the pope resisted and it was saved but concealed by draperies. After Michelangelo died, a law was issued to conceal genitals in art, so Daniele da Volterra, one of Michelangelo's apprentices, painted perizomas (a sort of loincloth) over the genitals. However, an uncensored copy of the original, by Marcello Venusti, is now in Naples, at the Capodimonte Museum.

Last Supper, The

The Da Vinci Code

The painting of *The Last Supper* by Leonardo Da Vinci (see Leonardo Da Vinci) represents Jesus's supper with his apostles on the night before his Crucifixion, the basis for the Christian sacrament of Holy Communion, or the Eucharist. It was painted onto the walls of the dining hall at the Dominican Convent of Santa Maria delle Grazie near Milan for Leonardo's patron Duke Lodovico Sforza. It took the artist from 1495 to 1498 to paint *The Last Supper*, and when the prior of the convent complained about the lengthy process, Da Vinci is said to have bought additional time by threatening to paint the prior as Judas.

Though *The Last Supper* is often called a fresco, in rendering it Leonardo did not use the *buon fresco* (Italian for "really fresh") technique of painting on wet lime plaster that bonds the painting to the wall. Fresco painting limited the color palette and didn't allow for changes or retouching once it had dried. Instead, Leonardo experimented with *in secco* (Italian for "on dry surface") painting using tempera (egg yolk and vinegar) and oils on dry plaster.

Unfortunately, the humidity combined with the medium he used meant that the painting began deteriorating within twenty years. By 1556 it had so deteriorated that the figures were unrecognizable, and a doorway was cut through it in 1652, then later bricked up. A number of failed restorations were attempted over the next three hundred years, but often damaged the painting or diverted from Leonardo's original vision.

The final restoration, which took over twenty years, was finished in 1999 by Pinin Brambilla Barcilon. The refectory was converted to a sealed, climate-controlled environment and restorers used scientific techniques and study of the original cartoons preserved in the Royal Library at Windsor Castle to determine the painting's original form. The areas deemed unrestorable were repainted in subdued watercolor tones to indicate they were not original work. This restoration generated considerable controversy because some art critics claim that the colors are now too bright and that some facial shapes have been changed.

Though Dan Brown and others have suggested that the person to Jesus's right in the painting is Mary Magdalene, others believe it is the apostle John, who is usually portrayed as beardless with a feminine appearance.

Le Bourget

The Da Vinci Code

Le Bourget, from where Sir Leigh Teabing flies out of France, is a suburb of Paris and the site of Le Bourget airport. Charles Lindbergh landed here in 1927 after his transatlantic flight.

Learjet 60

Digital Fortress

The largest model in the Learjet family, the Learjet 60 first flew in June 1991 as an experimental model, and was formally certified in January 1993. The midsize luxury jet has a number of possible cabin arrangements, and requires a crew of two with room for six to ten passengers, depending on cabin layout. The plane is roughly 55 feet long and has a wingspan of roughly 44 feet. Its cruising speed is 515 miles per hour, and its maximum ceiling for flight is 51,000 feet. It has the range to go cross-country—it can travel 2,800 miles nonstop.

The model's high price tag keeps its numbers small, and the planes are generally found in the hands of Fortune 500 business moguls, high-end air charter services, and the occasional rock star or movie A-lister. A ten-year-old used Learjet 60, to give an idea of the general cost to buy this plane, starts at over six million dollars. New versions have no set and final price, but the base price of over ten million generally climbs astronomically as prospective purchasers customize the interior.

The United States government demonstrated an unusual measure of common-sense frugality in 2002: rather than buying a whole Lear 60, it purchased only a fractional share in one, roughly equal to 450 hours of flight time per year, for use by NASA. Apparently even pork-barrel political considerations balk at paying for a whole Learjet 60. David Becker's trip on such a plane indicates the high priority the government placed on his mission.

Lemaître, Georges

Angels & Demons

Georges Henri Lemaître (1894–1966) was a Belgian astrophysicist, mathematician, and Catholic priest. As a lecturer of astrophysics at the University of Louvain in 1927, he proposed a theory of the origin of the universe to help link Einstein's theory of relativity to evidence of an expanding universe. Though Lemaître described his theory as "the Cosmic Egg exploding at the moment of the creation," Fred Hoyle coined it the Big Bang theory, and that name stuck.

Albert Einstein originally refused to accept the idea of an expanding universe because it strongly resembled the Christian dogma of creation, though Lemaître tried to separate science from faith. However, in 1933, Einstein applauded the Belgian's theory at a number of seminars in California and said, "This is the most beautiful and satisfactory explanation of creation to which I have ever listened." Indeed, Einstein, along with Charles de la Vallée-Poussin and Alexandre de Hemptinne, recommended Lemaître for the Francqui Prize, the highest Belgian scientific distinction, which he received in 1934 from King Léopold III.

Lemaître died in 1966 shortly after learning that cosmic microwave background radiation had been discovered, which proved his theory about the birth of the universe.

Leonardo Da Vinci

Angels & Demons and *The Da Vinci Code*

Leonardo Da Vinci (1452–1519) was an Italian Renaissance man with many talents in many fields, including painting, sculpture, music, architecture, engineering, geology, hydraulics, anatomy, geometry, and the military arts. Best known for his paintings the *Mona Lisa* and *The Last*

Supper, he is generally referred to as Leonardo rather than da Vinci, because his name means Leonardo from Vinci.

He made many important scientific discoveries during his lifetime, yet never published his ideas, preferring to write his notebook entries and diaries in a mirror script that kept his work from being known until many years after his death. Some of these discoveries included inventions that anticipated modern technology, such as parachutes and flying machines that weren't constructed until the nineteenth and twentieth centuries.

Leonardo Da Vinci International Airport

Angels & Demons and *The Da Vinci Code*

The Leonardo Da Vinci International Airport lies sixteen miles southwest of Rome, at Fiumicino, and is also known as Fiumicino International Airport. Completely nonsmoking, it has an ongoing rivalry with Milan's Malpensa International Airport as each strives to become the chief international gateway into Italy.

Les Demoiselles d'Avignon

The Da Vinci Code

Les Demoiselles d'Avignon, by Pablo Picasso, is a cubist painting depicting five prostitutes in a brothel. Completed in 1907, *Les Demoiselles* was a radical departure from prevailing artistic ideas of the times and is considered the most significant milestone in the development of modern art. The painting was acquired in 1939 by the Museum of Modern Art in New York City, where it now hangs.

Letter to the Grand Duchess Christina

Angels & Demons

In 1613, a dinner party was hosted by Christina, the Grand Duchess of Tuscany, whose deceased husband, the Grand Duke, had appointed Galileo (see Galilei, Galileo) to the professorship of mathematics at the

University of Pisa in 1588. At the dinner, Cosimo Boscaglia, a professor of philosophy, argued against the heliocentric theory of the Earth revolving around the sun, since it didn't agree with the Bible. Curious, the Grand Duchess asked Benedetto Castelli, a Benedictine monk and Galileo's former student, about it. Castelli subsequently wrote to Galileo of this conversation, and Galileo responded with a long letter detailing his position on the relation between science and the Bible.

Galileo revised and expanded the letter in 1615, when it became known as the *Letter to the Grand Duchess Christina*. It was first circulated in manuscript form, then printed after the Inquisition condemned Galileo for heresy. As with all of Galileo's works, it was placed on the *Index of Prohibited Books* by the Catholic Church.

Leukotriene

Angels & Demons

Though Dan Brown implies that leukotriene is a drug that Kohler uses to help him breathe again, leukotriene is actually a type of chemical involved in inflammation that constricts the airways of asthma sufferers. It is more likely that Kohler used a leukotriene modifier or inhibitor to reduce the inflammatory response.

Libation tubes

Angels & Demons

Libation tubes were tubes leading from ground level down into the grave that allowed people to give libations (an offering of food or drink) to the deceased. The pagan practice originated in the Mediterranean cultures and was widespread among the Romans and in other parts of Europe, though mostly died out a couple of centuries after Christianity took root.

The practice still survives in revised form in Europe and Mexico, where families have picnics near family gravesites on The Day of the Dead or All Saints' Day, to let the dead know they have not been forgotten.

Lincoln Bedroom

Deception Point

The Lincoln Bedroom in the White House was originally part of the second-floor private quarters, used as a study and cabinet room by American presidents between 1830 and 1902. President Abraham Lincoln used the room to chart the progress of the Civil War and signed the Emancipation Proclamation there as well.

In 1902, the second-floor offices were moved to the West Wing during the Roosevelt renovation and the room became a bedroom. The room received its current name in 1945 when President and Mrs. Truman moved a large bed (eight feet long by six feet wide) made of carved rosewood there, which had been originally purchased by Mary Todd Lincoln for the Prince of Wales room.

Though President Lincoln never used it himself, his son Willie died in the bed of typhoid fever at age eleven, in 1862. Ever since, numerous sightings of Abraham Lincoln's ghost in the room have been reported by White House guests.

The most often-requested guest room for visitors to the White House, the Lincoln Bedroom was recently renovated by First Lady Laura Bush, who worked in concert with the Committee for the Preservation of the White House and White House curator William Allman to decorate it in Victorian splendor.

Logan Airport

Angels & Demons

Logan Airport is located in East Boston, Massachusetts, and was originally called Boston Airport when it opened in 1923. It was renamed Lieutenant General Edward Lawrence Logan International Airport in 1956, after a Spanish-American War hero. It is the nation's nineteenth-busiest and the world's thirty-fifth busiest, encompassing approximately 2,400 acres—1,800 of those landfill in Boston Harbor.

This is the airport the fictional Langdon uses to fly out of, and is also the departure point of American Airlines Flight 11 and United Airlines

Flight 175, which crashed into the World Trade Center towers in the September 11, 2001, terrorist attack.

LoJack

The Da Vinci Code

The LoJack Corporation provides products and services for locating, tracking, and recovering stolen vehicles. The company hides a transmitter in the vehicle, and when it is reported as stolen, a radio signal activates the transmitter. The LoJack Police Tracking Computer then receives the signal and leads the police to the vehicle. The company reports that approximately 90 percent of stolen vehicles installed with LoJack are recovered—more than 150,000 vehicles to date.

Long-range stun guns

Angels & Demons

Most commercial stun guns work at close quarters and target one person at a time. Long-range stun guns, developed for the police and military for nonlethal crowd control, can incapacitate many people at a greater distance by sweeping a beam of electricity across them. The guns will also interfere with electronic ignition systems and stop vehicles.

To do this, an electrically conductive path must be created between a gun and a target without using wires. Some long-range stun guns that have been developed or are still in development squirt tiny conductive fibers, ionized gas or plasma, or conductive liquid through the air at the victim.

Louvre museum

The Da Vinci Code

The Louvre museum (Musée du Louvre) is one of the largest and most famous art museums in the world. It is situated in the center of Paris, between the Seine river and the Rue de Rivoli.

The building was originally a royal fortress built by Philippe II in 1190. In the fourteenth century, Charles V installed his private library in one of the towers and turned the Louvre into a palace. François I reworked the old citadel in 1528, then commissioned Pierre Lescot to renovate it and design a new facade in 1546. Lescot's renaissance design made the building the primary royal palace where the royal family stayed when in Paris. François I later dispersed Charles V's library to form the basis of the Bibliothèque Nationale and began a new collection of art with twelve paintings from Italy, including works by Titian, Raphael, and Leonardo Da Vinci, the most famous being the *Mona Lisa*.

In 1564, Catherine de Medici commissioned Philibert Delorme to connect her pleasure palace at the Tuileries to the Louvre by a long gallery. In 1606, Henry IV added the Grande Gallery, more than a quarter of a mile long and one hundred feet wide, to further connect the two palaces. He treated it as a huge royal city, hosting royal servants and nobles as well as the hundreds of artists and craftsmen he invited to live and work on the building's lower floors—a tradition which continued for two hundred years until Napoleon ended it.

Louis XIII followed in his father's footsteps and increased the Louvre by four times its size. Jacques Lemercier expanded Lescot's designs in 1624, and under Louis XIV, the Petite Gallery was renovated, the magnificent colonnade and eastern wing were added, the size of the Louvre doubled, and a facade was added.

But in 1682, Louis XIV chose to leave the Louvre where he felt surrounded by the crowd, and moved his court to Versailles where he felt more at ease. The art collection at the Louvre was strictly for the private pleasure of the court until 1793, when the Grande Gallery of the Louvre was officially opened to the public.

Napoleon I's conquests added to its collections, though many were returned after his downfall. The museum became the property of the State in 1848, Napoleon III added a new wing in 1857, and work continued until 1876.

Work to expand the Louvre underground was begun in 1984 and completed in 1993, opening the north wing, which used to house government offices, and covering over some courtyards. The famous glass pyramid designed by I.M. Pei was constructed in 1989, and sits atop the entrance to the underground space.

Among the Louvre's thousands of priceless works of art are the *Mona Lisa*, *Venus de Milo*, *Whistler's Mother*, and the *Winged Victory of Samothrace*. It also houses works by artists such as Fragonard, Rembrandt, Rubens, Titian, and Poussin, and has other exhibits covering archeology, history, architecture, and a large furniture collection.

Lymphoma

Deception Point

In Dan Brown's novel, Michael's wife died of lymphoma, a malignant tumorous cancer of the lymph nodes. Lymphoma is one of the four major types of cancer and accounts for about five percent of all cancer cases in the United States. Hodgkin's disease, a type of lymphoma, accounts for less than one percent.

Lyonnais

The Da Vinci Code

Lyonnais, where Teabing says Rémy is from, is an historical region and former province of east central France, located in the modern-day Rhône département. It was a county during medieval times and became part of the French royal domain circa 1307 when Phillipe IV acquired it. Lyonnais included the region around Lyons, the former counties of Forez and Beaujolais that were acquired in 1531, and the tiny dependency of Franc-Lyonnais.

Madonna of the Rocks, The

The Da Vinci Code

There is some controversy over whether *The Madonna of the Rocks* or *The Virgin of the Rocks* (which is very similar) came first. However, the consensus seems to be that *The Madonna of the Rocks* oil painting that hangs in the Louvre was painted by Leonardo Da Vinci from 1483 to 1486. Both paintings illustrate the infant Jesus meeting John the Baptist, who is in the care of the angel Uriel.

In April 1483, the Confraternity of the Immaculate Conception commissioned Leonardo to do a painting that was to be the centerpiece of a three-panel altarpiece for the chapel of the Immacolata at the church of San Francesco Grande in Milan. The de Predis brothers were commissioned to complete the altar and the two side panels, and Giacomo del Maino was commissioned to carve the framework. The monks' contract was very precise in detailing exactly what they wanted.

However, Leonardo failed to deliver the images they expected and did not meet their short deadline. This resulted in lengthy lawsuits, eventually settled in 1506, determining that the work was unfinished, which means Leonardo was not paid for *The Madonna of the Rocks* but ownership of the work reverted to him. He agreed to do a second work for half the additional payment he was supposed to get for the first painting. This second painting, on wood, was *The Virgin of the Rocks*, and was delivered in August 1508.

The controversy over which painting came first, the Virgin or the Madonna arises from the fact that *The Virgin of the Rocks* can be traced from its origins in Milan to the present day in London, but *The Madonna of the Rocks* is not as well documented. However, experts have examined both paintings and believe (based on the style of painting and the depiction of nature) that *The Madonna of the Rocks* is by Leonardo, but that *The Virgin of the Rocks* is not. Some speculate that de Predis completed this painting under Leonardo's direction.

Magdalene Diaries

The Da Vinci Code

The Magdalene Diaries purport to be Mary Magdalene's personal account of her relationship with Jesus, and Dan Brown says they are listed as part of the Templars' treasure. There is no evidence showing that these diaries actually exist outside anyone's imagination, though there is a novel by the same name.

Magma dome

Deception Point

Magma is what the molten rock of a volcano is called when it is still underground. A magma dome is formed when magma pushes its way toward the surface and causes the land to bulge under a great deal of pressure. When the surface collapses, magma flows onto the surface and is called lava. When a magma dome collapses under water, the massive pressure generates a great deal of steam very quickly, setting off an explosion like a pressure cooker exploding.

Málaga

Digital Fortress

Málaga is a city of southern Spain, in Andalusia, northeast of Gibraltar on the Guadalmedina River and the Costa del Sol. Founded by Phoenicians in the twelfth century BC, the city passed to the Carthaginians, Romans, Visigoths, and Moors (after 711). It was used from the thirteenth century on as a seaport of the Moorish kingdom of Granada, until it was conquered by Ferdinand and Isabella's troops in 1487. Its exports are olives, almonds, dried fruits, Málaga wine, and iron ore.

Manurhin MR-93

The Da Vinci Code

The Manurhin MR-93 is a French revolver manufactured by Manufacture du Haut Rhin (Manurhin), which has produced handguns since the end of World War II. After the war's conclusion, the French police force had poor handguns that had a tendency to over penetrate and injure or kill innocent victims.

Manurhin and the police collaborated on a new revolver at the beginning of the 1970s that would have high quality, great accuracy, and robustness. This resulted in the design of the MR-73, but it was too expensive to make. Manurhin worked with Ruger to produce a new revolver, the MR-88, then later produced a new revolver on its own: the

MR-93. Released in 1993, it is in common use by French and Swiss police forces.

Map Room

Deception Point

John L. McCrea, a naval aide to President Franklin D. Roosevelt, set up the White House Map Room. It was used by Roosevelt as a situation room to follow the course of World War II. The last situation map he used, from April 3, 1945, hangs above the mantel. Decorated in the Chippendale style, the Map Room now serves as a private meeting room for the president or the first lady.

This is also the room from which President Clinton spoke to the American people via live broadcast concerning charges of infidelity and perjury against him, on August 17, 1998.

Mark I

Digital Fortress

The IBM ASCC, the Automatic Sequence Controlled Calculator, called the Mark I, was the first large-scale fully automatic digital computer in the United States. Designed by professor Howard Aiken, it was built by IBM and installed at Harvard University in 1944.

The electromechanical machine strung 78 adding machines together and worked in decimal arithmetic, not binary, to perform three additions or subtractions per second. Made of 765,000 components, it was 51 feet long, 8 feet high, 2 feet deep, and weighed 5 tons. It used paper tape for input and typewriters for output, and could store 72 numbers. My, how things have changed!

Marseilles

The Da Vinci Code

The city of Marseilles is in southeast France on the Gulf of Lyons, on an arm of the Mediterranean Sea, west-northwest of Toulon. The oldest

French city, it was settled by Phocaean Greeks from Asia Minor, circa 600 BC, and overrun by barbarian tribes in the fifth and sixth centuries AD. Marseilles was taken by Charles I of Anjou in the thirteenth century, then bequeathed to the French Crown in 1481. Today it is a major seaport and industrial city where flour, vegetable oil, soap, cement, sugar, sulfur, chemicals, and processed foods are produced.

Mary Magdalene

The Da Vinci Code

Mary Magdalene's past is shrouded in controversy. The New Testament portrays her as the woman Jesus cured of evil spirits, as a watcher at the Cross, as an attendant at Christ's burial, and as one of those who found his tomb empty. Tradition in the Catholic church as early as the third century also identified Mary Magdalene as the repentant prostitute who washed the feet of Jesus, and as Mary of Bethany, the sister of Martha and Lazarus. Though no assertion is made in the New Testament that Mary Magdalene was unchaste, this idea (complicated by the fact that there were so many Marys) was put forth by the early church fathers of the third and fourth centuries and is still believed by many Catholics today. Indeed, in Catholic representations of the crucifixion, Mary Magdalene is often left out or replaced by John.

Others believe that Mary Magdalene was a leader of the early Church and perhaps even the unidentified "disciple whom Jesus loved," to whom the fourth gospel, commonly called the Gospel of John, is attributed. Early Christian Gnostic writings show a power struggle between Mary and the apostle Peter, who was appalled that Mary thought she had the authority to teach as if she were one of the apostles. Instead he promoted the hierarchical, male, formal authority that is an integral part of the Catholic church today. Since Peter obviously won the power struggle, some believe that the Catholic church simply suppressed any mention of Mary Magdalene's authority. Indeed, since the papacy traces itself back to Peter, it was in the best interests of the Catholic church to do so.

Some modern writers also believe that Mary Magdalene was the wife of Jesus, and that this fact was omitted by revisionist editors of the gospels. To support their argument, they use Gnostic writings like the ones mentioned above, which show Mary Magdalene as being closer to Jesus than any other disciple. In addition, they point to the fact that it was unusual for Jewish males of Jesus's time to be unmarried, especially rabbis (teachers) like Jesus. They hold that Mary Magdalene fled to France with the Holy Grail, which was not a cup but Jesus's bloodline in the form of a child, Sarah.

Detractors of this theory say there is no ancient document that claims Mary Magdalene to be Jesus's wife, and that Judaism of that time was diverse and the role of the rabbi wasn't uniform. In any case, none of this can be proven one way or the other.

Mary Magdalene is considered a saint by Roman Catholic, Eastern Orthodox, and Anglican churches.

Mary, Queen of Scots

The Da Vinci Code

Mary, Queen of Scots, also known as Mary I of Scotland or Mary Stuart (1542–1587), was Queen of Scotland from 1542 to 1567. She was forced to abdicate in favor of her son, James VI of Scotland, during the Scottish Reformation. After fleeing to England in 1568, she was imprisoned at Chartley Hall by her cousin, Queen Elizabeth I, who feared Mary's strong claim to the English throne, and her Catholicism. Catholics considered Mary the rightful heir, and the Church of England and Parliament had declared Elizabeth illegitimate. Elizabeth's claim to the throne depended solely on her father's will, which many believed invalid.

Elizabeth's ministers tried to persuade her to have Mary killed, but Elizabeth could not bring herself to do so. To further protect Elizabeth, her Privy Council signed a "Bond of Association" in 1584, which required that if anyone plotted against Elizabeth on behalf of any claimant to the throne, that claimant would be excluded from the succession and put to death . . . even if he or she was ignorant of the plot. When the bond was put into law the following year, it required that the claimant be privy to the plot.

After being held captive for eighteen years, Mary exchanged letters with Anthony Babington, a devout Catholic who wanted to free Mary and murder Elizabeth. They used a simple cipher with symbols to replace letters and words, putting the letter in the bung of a beer barrel to sneak it past Mary's guards. His conscience chiding him for plotting to kill a monarch, Babington wrote to Mary to get her approval for the assassination before it was attempted. She didn't grant it one way or the other, leaving it up to his discretion, but stressed that a rescue attempt would be welcome and rewarded.

However, Sir Francis Walsingham, Elizabeth's secretary of state and chief of espionage, learned of the plot and contrived to use a double agent to intercept the letters. His chief code breaker was able to decipher the correspondence, and they made alterations to Mary's letter to Babington, forging a postscript saying that she offered to take an active part in the assassination.

This allowed Walsingham to try Mary for sedition. Though the English court had no jurisdiction over her, she attended the trial to assert her innocence in plotting to kill Elizabeth, admitting only to escape attempts and a promise to reward her rescuers. Though Mary's original letter wasn't produced in evidence, a copy was read at the trial. The result was a foregone conclusion. The court illegally convicted her, and she was beheaded at Fotheringay in 1587. Ironically, Elizabeth eventually recognized Mary's son as her heir, and James VI of Scotland became James I of England.

Maupassant, Guy de

Angels & Demons

Henri René Albert Guy de Maupassant (1850–1893) was a popular nineteenth-century French novelist and short-story writer from an ancient Norman family. A protégé of Gustave Flaubert, he crafted stories characterized by their realism, simplicity, and objectivity. Guy de Maupassant wrote over three hundred short stories, as well as novels, plays, and travel sketches during his lifetime, and had a tremendous influence on European literature.

Having contracted syphilis early in life, he spent his last years in solitude with a fear of death and persecution, slowly going mad. He died in 1893 in a sanitarium.

It is said that after viewing Michelangelo's *Last Judgment,* de Maupassant quipped, "It looks like a canvas of a fair, painted for a wrestling booth by an ignorant coal heaver."

Mecca

Angels & Demons

A city in western Saudi Arabia near the coast of the Red Sea, Mecca is the birthplace of Muhammad the Prophet in 570 AD. It is the holiest city of Islam and only Muslims are allowed to reside there. Muslims face in the direction of Mecca when they pray, and are expected to embark on a pilgrimage to Mecca—the hajj—at least once in their lives. Over two and a half million pilgrims visit Mecca during the annual hajj.

The Hegira, Muhammad's flight from Mecca in 622, was the beginning of the rise of Islam. He returned shortly thereafter to recapture the city and it has had a turbulent history ever since.

Megaplume

Deception Point

A megaplume is much like an underwater cyclone, with warm water spinning slower than a tornado, but soaring up to several thousand feet off the sea floor. They can be twelve miles across and travel hundreds of miles over several months.

Megaplumes were first discovered in 1986 when a research ship off the Juan de Fuca Ridge was lucky enough to happen upon one about a week after its first eruption. The phenomenom interests researchers because it stirs up huge amounts of the ocean floor, moves sea animals and plant life over vast distances, and carries food to animals in shallow water. Researchers have different opinions about what exactly causes a megaplume, though they know it comes from an underwater volcano eruption. Some see the megaplume erupting from the sea floor like the release of a pressure cooker, others as a sort of hot plate heating the water above.

Studies are still ongoing, though they aren't easy to conduct since it is difficult to predict when and where they will occur, but they are changing the way we understand the energy of the oceans.

Menwith Hill, England

Deception Point

The 560-acre Menwith Hill base, eight miles northwest of Harrogate, in North Yorkshire, England, is the largest electronic monitoring station in the world. Run by the United States National Security Agency (NSA), it is one of a global network of Signals Intelligence bases that monitor the world's communications using high-altitude signals intelligence satellites.

The base, now jointly operated with the United Kingdom's Government Communications Headquarters (GCHQ), was established in 1956 by the US Army Security Agency (ASA), which ran it until it was turned over to the NSA in 1966. Menwith Hill originally focused on monitoring international cable and microwave communications passing through Britain. It now has the capability to sift through satellite, electronic, telephone, and cable communications to extract information at the rate of two million intercepts per hour.

Because of its nature, Menwith Hill is the regular target of international protesters and saboteurs, many of whom consider it to be the "Area 51" of the UK.

Meridian

The Da Vinci Code

A meridian is an imaginary circle on the Earth's surface, passing through the North and South geographic poles. All points on the same meridian have the same longitude.

The prime meridian is the zero meridian used as a reference line from which all other longitudes are measured. It currently passes through the original site of the Royal Observatory in Greenwich, England, though that wasn't always the case.

Until 1871, each town or country used its own system of time measurement. With the expansion of railway and communications networks during the 1850s and 1860s, it became necessary to set an international time standard and there were several attempts to do so. The first International Geographical Congress took place at Antwerp in 1871 and expressed the need for all nations' passage charts to match. Most of them agreed on making Greenwich the prime meridian and asked that it be compulsory within fifteen years. A second congress took place in Rome but there was no consensus, though France did say that if the United Kingdom accepted the metric system, it would accept Greenwich as the prime meridian.

At the request of United States President Chester A. Arthur, an International Meridian Conference was convened in Washington, D.C., in 1884, with 41 delegates from 25 nations. In a vote of 22 to 1 (the Dominican Republic voted against and France and Brazil abstained), they agreed to adopt Greenwich as the prime meridian. They came to this conclusion because 72 percent of the world's commerce depended on sea charts, which used Greenwich as the prime meridian, so this standard would be advantageous to the largest number of people. However, Algeria, a French dependent, objected to the phrase "Greenwich Mean Time" and proposed "Paris Mean Time diminished by 9:21 seconds" instead. The French did not adopt the Greenwich meridian until 1911.

The International Date Line is on the opposite side of the world from the Prime Meridian.

Meridian medallions

The Da Vinci Code

The meridian medallions in Paris mark the imaginary meridian line running North-South through Paris (now longitude 2°20 east). In 1667, the median line of the Observatory of Paris defined the meridian of Paris, and was used by everyone in France from 1667 until 1884 when the world powers agreed upon Greenwich as the prime meridian (see Meridian). France abstained at the vote, and continued to keep its own Paris meridian as the prime meridian until 1911 for timekeeping purposes and until 1914 for navigation.

François Arago was director of the Paris Observatory at the height of the meridian issue and the French honored him with a statue which once stood where the meridian intersects the boulevard Arago. However, it was melted down during World War II, so in 1994, the Arago Association, the Ministry of Culture, and the city of Paris commissioned Dutch conceptual artist Jean Dibbets to create a new memorial. He used 135 bronze plaques, each about five inches in diameter and marked with the name Arago plus north and south pointers, and set them in the ground to mark the imaginary meridian line across Paris.

Interestingly enough, as part of its millennium celebration, France began planting a line of a thousand trees across the country to mark the Paris meridian. Each tree was to represent one year of the millennium, and collectively they were called the Green Meridian. However, more than 10,000 trees have been planted on the line to date, and on Bastille Day, July 14, 2000, the French were invited to a giant picnic all along the line, where they celebrated the national holiday, the millennium, and the Paris meridian.

Merovingians

The Da Vinci Code

A dynasty of Frankish kings that ruled from circa 450 to 751, the Merovingians originated with Merovech (or Merovée, Meroveus, or Merovius), leader of the Salian Franks in the mid-fifth century, whom legend says was the son of two fathers. When his pregnant mother went swimming in the ocean, she was raped by a "Quinotaur," a mysterious aquatic creature that supposedly endowed Merovech with magical powers. Known as the long-haired sorcerer kings, the Merovingians were believed to have miraculous powers (primarily invested in their long hair which they were forbidden to cut), and royal blood credited with a divine nature.

The bloodline was brought to prominence by Clovis I, who was dubbed the New Constantine, and presided over a unified empire—the Holy Roman Empire—establishing the capital of France in Paris. In 496, the Catholic Church officially bound itself indissolubly to his bloodline in perpetuity. He then expanded the Frankish kingdom to encompass most of France and much of Germany. When Clovis died in 511, his empire was divided, according to Merovingian custom, among his four sons, but was still thought of as a single realm ruled collectively by several kings.

This practice led to infighting among the Merovingians, and by the seventh century the kings had ceased to wield effective political authority. They had become symbolic figures, allotting more and more administration to a powerful household official called the Mayor of the Palace, an office that became hereditary in the Carolingian family. Soon the mayors were the real military and political leaders of the Frankish kingdom.

Clovis's direct descendant, Sigisbert III, died in 565, and the nobles ordered the death of his five-year-old son, Dagobert II. However, he was spirited away, then returned in 676 to take the throne, from where he curbed the expansion of the Church.

Dagobert II was assassinated three years later, and many believe that his son was killed with him, so that was the end of his line. After Dagobert II's assassination, the Church did everything it could to remove him from history and deny that he ever existed.

In 751, Mayor of the Palace Pepin III, who carried the real military and political power, sought the support of the nobles and the Church to sanction his coronation in exchange for military assistance. The pope betrayed the Church's pact with Clovis and condoned Pepin III's usurpation of the throne, thereby assuming the Church's prerogative of king-making, by creating the coronation and anointment ceremonies to confer divine grace upon a ruler who did not inherit it through a royal bloodline.

Endorsed by Rome, Pepin III took the throne, thereby inaugurating the Carolingian dynasty. He deposed the last vestige of Merovingian royalty, Childeric III, cut off his sacred hair, and had him confined to a monastery.

Though many believe Childeric III was the last surviving member of the Merovingian dynasty, others say that Dagobert's three-year-old son, Sigisbert IV, survived and was smuggled out of the country to the village of Rennes-le-Château, in Southern France. Sigisbert assumed the name of "the Plant-Ard" (which evolved into the surname Plantard) and the title of the Count of Razes. He passed the bloodline down to Guillem de Gellone, whose father had been recognized as belonging to the House of David, and the line continued, culminating at one point in Godefroi de Bouillon (see de Bouillon, Godefroi).

Those who believe that inheritors of the Merovingian bloodline are direct descendants of a marriage between Jesus Christ and Mary Magdalene believe that the Holy Grail Mary brought to France was Christ's bloodline in the form of their child. To support their hypothesis connecting the Merovingians to this line, they point to the divine nature of the Merovingian bloodline, the legend of Merovech's birth which symbolized the combining of two dynasties (including Jesus's symbol of the fish), the pope's bond with the bloodline of Clovis, the family's association with the Grail family, and their descent from the House of David, among other things.

MH-60G PaveHawk Helicopter

Deception Point

The Sikorsky MH-60G Pave Hawk twin-engine medium-lift helicopters are an upgrade of the Black Hawk helicopters and are used by the United States Air Force, National Guard, and Air Force Reserve to perform special operations and search-and-rescue missions worldwide. The helicopters' primary wartime missions are infiltration, exfiltration, and resupply of special operations forces in day, night, or marginal weather conditions for deep insertion behind enemy lines. During Desert Storm, Pave Hawks provided combat recovery in Iraq, Saudi Arabia, Kuwait, and the Persian Gulf, as well as emergency evacuation for United States Navy SEAL teams penetrating the Kuwait coast before the invasion.

Michelangelo

Angels & Demons and The Da Vinci Code

Michelangelo Buonarroti, known simply as Michelangelo (1475–1564), was an Italian sculptor, architect, painter, and poet in the period known as the High Renaissance. Considered one of the greatest masters in the history of European art, Michelangelo worked primarily for the Catholic church. His best-known works include the statue of the Biblical figure David in Florence, the *Pietà*, the ceiling of the Sistine Chapel (commissioned by Pope Julius II), the fresco of *The Last Judgment* for the Sistine Chapel, his sculpture of *Moses* on Julius's tomb, and the dome of St. Peter's Basilica. Though censorship followed Michelangelo for his choice in painting and sculpting nudes, his influence in painting, sculpture, and architecture has been immense.

Micro Electro Mechanical Systems (MEMS)

Deception Point

Microelectromechanical systems, or MEMS, are tiny mechanical devices that are built onto semiconductor chips and generally range in size from a micrometer (a millionth of a meter) to a millimeter (thousandth of a meter). Common applications include sensors, light reflectors, optical switching, ink jet print heads, accelerometers for airbag deployment in collisions, car tire pressure sensors, disposable blood pressure sensors, pacemakers, and games.

MEMS and nanotechnology, though both deal with microminiaturized objects, differ. MEMS deals with devices that are measured in micrometers, whereas nanotechnology deals with manipulating atoms at the nanometer level.

Microbot

Deception Point

Microbots are constructed using micromechanics—the microminiaturization of mechanical devices (gears, motors, rotors, valves, etc.) less than one millimeter across—and are operated by microcontrollers. Though the microcontroller is very portable and the microbot is very mobile, the latter has limited computing power. However, with the advent of wireless connections, the microbot's processing capacity has risen, so it can complete more complex tasks.

Microcosm, Inc.

Deception Point

Dan Brown's book mentions Microcosm, Inc. as one of the private aero-space companies that offered bribes to Senator Sexton to put space exploration in the hands of the private sector. Microcosm, Inc., estab-lished in 1984, specializes in space mission analysis and design, space-craft orbit attitude control systems, space-related software for autonomous navigation, and low-cost launch vehicles.

Millennium Eye

The Da Vinci Code

The Millennium Eye, or the British Airways London Eye, is a giant Ferris wheel on the South Bank of the River Thames in London offering a spectacular view of the city. It was opened in 1999, but didn't begin operation until 2000. Designed by architects David Marks and Julia Barfield, the wheel stands 443 feet high and carries 32 sealed, air-conditioned passenger capsules. It rotates very slowly, allowing passengers to walk on and off at ground level, so it usually doesn't stop.

A major landmark and tourist attraction, the Millennium Eye is currently listed in the Guinness Book of Records as the tallest obser-vation wheel in the world. But it may not keep that distinction for long—plans are in the works to build larger ones in Las Vegas and Shanghai.

Milne Glacier

Deception Point

The Milne Glacier is a huge mass of ice slowly flowing over Ellesmere Island in northern Canada, formed from compacted snow. It appears that the Milne Glacier is a surging glacier, advancing in surges outward and downward by the force of gravity and its accumulated mass, though it moves more slowly than other glaciers of the same type.

Milne Ice Shelf

Deception Point

The Milne Ice Shelf is the second-largest of the ice shelves on Ellesmere Island in northern Canada. It is a thick, floating platform of ice that forms where the Milne Glacier flows down to the coastline and onto the ocean surface. The boundary between the two is called the grounding line. An ice shelf will flow out over the water for years or decades before losing mass due to ice calving (see ice calving).

Milton, John

The Da Vinci Code and *Angels & Demons*

John Milton (1608–1674) was an English poet and scholar best known for the epic blank-verse poem *Paradise Lost*, an account of humanity's fall from grace, which he dictated after he went blind. He is considered one of the greatest of all English poets.

Mithras

The Da Vinci Code

Mitra or Mithra was an ancient Persian who became the principal Persian deity in the fifth century BC, the god of light and wisdom and the guardian against evil, often identified with the sun. His cult expanded through the Middle East into Europe and became a worldwide religion, where the Greeks changed his name to the masculine Mithras and altered some of his aspects. Mithras was worshipped in the Roman Empire from the first century BC to the fifth century AD and his religion was at times more widespread than Christianity.

Mithraism had many similarities to Christianity: Mithras was born of a virgin and had twelve followers with whom he shared a last sacramental meal; he sacrificed himself to redeem mankind and rose again on the third day; his birth was celebrated on December 25; his followers practiced baptism and a communion rite; and he was called "the Truth," "the Light," and "the Good Shepherd."

Some see this as evidence that Christianity evolved out of pagan myths or was combined with Mithraism to make it more palatable to the pagans. Others believe that there was no evidence that these elements were present in Mithraism prior to Christianity, saying that Mithras borrowed from Christianity. Mithraism declined rapidly in the late third century.

Möbius strip

Angels & Demons

A Möbius strip is a topological object with a continuous one-sided surface. It can be formed by taking a rectangular strip of paper, rotating one end 180 degrees, and attaching it to the other end to form a single strip. It was discovered independently by German mathematicians August Ferdinand Möbius and Johann Benedict Listing, in 1858.

Mona Lisa

Angels & Demons and The Da Vinci Code

The Mona Lisa is a famous sixteenth-century oil painting on poplar wood by Leonardo Da Vinci. Perhaps the most famous painting in art history, the portrait shows a woman looking out at the viewer with an enigmatic smile.

Leonardo began the portrait in Florence in 1503, continued work on it through 1506, then kept the painting until his death in 1519. It passed through many hands over the next three centuries, but since 1804, the Mona Lisa has resided in the Louvre museum in Paris. At some point after Leonardo's death, the painting was cut down by having part of the panel at both sides removed. It has been restored numerous times, and x-ray examinations show three versions of the Mona Lisa beneath the present one.

The Mona Lisa was stolen from the Louvre in 1911 by an employee, Vincenzo Peruggia, who walked out with it under his coat. After keeping the painting in his apartment for two years, Peruggia attempted to sell it to a Florence art dealer and was caught; it was exhibited all over Italy and returned to the Louvre in 1913.

The lower part of the painting was damaged by an acid attack in 1956, and later someone threw a stone at it. It is now displayed in a climate-controlled enclosure behind unbreakable glass and was moved to its current spot in the Louvre's Salle des États in April 2005.

The true identity of the woman pictured in the portrait remains unknown, despite intensive research by art historians. Leonardo's first biographer, Vasari, described the portrait as being of Lisa Gherardini Giocondo (Madam Lisa, or Mona Lisa), the wife of wealthy Florentine merchant Francesco del Giocondo (which is why she is known in Italy as *La Gioconda*). Others have suggested the subject was a mistress of Leonardo's; a portrait of a Florentine lady requested by Giuliano de' Medici; Isabella of Aragon, the Duchess of Milan; or even a self-portrait, since the features of the Mona Lisa and Leonardo's self-portrait are said to line up perfectly.

Mozart

The Da Vinci Code

Wolfgang Amadeus Mozart (1756–1791) was an Austrian composer, one of the greatest and most prolific in history. A child prodigy who wrote his first symphony at age eight, Mozart wrote more than 600 pieces of music in almost every genre during his thirty-five-year lifetime. Best known for *A Little Night Music*, and the operas *Don Giovanni* and *The Magic Flute*, he used phi, the golden ratio, in his music and was an acknowledged Freemason.

Mullin, Chris

Angels & Demons

Christopher John Mullin is a United Kingdom Labour politician, currently the member of Parliament for the English constituency of Sunderland South. As a member of a Parliament committee, Mullin became suspicious that Freemasons had played a part in miscarriages of justice and other major scandals such as the corrupt West Midlands Serious Crimes Squad, the John Stalker affair, and the Birmingham Six pub bombings, saying Freemasons had operated within the police as "firms within firms." He further accused Freemason police officers of promoting or defending fellow Freemasons unjustly, and judges of exonerating guilty criminals simply because they were fellow lodge members.

Mullin required the United Grand Lodge of Freemasons in England to identify which of 161 police officers and judges on his list were Freemasons. The lodge at first refused, then later complied, with the stipulation that only a select few would see it. Mullin said that 96 of the 161 names on the list were former members of the West Midlands Serious Crime Squad, which was disbanded in 1989 for corruption, and about 60 were involved with the investigation that led to the "wrongful conviction" of the Birmingham Six. At that time, the Home Affairs Select Committee called for the registration of police officers and justice officials who held membership in a Masonic lodge.

Nanotechnology

Deception Point

Nanotechnology is the science and technology of building electronic circuits and devices at the atomic and molecular level. It usually deals with devices less than 100 nanometers in size. (One nanometer is one billionth of a meter.) Nanotechnology, fabricated using chemical processes, is expected to make a significant contribution to the fields of electronics, computer storage, semiconductors, biotechnology, surgery, custom-tailored pharmaceuticals, manufacturing, and energy.

NASA

Deception Point

The National Aeronautics and Space Administration (NASA) is a civilian agency of the United States federal government responsible for international cooperation in space matters, conducting research into both civilian and military aerospace systems, and developing operational programs in the areas of space exploration, artificial satellites, rocketry, space telescopes, and observatories.

The agency's stated mission is to "understand and protect our home planet; to explore the Universe and search for life; and to inspire the next generation of explorers." NASA has four divisions: Space Flight, Space Science Programs, Aeronautics Exploration and Technology, and Tracking and Data Acquisition.

NASA came into existence after the Soviet Union launched the first man-made satellite (Sputnik 1) on October 4, 1957. Alarmed by the perceived threat to American security and technological leadership, President Dwight D. Eisenhower signed the National Aeronautics and Space Act of 1958 on July 29, 1958, establishing the National Aeronautics and Space Administration (NASA). NASA began operations on October 1, 1958, with its early programs (including the Mercury program) researching the possibility of manned spaceflight. On May 5, 1961, astronaut Alan B. Shepard Jr. became the first American in space, on February 20, 1962 and astronaut John Glenn became the first American to orbit the Earth.

NASA's installations include the Lyndon B. Johnson Space Center (Houston, Texas), the John F. Kennedy Space Center (Cape Canaveral, Florida), Dryden, Glenn, Goddard, Stennis, and NASA headquarters (Washington, D.C.).

National Medal of Science

Deception Point

The National Medal of Science, also called the Presidential Medal of Science, was established in 1959 as a United States presidential award to be given to people in science and engineering who have made special contributions to the advancement of knowledge in physics, biology, chemistry, mathematics, or engineering. In 1980, this was expanded to include the social and behavioral sciences as well. A twelve-person committee composed of scientists and engineers is appointed by the president to evaluate the nominees for the award. There have been over four hundred recipients of the medal to date.

National Reconnaissance Office (NRO)

Deception Point

The National Reconnaissance Office (NRO) is a department of the US Department of Defense (DoD), which is tasked to ensure that the United States has the technology and the spaceborne and airborne assets needed to acquire intelligence worldwide. Through research and development, acquisition, and operation of spaceborne and airborne intelligence data collection systems, NRO designs, builds, and operates the reconnaissance satellites, and coordinates the collection and analysis of information from airplane and satellite reconnaissance.

National Security Adviser

Deception Point

The assistant to the president for national security affairs, commonly referred to as the national security advisor, serves as the chief advisor to the president of the United States on national security issues and foreign policy, and serves on the National Security Council.

The National Security Council was established in 1947 under President Harry S. Truman and is chaired by the president. Besides the national security advisor, members of the committee include the vice president, the secretary of state, the secretary of the treasury, and the secretary of defense. The national security advisor position was created in 1953 under President Dwight D. Eisenhower.

Since the national security advisor is appointed by the President without confirmation by the United States senate, in theory the person in the position is not connected to politics and is therefore able to offer independent advice. The power and role of the national security advisor varies from administration to administration. In times of crisis, the national security advisor remains in the White House Situation Room, keeping the president updated on the crisis.

National Security Agency (NSA)

Digital Fortress and *Deception Point*

The National Security Agency (NSA) is an independent agency within the United States Department of Defense, headquartered in Fort Meade, Maryland, that was founded by presidential order in 1952. The largest employer of mathematicians in the country, it is responsible for the collection, decoding, and analysis of message communications, and for the encoding and security of United States government communications. It also performs cryptanalytic research and participates in the production of semiconductors and communications hardware and software when necessary.

The NSA includes the Information Systems Security department (INFOSEC), which protects classified and sensitive information on government computers; and the Central Security Service (CSS), which coordinates cryptological elements between NSA and the armed forces.

For many years the NSA was very secret and its existence wasn't even admitted by the United States government, which prompted many to say NSA stood for "No Such Agency."

Nazca sand drawings

Angels & Demons

The Nazca sand drawings are the famous lines and giant drawings etched across nearly four hundred miles of desert on the desolate Nazca plains near Peru's southern coast. Supposedly made by an ancient civilization called the Nazca that flourished from 200 BC to about 600 AD, the stylized drawings consist of geometric lines and about three hundred huge figures of various beings made of straight lines and other geometric shapes.

Since the area is one of the driest on Earth, and there is little rain or wind to erode the drawings, they have lasted hundreds of years. The desert crust is darker than the subsoil beneath it, so when the top gravel is removed, it contrasts with the color underneath, making the drawings stand out in high relief.

No one knows for sure who made them or why, but since the drawings are most visible from the air, theories include construction by ancient gods, a landing strip for returning aliens, a celestial calendar, ritual symbology to confirm the functions of various clans, or a map of underground water supplies.

Necropolis

Angels & Demons

A necropolis (city of the dead) is a cemetery or burying place, primarily used to refer to burial grounds near ancient cities. The Vatican Necropolis below Saint Peter's Basilica was excavated between 1939 and 1950 and revealed part of a Roman necropolis dating back to the second century. The pagan cemetery spread out over the Vatican hillside extended from the Via Cornelia and flanked Nero's Circus. This well-preserved underground city consists of streets in two parallel rows lined with brick mausoleums and tombs rich in decoration.

The northern section encompasses Christian tombs, including Saint Peter's. Nero crucified Saint Peter in the Circus during the first persecution of the Christians, around 67 AD, and the Christians immediately took his body and buried it in the cemetery near the Circus. Peter's immediate successor, Pope Anacletus, built a small *memoria* over the Apostle's tomb. Emperor Constantine replaced the *memoria* with an altar and built a basilica around Saint Peter's tomb in the fourth century, and the basilica's floor was raised in the sixth century, making the grave accessible by two stairways that came down into the circular hall of the crypt. The actual vault in which St. Peter's body lies (beneath the altar) has been inaccessible since the ninth century.

Neptune and Apollo

Angels & Demons

In the novel, Langdon wonders if the statue *Neptune and Apollo* represented the altar of science for water, then said it couldn't because it was in London's Victoria & Albert Museum.

It appears Dan Brown was confused, or a typographical error was made. The Bernini statue in London that he refers to is actually *Neptune and Triton* (not Apollo), sculpted in marble by Bernini in 1620 and depicting the scene in Virgil's *Aeneid* where Neptune and Triton calm the seas to ensure Aeneas's safe passage. It was commissioned by Cardinal Peretti Montalto for the garden of his Villa Montalto and was later purchased by an Englishman.

Nero

Angels & Demons

Nero Claudius Caesar (37–68 AD) was originally named Lucius Domitius Ahenobarbus and was the son of Cnaeus Domitius Ahenobarbus (consul in 32 AD) and of Agrippina the Younger, who was the great-granddaughter of Augustus Caesar. Agrippina later married Claudius I in 49 AD and persuaded him to adopt Nero.

Some believe Agrippina poisoned Claudius so her son could succeed to the throne, which he did in 54 AD when he was only seventeen. His early reign was dominated by his mother but in 55 AD, seeing her control weakening, Agrippina intrigued in favor of Claudius' son, Britannicus. Nero poisoned the boy, then later murdered his mother and his wife, Octavia.

The Great Fire of Rome in 64 AD destroyed much of the city, and many believe Nero himself ordered the fires set. The historian Suetonius wrote that Nero sang as he watched the flames from a tower, but other historians say these are merely rumors. In any case, Suetonius is the origin of the belief that Nero "fiddled while Rome burned," though the violin wasn't invented until the sixteenth century. Nero accused the Christians of setting the fires, thus setting the stage for years of their persecution by Romans.

Nero's high living, self-indulgence, whimsical cruelty, and irresponsibility alienated everyone, provoking widespread revolts, including one by his own Praetorian Guard. In 68 AD he was forced to commit suicide and was replaced by the emperor Galba.

Neutron activation analyzer

Deception Point

Neutron activation analysis was discovered in 1936 when researchers found that samples with rare earth elements became highly radioactive after exposure to a source of neutrons. The method radiates the sample with neutrons in a nuclear reactor, then measures the gamma rays emitted from radioactive isotopes produced in the sample. This sensitive analytical technique is the most accurate and reliable method for analyzing the precise concentrations of all elements in a sample, accurate to the nanogram level and below, and is the method used to determine the meteorite's content in the novel.

Newfoundland

Deception Point

Newfoundland is a province of eastern Canada that includes the island of Newfoundland and the mainland area of Labrador with its adjacent islands. The world's fifteenth-largest island, Newfoundland is separated from the Labrador Peninsula by the Strait of Belle Isle and from Cape Breton Island by the Cabot Strait, blocking the mouth of the Saint Lawrence River to create the Gulf of Saint Lawrence.

The remains (circa 1000 AD) of possible Viking settlements have been found in Newfoundland, but the area wasn't known to European fishermen and explorers until Frenchman John Cabot's voyages in the late fifteenth century. England claimed Newfoundland as its first overseas possession in 1583, though the claims were disputed by France until the Treaty of Paris in 1763. The province of Quebec continued to claim Labrador until 1927, and Newfoundland became Canada's tenth province in 1949. The provincial capital and largest city, St. John's, is located on the southeastern tip of the island.

Newton, Sir Isaac

Angels & Demons and The Da Vinci Code

Isaac Newton (1642–1727) was an English mathematician and scientist who co-founded the field of calculus, defined the laws of gravity and planetary motion, explained the laws and nature of light and color in optics, and developed the three laws of motion, among other discoveries.

His theory of gravity was supposedly inspired by the sight of an apple falling from a tree, though no proof of this exists. He was knighted in 1705 and was the first scientist given the honor of burial in Westminster Abbey. Many consider him the father of modern science.

Nicene Creed

The Da Vinci Code

The Nicene Creed is a formal statement of doctrine of the Christian faith adopted at the first Ecumenical Council, which was also the First Council of Nicaea (see Council of Nicaea), in 325 AD, and accepted by the Roman Catholic, Eastern Orthodox, Anglican, and most Protestant churches.

The creed establishes a set of beliefs that Christians adhere to and was designed to identify heresies or those who did not conform. It was primarily created to respond to the Arian heresy that believed in Jesus's mortality; the creed sought to firmly establish his divinity. In 381, the second Ecumenical Council, which was also the First Council of Constantinople, added additional text to what is also called the Nicene-Constantinopolitan Creed. The third Ecumenical Council, the Council of Ephesus in 431, reaffirmed the 381 version, and forbade any further changes to it, except in another such council.

The Nicene Creed states that the Holy Spirit "proceeds from the Father." However, the *filioque* clause "and the Son" was added to the creed by the Synod of Toledo in Spain in 447 to stress more clearly the connection between the Son and the Spirit. The Bible doesn't explicitly state that the

Holy Spirit proceeds from the Son, so many challenged the addition of the *filioque* clause.

This argument was one of the main contributors to the Great Schism of the East and West in 1054. The East and the West met at the Council of Florence in the fifteenth century in hopes of reconciliation. All but one of the Orthodox bishops present agreed that the Western usage of the *filioque* clause was held not to be a heresy. However, many Orthodox adherents and bishops rejected the union between the Catholic and the Orthodox churches and the *filioque* clause is still not widely accepted. In modern day, the Orthodox Church uses the Nicene Creed of 381 without the *filioque* and eastern churches have rejected the phrase as an unauthorized interpolation.

Niche of the Palliums

Angels & Demons

In the center of Saint Peter's Basilica, Bernini's magnificent bronze baldachin rises above the papal altar that is built atop Saint Peter's tomb in a horseshoe-shaped sacellum. The area is beautifully illuminated along the balustrade by the perpetually burning flames of lamps supported by elegant bronze cornucopias by Mattia de' Rossi. Sources disagree on the number of lamps surrounding the niche—anywhere from 89 to 100.

In the niche over the grate that covers the tomb is a silver-gilt coffer containing palliums, or narrow white stoles that the Pope bestows upon new archbishops (see palliums).

NightSight

Deception Point

Raytheon's NightSight thermal imaging system applies infrared technology developed in the 1960s for military purposes to allow users to "see" in the dark. The infrared imaging system works by detecting slight temperature variances between objects and people, then creating "thermal landscapes" of the area on display.

Though widely used in surveillance, the system has been used by commercial fishermen since 1995, and NightSight products are now available to offshore sport fishermen, providing increased safety measures for crews who must cross unfamiliar waters at night.

Normandy

The Da Vinci Code

A geographic and historical region and former province of northwest France bordering on the English Channel. It now includes five departments: Manche, Calvados, Eure, Seine-Maritime, and Orne.

Part of ancient Gaul, the region was successively conquered by the Romans, Franks, and Norse; passed to England after the Norman Conquest in 1066; was joined to France in 1204 after the invasion and conquest by Philip II; was devastated by the Hundred Years' War (1337–1453); and was permanently restored to France in 1450 (with the exception of the larger Channel Islands). Its beaches were the scene of the Allied invasion of Europe in 1944, in World War II.

North Sea

Deception Point

The North Sea is an arm of the Atlantic Ocean surrounded by Great Britain, Norway, Denmark, Germany, the Netherlands, Belgium, and the northern tip of France. The North Sea connects with the Atlantic Ocean in the south by the Strait of Dover to the English Channel and in the north through the Norwegian Sea. The Kiel Canal, one of the world's busiest artificial waterways, connects the North Sea with the Baltic.

Obelisk

Angels & Demons

An obelisk is a tall, slender four-sided stone shaft that tapers to a pointed pyramidal top. Ancient Egyptian obelisks were made of a single piece of stone, most commonly of red granite, and dedicated to the sun god. Obelisks of colossal size were first raised in the Twelfth dynasty, and many of the historic monoliths were moved from Egypt to foreign locations, including Rome, Florence, Paris, London, and New York.

Oculus

Angels & Demons and The Da Vinci Code

An oculus (the Latin word for eye) is an eyelike opening or ornament, especially referring to a round window or the circular opening at the apex of a dome. The oculus in the dome of the Pantheon in Rome is open to the weather. Rain falls to the floor, where it is carried away through drains.

Office of the Pope

Angels & Demons

Though Dan Brown uses this term to describe the physical space of the pope's office, it is usually used to refer to the position held by the pope. The Roman Catholic pope's formal title is "Bishop of Rome, Vicar of Jesus Christ, Successor of the Prince of the Apostles, Supreme Pontiff of the Universal Church, Patriarch of the West, Primate of Italy, Archbishop and Metropolitan of the Roman Province, Sovereign of the State of the Vatican City, Servant of the Servants of God."

OH-58D Kiowa Warrior Helicopter

Deception Point

The OH-58D Kiowa Warrior used by the Delta Force in Dan Brown's novel is a two-man single-engine armed reconnaissance helicopter. It has a highly accurate navigation system, an infrared thermal imaging capability, and Air-to-Air Stinger missiles. Though the primary mission of the Kiowa Warrior is armed reconnaissance in air cavalry troops and light attack companies, it may be called upon to participate in Joint Air Attack (JAAT) operations, air combat, limited attack operations, and artillery target designation.

To counter the threat of a hostile nighttime gunboat presence in 1987 in the Persian Gulf, the OH-58D Kiowa Warrior was developed in less than 100 days in cooperation between Bell Helicopter Textron, Inc. and the United States Armed Forces.

O'Keeffe, Georgia

The Da Vinci Code

Georgia O'Keeffe (1887–1986) was a well-known artist of the twentieth century. Though she grew up in the American Northeast, she settled in the Southwest later in life. Using the motifs of the region, she painted desert landscapes and bleached cow skulls, but is especially known for her sensuous close-up paintings of flowers and plants, utilizing sexual symbolism.

Old Masters

The Da Vinci Code

Old Masters refers to European artists of the period from about 1500 to 1800, especially the great painters of this period. It can also refer to a painting by one of these painters. The list of Old Masters includes Leonardo Da Vinci, Michelangelo, Titian, Raphael, Tintoretto, El Greco, Caravaggio, Rubens, Poussin, Velázquez, Rembrandt, and Vermeer.

Olivine

Deception Point

Olivine is a mineral silicate that crystallizes from magma rich in magnesium and iron but low in silica. Also called chrysolite, olivine's characteristic yellow-green to olive-green color gives the mineral its name. Transparent olivine can be cut into gemstones known as peridot. It is one of the most common minerals on Earth by volume and has been discovered in meteorites, on Mars, and on the moon.

Olympian Gods

Angels & Demons

Olympian Gods, from Greek mythology, were the principal gods (between twelve and fourteen) of the Greek pantheon, residing atop Mount Olympus for which they are named. The Olympian Gods always include Zeus, Hera, Poseidon, Ares, Hermes, Hephaestus, Aphrodite, Athena, Apollo, and Artemis, with status accorded sometimes to Hestia, Demeter, Dionysus, and Hades. The status of these four is less certain because Hestia gave up her position on Mount Olympus to Dionysus, Demeter left Olympus six months of the year to be with her daughter, and Hades' home is in the underworld.

Olympic Games

The Da Vinci Code

The Olympic Games were a pan-Hellenic festival in ancient Greece consisting of athletic games and contests of choral poetry and dance, in honor of the Olympian Zeus. The first recorded celebration was in 776 BC, but the contests mentioned in Homer's *Iliad* indicate an earlier tradition of the games. They reached their height in the fifth or fourth century BC, but became more professionalized until they were discontinued by Emperor Theodosius I of Rome (when Greece was under Rome's rule), who condemned them as a pagan spectacle at the end of the fourth century BC. They continued to be held periodically in Greece until 393 AD for four days every fourth summer.

The Greeks took their games seriously. Before participating, contestants were required to train for ten months, to remain under the watchful eyes of the games officials for thirty days, and to take an oath that they had fulfilled the training requirements. States were often more proud of Olympic victories than military ones, and champions were accorded many honors and privileges.

Women, foreigners, and slaves could not compete. Since Greek women were also forbidden to watch the Olympics, they held games of their own, called the Heraea, as early as the sixth century BC.

The modern Olympic Games were revived in the late nineteenth century as a series of international sports contests with goals of peace and fellowship modeled on those of the ancient Olympics.

Opus Dei

The Da Vinci Code

Opus Dei (the work of God) was founded in 1928 by Josemaría Escrivá (see Escrivá, Father Josemaría), a Spanish priest who objected to the liberal atmosphere at the University of Madrid. A Roman Catholic lay order dedicated to promoting traditional Catholic values and opposing liberalism and immorality, Opus Dei was given the status of Personal Prelature by Pope John Paul II in 1982 and is considered a separate diocese with its own bishop.

Opus Dei has about 85,000 members worldwide.

The lay spirituality of Opus Dei members sanctifies the value of daily work in ordinary lives, saying they can serve God in worldly vocations and lead a holy life without taking religious vows. Opus Dei asks members to do their work with a spirit of excellence, respect the freedom of others, be open to a pluralism of opinions, and practice human virtues. They do these things through love, nurtured by constant prayer, mortification of the senses, and charity. Numeraries of the church (fewer than twenty percent) consider Opus Dei their family, donate all their earnings to the organization, live in Opus Dei centers, and practice celibacy and mortification of the flesh.

Opus Dei has been criticized for its secretive nature, emphasis on discipline, wealth, overly conservative vision, and inflexibly traditionalist approach to women, and for its infiltration of professional organizations and influential positions in politics, the economy, and the arts. Critics describe Opus Dei as a cult-like sect that uses secrecy and manipulation to attempt to increase its power and influence to dominate the world (see Opus Dei Awareness Network).

Opus Dei defends itself by saying it has become a victim of Christianphobia, and that anti-cult movements have become obsessed with Opus Dei's use of the cilice (see cilice). They say that mortification of the flesh is a voluntary choice for each adult, that it was practiced by Christ himself and secularists can't understand "the need for suffering." The secretism is explained as an obligation to respect its members' privacy and the order says it does not take sides in politics and does not need to infiltrate influential positions, since it received God's call.

When Pope John Paul II canonized Escrivá on October 6, 2002, critics said that the process of canonization was too fast and had too many irregularities, accusing Opus Dei of pressuring bishops to recommend Escrivá. But Catholic officials disagree, saying that it was the Vatican reforms of the canonization process that made it seem faster than normal.

Opus Dei Awareness Network (ODAN)

The Da Vinci Code

The Opus Dei Awareness Network, Inc. (ODAN) was founded in 1991 to "meet the growing demand for accurate information about Opus Dei and to provide education, outreach and support to people who have been adversely affected by Opus Dei." It was founded by Diane DiNicola who saw unusual behavior in her daughter, Tammy, who was a numerary of Opus Dei. Diane received help from counselors to "deprogram" her daughter and Tammy is now the executive director of ODAN.

ODAN is a worldwide community of people who have had negative experiences with Opus Dei and provides a venue for them to discuss their views, saying that Opus Dei's radical demands make it act as a religious cult within the Church. ODAN points to Opus Dei's aggressive recruitment methods, its exerting undue pressure to join, the lack of informed consent for new recruits, its violation of members' personal freedom by controlling the lives of numeraries, threatening members when they try to leave, requiring numerary members to use corporal mortification (see cilice), and systematic alienation of families.

Opus Dei responds by saying that ODAN uses personal grievances to take the order's practices out of context in an attempt to make it look evil.

Original Sin

The Da Vinci Code

Original Sin, in Christian theology, was the eating of the forbidden fruit by Adam and Eve in the Garden of Eden, causing them to be expelled from Eden by God. As a result, all humankind fell from divine grace and requires redemption to be saved and enter the kingdom of Heaven. The purpose of baptism is to wash away the original sin and to restore the person's innocence.

Osiris

The Da Vinci Code

Osiris is the ancient Egyptian god of death and the underworld who brought knowledge of agriculture and civilization to the world. In Egyptian myth, he was the son of the sky goddess Nut and the Earth god Geb and married his sister Isis. Though Osiris was slain by his evil brother Set who cut his body into pieces and spread them throughout Egypt, Isis found all but one of the pieces and brought him back to life; their son, Horus, later killed Set. As a result, Osiris's annual death and resurrection symbolized the creative and fertile forces of nature and the imperishability of life.

First mentioned in the Fifth Dynasty, the worship of Osiris gradually spread throughout the Mediterranean world and was active during the time of the Roman Empire. Attempts to merge Greek philosophy with the cult of Osiris and his resurrection resulted in a mystery religion that merged Osiris with similar local gods. Later, Ptah, the Egyptian creator god, had an increased association with death and was combined with Seker (god of reincarnation) and Osiris to become Ptah-Seker-Osiris.

Osprey tilt-rotor airplane

Deception Point

The V-22 Osprey aircraft is a joint service aircraft with tilt rotors that allow it to take off vertically like a helicopter, then tilt the wings to fly like fixed-wing aircraft. Faster than traditional helicopters, the Osprey has the long-range abilities and cargo capacities of a twin turboprop aircraft.

The MV-22A is used as an assult transport by the United States Marine Corps, and for combat search and rescue by the Navy. The United States Air Force CV-22A will conduct long-range special operations missions.

Oval Office
Deception Point

The Oval Office is an oval-shaped room in the West Wing of the White House (see White House) that serves as the formal workspace of the president of the United States. The current Oval Office wasn't part of the original White House; the West Wing was built in 1902 by President Theodore Roosevelt, and President William Howard Taft had the oval office built in the center of the West Wing in 1909.

When Franklin Delano Roosevelt became president in 1933, he disliked the lack of windows in the first Oval Office and had a new one constructed at the southeast corner of the West Wing, where it is today. Typically, each new administration redecorates the office to suit the new president's tastes.

According to the White House curator, there is only one Seal of the President at any given time, and it doesn't change according to whether or not the United States is at war. However, the original seal had the eagle's head facing left, toward the arrows, symbolic of war. In 1945, President Truman modified the seal to turn the eagle's head to its right, toward the olive branches of peace. The eagle has faced to its right ever since, but some items in the White House collection that were made before 1945 still display the eagle facing to its left.

Overshooting
Deception Point

Overshooting is an interrogation technique designed to elicit confessions from criminals suspected of lying. This technique has the interrogator stating the information he wants confessed as fact, then alleging something far worse. The prisoner will often willingly confess the lesser of two evils—the truth—to keep from being punished for the greater evil. For example, an interrogator might accuse a prisoner of treason or conspiracy to assassinate a world leader in order to get him to confess to the lesser crime of embezzling government funds.

Oxford University

The Da Vinci Code

Oxford University, located at Oxford, England, is one of the oldest English-language universities in the world. The actual founding date is unknown, since the university gradually came into existence through the combination of independent learning institutions. There is evidence it existed as early as 1096 and the university was a leading center of learning throughout the Middle Ages.

The first halls of residence, which later became colleges, were founded then, leading to its collegiate system of seven permanent private halls and thirty nine colleges that are not only houses of residence, but have responsibility for teaching students.

Cambridge University was founded by students who left Oxford, generating a long history of rivalry between the two. They are sometimes referred to collectively as Oxbridge.

Pagan

The Da Vinci Code

Pagan refers to a person who is a worshiper of an ancient polytheistic pre-Christian religious tradition such as Egyptian, Greek, Norse, Roman, Sumerian, and Celtic. To make sense of an illogical universe, people in ancient times used the vagaries of gods and goddesses to explain the mysteries of nature.

Pagans in today's world are often referred to as neopagans. It is difficult to characterize neopaganism because beliefs and practices are extremely diverse, and tend to combine different traditions and belief systems. However, most neopagan religious beliefs tend toward individualism, a reverence for the sanctity of nature, belief in a Goddess and/or God (often with more than one aspect), use of ancient mythologies, and the belief in "magick." Some of the more popular traditions are Wicca, Heathenism, Celtic-based, Slavic, Baltic, Ancient Near East-based, Solitary Paganism, Christo-Paganism, and Unitarian Universalists.

Paleontology

Deception Point

Paleontology is the science that studies the early forms of life existing in prehistoric or geologic times by examining fossils from the past 600 million years. Paleontologists study the fossils of plants, animals, and micro-organisms as well as the global geographic and climatic changes to see how each affected each other in the evolution of life.

Palliums

Angels & Demons

The pallium (from the Roman meaning a woolen cloak) is a vestment worn by the pope, who confers it on archbishops in token of their union with and obedience to him. It is a stole worn around the neck whose usage dates from the sixth century.

Two lambs, raised by the Trappist Fathers of the Abbey of the Three Fountains, are blessed by the pope on January 21, the feast of Saint Agnes. One lamb is crowned with white roses to signify Agnes's virginity, and one with red roses to signify martyrdom. After the lambs are blessed, they are transferred to Castel Gandolfo where a Vatican shepherd cares for them. They are sheared in late May and the wool is transferred to the Benedictine Sisters of Saint Cecilia who use it to make the palliums.

The sisters used to hand-weave the wool, but now, due to their diminished numbers, they commission a textile company to supply the unfinished wool strips. The sisters stitch the stoles, measuring about two inches in width, with six black crosses. Three gold jeweled pins are added and each pallium is then blessed by the Pope and placed in a silver-gilt box in the niche of the palliums (see Niche of the Palliums).

Conferral of the palliums takes place each year on June 29, the feast of Saints Peter and Paul, where the pope presides at a mass with the new archbishops. After the homily, the pope places a pallium on the shoulders of each archbishop, symbolizing the jurisdiction delegated to him by the Holy See and reminding the archbishop to be a good shepherd and care for the flock entrusted to him.

Only the pope and metropolitan archbishops may wear the pallium, which is required for some liturgical functions such as ordination, and it must be bestowed before the archbishop can exercise his office.

Pope Benedict XVI reverted to an earlier form of the pallium for his inauguration. It is wider than the standard pallium, made of wool with black silk ends, and decorated with five red crosses and three pins.

Panspermia

Deception Point

Panspermia is the theory that life on Earth was seeded from microorganisms or biochemical compounds from outer space. It postulates that the seeds of life are prevalent throughout the universe and have propagated where suitable conditions exist.

The theory hasn't been proven or disproven, but most believe that panspermia is unlikely because of the difficulty in life forms surviving travel through the harsh environment of space, the immense heat of passage through the atmosphere, and the force of the impact on the planet.

Pantheism

Angels & Demons

Pantheism, which means "God is all" or "All is God," is the philosophical belief that God and the universe are one and the same. Though it can encompass the belief in many gods who are really one because they are all aspects of the single creative force, it does not mean the worship of many gods as Dan Brown mentioned in his novel; that is polytheism.

Pantheon

Angels & Demons and The Da Vinci Code

The term pantheon was originally used to refer to any temple dedicated to all the gods. The Pantheon on the Piazza Rotond in Rome was built by Agrippa in 27 BC as a temple to the Roman gods but was damaged by fire in AD 80 and restored by Domitian. Hadrian rebuilt it in the second century; it was closed in the fourth century by the first Christian emperors, along with all pagan places of worship; and sacked by barbarians in 410. However, the Pantheon was saved from destruction by Pope Boniface IV who received it as a gift from the emperor in Byzantium and converted it to a Christian church dedicated to Saint Mary in 609.

The Pantheon is a great hemispherical dome built on hollow concrete walls sporting a portico with Marcus Agrippa's inscription, "Marcus Agrippa, son of Lucius, consul for the third time, built this." It was originally covered in bronze, but 356 tiles were taken for embellishment of Constantinople, and Pope Urban VIII removed nails and bronze plates to fortify Castel Sant'Angelo with cannon and make the baldachin in Saint Peter's Basilica.

Two belfries were added in Alexander VII's reign by Bernini and dubbed "Bernini's ass' ears." They were removed in 1883. The interior is a perfect circle with the diameter equal to the height of the building. An oculus at the apex of the dome lets in light and weather.

The Pantheon has been used as a tomb since the Renaissance; Raphael, Annibale Caracci, Baldassare Peruzzi, Vittorio Emanuele II, Umberto I, and Queen Margherita are buried there.

Papal Apartments

Angels & Demons

The Papal Apartments are a series of private and state rooms on the top floor of the Apostolic Palace. The Papal Apartments consist of seven large rooms plus a private chapel, a roof garden, and quarters for the nuns who run the household.

These apartments have served as the religious residence of the pope since the seventeenth century. Before 1870, the pope's official secular residence was the Quirinal Palace, which is now the official residence of the president of Italy. The pope is in residence in the apartments from October to June, and spends July to September at Castel Gandolfo.

Particle physics

Angels & Demons

This branch of science studies subatomic particles and their interactions. It is also called high-energy physics because many elementary particles can only be created during the collisions of other particles in particle accelerators. Subatomic particles include electrons, protons, neutrons, quarks, photons, neutrinos, and muons.

Passetto, Il

Angels & Demons

Il Passetto (the Little Passage), also known as Passetto di Borgo (for Borgo district's corridor), is the secret passageway disguised as an aqueduct built between the Castel Sant'Angelo and the Vatican. It was constructed around 850 by Pope Leo IV after the Saracen attack on Rome in 846 so the pope could reach the fortress in case of siege, and was actually used by Pope Clement VII to flee to safety when Rome was sacked by German mercenaries sent by Charles V.

Pearl Harbor

Digital Fortress

An inlet of the Pacific Ocean on the southern coast of Oahu island, Hawaii, west of Honolulu. Its name comes from the fact that it was filled with pearl-producing oysters until the late 1800s.

Pearl Harbor became the site of a naval base after the United States annexed Hawaii in 1900. On Sunday, December 7, 1941, Japanese planes attacked the base without warning, sinking or severely damaging nineteen naval vessels and destroying 188 United States aircraft with significant casualties and loss of life. The next day, the United States declared war on Japan and entered World War II.

Pei, I.M.

The Da Vinci Code

Ieoh Ming Pei (born 1917) is a Chinese-born American Pritzker Prize-winning architect, known as the last master of modernist architecture. Pei is renowned for working with abstract shapes, using stone, marble, concrete, steel, and glass and turning them into breathtaking sculptural structures with soaring interior spaces.

Best known for his controversial glass Pyramide at the Louvre in Paris, Pei also designed the East Building of the National Gallery in Washington, D.C., and the Mile High Center in Denver. His involvement in urban renewal schemes of the 1960s includes such structures as the Government Center, Boston; Society Hill, Philadelphia (with Edmund N. Bacon); the John Hancock Tower, Boston; the John F. Kennedy Memorial Library, Boston; the Jacob Javits Exposition and Convention Center, New York City; the Rock and Roll Hall of Fame, Cleveland; the Miho Museum, Kyoto; and a new wing of the German Historical Museum, Berlin. Pei retired in 1990.

Pentacle

The Da Vinci Code

A five-pointed star (a pentagram) enclosed in a circle. In pagan usage, it is most often shown with one point of the star pointing up and two down. The inverted version is sometimes associated with Satanism.

As a pagan symbol the pentacle has mystical significance, with some people equating the five points of the star to the five elements of air, earth, fire, water, and spirit.

Pepin d'Heristal

The Da Vinci Code

Pepin of Heristal (or Pepin II or Pepin the Younger or Pepin the Fat) (circa 635–714) was Mayor of the Palace from 680 to 714 in the Frankish territory of Austrasia, grandson of Pepin the Elder (Pepin of Landen), and father of Charles Martel.

With the approval of the Roman Catholic church, Pepin II ordered the assassination of Merovingian king Dagobert II in 679, then further consolidated his power with a military victory at Tertry in 687. He became the actual ruler of Austrasia, with the Merovingian king Theuderic III ruling in name only.

Pepin's descendants continued to serve as Mayors of the Palace and the real power behind the throne. They eventually became the legal rulers of the Frankish kingdoms, thus laying the foundation for the Carolingian dynasty.

Pepin the Short

The Da Vinci Code

Pepin the Short (or Pepin III) (circa 714–768) was the Mayor of the Palace in the Frankish territory of Austrasia who schemed with the nobles and the Catholic Church in 751 to depose Childeric III, the last of the Merovingian kings, and place himself on the throne. Son of Charles Martel and father of Charlemagne, he was the first king of the Carolingian dynasty.

Peter, Saint

Angels and Demons and The Da Vinci Code

Saint Peter, also known as Peter, Simon ben Jonah/BarJonah, Simon, Simon Peter, Cephas, and Kepha, was a Galilean fisherman and chief of the twelve disciples or apostles of Jesus. His original name was Simon, but Jesus gave him the nickname Peter (from the Greek petros, meaning rock), saying, "On this rock I will build my church."

A staunch defender and teacher of Christianity, Peter, as head of the local church, was crucified upside down in Nero's circus in 64 or 69 AD. He was buried nearby, and his successor, Pope Anacletus, built a *memoria* atop the site. Emperor Constantine erected a basilica around the tomb in the fourth century. It is now the centerpiece of the Vatican palace where Saint Peter's remains are believed to lie.

In Roman Catholic tradition, Peter is traditionally considered the first bishop of Antioch and the first bishop of Rome, and therefore the first pope. As prescribed in the Gospel of Matthew, Peter is often depicted as holding the keys to the gates of heaven, which also represent his papal power. The Roman Catholic Church cites these details as the foundation for papal primacy, saying the popes are Peter's successors and therefore retain the privileges given to him by Jesus in the Gospel of Matthew. Others say the primacy is of honor only and does not confer rulership of the whole church.

In honor of Peter's previous occupation, the popes wear the Fisherman's Ring, depicting Peter casting his nets from a fishing boat. The Papal Keys, received by Peter from Jesus, are also used as a symbol of the Pope's authority.

Phi

The Da Vinci Code

Phi is a number (1.618033988749895 . . .) with many unusual mathematical properties. Also known as the golden section, the golden ratio, the divine proportion, or the golden mean, it is a mathematical proportion wherein the ratio between a small section and a larger section is equal to the ratio between the larger section and both sections put together.

The ratio was given the symbol phi at the beginning of the twentieth century in honor of Greek sculptor Phidias (circa 490–430 BC), who made extensive use of the golden ratio in his works. Phi can be found throughout nature in the spirals of galaxies; the spiral of a Nautilus seashell; the growth pattern of flowers, seed heads, pine cones and other plants; the ratios of the human body; and the breeding of rabbits.

Many find the proportion aesthetically pleasing, leading artists throughout history to consciously use it to create harmony in their works. It has been used in music by composers such as Mozart, Beethoven, Bach, Debussy, and Bartók; in paintings by Michelangelo, Raphael, and Leonardo Da Vinci; and in construction of the great pyramids.

Philippe IV

The Da Vinci Code

King Philippe IV (1268–1314) or King Philip IV, known as Philip the Fair for his handsome appearance, was King of France (1285–1314) and of Navarre (1284–1305). Phillipe's reign was marked by controversy with the papacy, transition to a bureaucratic kingdom, expansion of royal prerogative, and strengthening of the monarchy.

To fund his wars and spendthrift lifestyle, Phillipe arrested Jews so he could seize their goods and levied exorbitant taxes on the French clergy. This caused an uproar within the Roman Catholic Church until a French archbishop was made pope (Clement V) and Phillipe was able to control him.

Seeking to cancel his debts to the Knights Templar and seize their treasure, Philippe conspired with Pope Clement V to have them all simultaneously arrested on October 13, 1307, the infamous Friday the Thirteenth (see Friday the Thirteenth). He subsequently tried and tortured Jacques DeMolay, the Templar grand master, and Geoffrey de Charney, the preceptor of Normandy, then had them convicted and burned at the stake in 1314.

Not only did Philippe IV's reign cause the decline of the Knights Templar, but it signaled the decline of the papacy's power as well.

Piazza Barberini

Angels & Demons

Piazza Barberini is a square in Rome that lies at the end of several streets, including Via Barberini, Via Sistina, and Via Vittorio Veneto. At the center of the piazza is Bernini's *Triton Fountain*, commissioned by Pope Urban VIII (a Barberini). The fountain shows a vast open clam supported by dolphins. Triton sits in the center, blowing a cascade of water through a conch shell. In a corner of the piazza is another small fountain by Bernini, the *Fountain of the Bees*, a prominent symbol of the Barberini coat of arms.

Piazza del Popolo

Angels & Demons

The Piazza del Popolo is a large oval square near Borghese Park in Rome. According to legend, Nero's ashes were enshrined here until residents complained to the pope about his ghost in the eleventh century. The Porta del Popolo, built in 1562 by Pope Pius IV, is on the north side and leads to the Via Flaminia, which was built in 220 AD to connect Rome with the Adriatic coast. During the Middle Ages it was the main entrance to the city for travelers.

In 1589, Pope Sixtus V had the area turned into a square, and had an Egyptian obelisk dating back to the thirteenth century BC moved from the Circus Maximus to the center of the square. The obelisk, removed from the Sun Temple in Heliopolis in 10 BC by Emperor Augustus, had been erected at the Circus Maximus to commemorate the conquest of Egypt.

Piazza del Popolo was used as a place of execution for centuries, and after Napoleon annexed Rome to his French empire, the French government set up a guillotine there, in 1813, to deter gangs of thugs who roamed the streets. The last execution took place in 1826.

The piazza as it is now was designed in between 1815 and 1816 by Giuseppe Valadier, the favorite architect and town planner of Pius VI, Pius VII, and Napoleon. He created two semicircles on the ends, turning it into an oval, and setting the Church of Santa Maria del Popolo at the north, opposite two symmetrical baroque churches at the south: the Santa Maria dei Miracoli and the Santa Maria in Montesanto, commissioned by Pope Alexander VII in 1658 and designed by Carlo Rainaldi.

Piazza della Rotunda

Angels & Demons

The Piazza della Rotunda in Rome takes its name from the medieval name of the Pantheon, which it surrounds. In front of the Pantheon is the obelisk of Pharaoh Ramses II, which was moved there by Pope Clement XI in 1711 from the Temple of Isis. The fountain supporting the obelisk was designed in 1478 by Giacomo Della Porta, decorated with faces and water-spouting dolphins.

Piazza Navona

Angels & Demons

The Piazza Navona in Rome is on the site of the emperor Domitian's Stadium, built in AD 86 for sport competitions modeled after the Greek games. It had completely deteriorated by the fifth century, but the piazza was built over its ruins by the family of Pope Innocent X in the early seventeenth century, following the plan of the ancient circus.

Fountains here include Bernini's *Fountain of the Four Rivers*, Giacomo della Porta's *Fountain of the Neptune*, and the *Moor Fountain*, which was designed by della Porta and redesigned by Bernini. The Church of Saint Agnes in Agony, whose facade was planned by Borromini, is on the square.

Piazza Sant'Ignazio

Angels & Demons

The Piazza Sant'Ignazio in Rome is a rococo square designed by Filippo Raguzzin in the eighteenth century in imitation of a theater set. People make their entrances and exits into the square like actors on a stage. It is dominated by the facade of the church of Sant'Ignazio.

Pinturicchio

Angels & Demons

Pinturicchio or Pintoricchio (1454–1513) was an Umbrian painter whose real name was Bernardino di Betto (or Betti). The prolific painter's more well-known works include the frescoes for the Sistine Chapel (which he assisted with), a series of chapels in the church of Santa Maria del Popolo that he decorated, the decoration of the cathedral library in Siena, and the paintings decorating the Borgia Apartments in the Vatican, done for Pope Alexander VI (Borgia).

Plantard

The Da Vinci Code

In his novel, Dan Brown says that Plantard is one of the surnames of the two remaining direct lines of Merovingian kings; the other is Saint-Clair. This information appears to have come from *Holy Blood, Holy Grail*, by Michael Baigent, Richard Leigh, and Henry Lincoln, who postulated that Jesus and Mary Magdalene married, had children, and founded the Merovingian bloodline, which was continued in secret by Dagobert II's son, Sigisbert IV, who took the name Plantard. The bloodline's secret is allegedly protected by the Priory of Sion, whose objective was to restore the Merovingian dynasty.

Pierre Athanase Marie Plantard de St.-Clair (1920–2000) was the son of a butler and worked as a low-ranking government worker. He claimed to be a descendant of Merovingian king Dagobert II, with a legitimate claim to the throne of France, substantiated by documents he asserted were part of a treasure found in Rennes-le-Château by Father Bérenger Saunière. (Note the surname is the same as the murdered curator in Dan Brown's novel.) The documents showed a genealogy of the descendants of the Merovingian kings and a decrypted message saying the treasure belonged to Dagobert II and the Priory of Sion.

In 1956, under the pseudonym Henri Lobineau, Plantard placed

Les Dossiers Secrets in the Bibliothèque Nationale in Paris eventually adding more papers over the years. These included the documents supposedly found in Rennes-le-Château and those related to the founding of the Priory of Sion, with a list of grand masters going back to the twelfth century that included many prominent names.

In 1983–84, French author Jean-Luc Chaumeil revealed Plantard's troubled past—he had served two terms in prison, first at the end of World War Two for trying to set up organizations without permission, and again in 1953 for fraud. Because of this history, most believe *Les Dossiers Secrets* to be a forgery.

Plantard subsequently made a reappearance in 1989 with a new mythology about the Priory and drew up a new list of its grand masters, claiming that Roger-Patrice Pelat was once a Grand Master. Since the deceased Pelat was a friend of François Mitterrand's and center of a financial scandal, a French court ordered a search of Plantard's home. They turned up many documents, including some proclaiming Plantard the true king of France. Under oath, Plantard admitted that he had fabricated everything, and Philippe de Chérisey admitted that he had forged the documents from Rennes-le-Château that Gerard de Sede reproduced in his book *L'Or de Rennes-le-Chateau*. Plantard was let off with a severe reprimand and ordered to cease and desist all activities related to the Priory of Sion.

Plaza De España

Digital Fortress

The Plaza De España in Seville is a semi-circular plaza on the edge of Maria Luisa Park, with a surrounding moat. It was built in 1929 for the Spanish-American Exposition, to display Spain's technology and industry, and features fountains, staircases, and fifty tiled alcoves, each named for a Spanish province. The buildings now house government offices.

This beautiful plaza was used as a filming location for the movies *Lawrence of Arabia* and *Star Wars Episode II: Attack of the Clones*.

Plum Brook Station

Deception Point

Plum Brook Station is a 6,400-acre NASA test site located south of Sandusky, Ohio. It is the home of Glenn Research Center's four world-class test facilities, including facilities for testing new rocket engines and verifying engine performance with the world's largest space environment simulation chamber.

Poets' Corner

The Da Vinci Code

Poets' Corner is the name given to a section in the South Transept of Westminster Abbey (see Westminister Abbey), which contains the remains of many famous poets, playwrights and writers, as well as memorials to others who are buried elsewhere.

Geoffrey Chaucer was the first to be buried in the Poets' Corner, primarily because of his position as clerk of works of the Palace of Westminster. However, after Nicholas Brigham erected a tomb in the abbey to Chaucer in the middle of the sixteenth century and Edmund Spenser was buried nearby in 1599, a tradition began of interring literary figures in Poet's Corner—though it also houses the tombs of several officials of the abbey.

Besides Chaucer and Spenser, those buried in Poets' Corner include Robert Browning, Charles Dickens, Thomas Hardy, Dr. Samuel Johnson, Rudyard Kipling, Laurence Olivier, and Alfred Tennyson, with memorials to literary figures such as Jane Austen, the Brontë sisters, Fanny Burney, Robert Burns, Lord Byron, John Keats, Henry Wadsworth Longfellow, Christopher Marlowe, John Milton, William Shakespeare, Percy Bysshe Shelley, Oscar Wilde, and William Wordsworth.

Preferiti

Angels & Demons

In his novel, Dan Brown refers to the four favorite cardinals for election to the papacy as the preferiti. However, there are no official candidates for the office of pope, nor would they be called the preferiti if there were. Vaticanologists coined the unofficial Italian word *papabile* to refer to a cardinal who is a possible or likely candidate for the papacy.

But in order to make Dan Brown's plot work and provide additional suspense, a little literary license was in order. . . .

Prime meridian

The Da Vinci Code

(see Meridian)

Priory of Sion

The Da Vinci Code

Les Dossiers Secrets, though widely believed to be a hoax, details a history for the Priory of Sion (or Prieuré de Sion) that was discussed in the book *Holy Blood, Holy Grail,* by Michael Baigent, Richard Leigh, and Henry Lincoln. Basically, the *dossiers* claim that the Ordre de Sion was founded in Jerusalem in 1090 by Godefroi de Bouillion (see de Bouillion, Godefroi), whom they believed was a Merovingian descendant and rightful heir of the throne of David through Jesus's bloodline.

The Priory of Sion worked alongside the Knights Templar until they had a parting of the ways during an incident known as "the cutting of the elm," in 1188. Though the rest of the Knights Templar organization was destroyed in the early fourteenth century, the Priory secretly continued operations with a series of renowned grand masters until the present day. The stated purpose of the Priory of Sion is to restore the Merovingians to the throne of France, saying that they have a divine right because of their descent from the union of Jesus and Mary Magdalene. The genealogies listed in the *dossiers* culminate in Pierre Plantard and his son.

Les Dossiers Secrets were deposited in the Bibliothèque Nationale in 1956 by Pierre Plantard under a pseudonym. When exposed as a fraud in 1984, Plantard withdrew his claims, then in 1989 tried once again, claiming that the Priory of Sion had actually been founded in 1681 at Rennes-le-Château, and giving a new list of grand masters, which became his downfall (see Plantard, Pierre). The Priory of Sion, at least as far as its existence in modern times, is generally believed to be a complete fabrication by Plantard.

Alleged grand masters of the Priory of Sion on Plantard's original list include such notables as Jean de Gisors, Nicolas Flamel, Botticelli, Leonardo Da Vinci, Isaac Newton, Victor Hugo, Claude Debussy, and Jean Cocteau.

Public-key encryption

Digital Fortress

Throughout the history of cryptography, those who ciphered and deciphered messages had to agree beforehand on a shared secret key to transmit messages secretly. The key had the potential for being lost or stolen, rendering the method useless. With public-key encryption, invented in the 1970s, computer users can communicate secretly over an insecure channel without agreeing on a key ahead of time.

Normally, a pair of keys is used: one secret, one public. The sender encrypts the message using the recipient's public key, which can be distributed via e-mail or the Internet. The receiver then decrypts it using the paired secret key.

Digital signatures are created using the reverse of this procedure: the signature is encrypted by a private key. If it can be decrypted with the corresponding public key, the receiver is assured of the sender's identity.

Pyramide, La

The Da Vinci Code

La Pyramide is a huge glass pyramid built by architect I.M. Pei (see Pei, I.M.) for the entrance to the Louvre museum in Paris. Commissioned by President Mitterrand as one of his grand building projects, it was the only one awarded without competition.

Pei hollowed out the Louvre's plaza and constructed underground connections to its various wings, adding about 650,000 square feet of much-needed support space below the museum. Aboveground, the controversial spectacular pyramid rises seventy-one feet as a sort of portico, a steel lattice structure sheathed in reflective glass that is lightly tinted to be compatible with the honey-colored stone of the Louvre. The story that it has 666 glass panes is a rumor; it actually has 673.

Pyramide Inversée, La

The Da Vinci Code

La Pyramide Inversée (The Inverted Pyramid) is a skylight built in an underground shopping mall in front of the Louvre museum in France, an upside-down smaller version of the pyramid framing the museum's entrance. The pyramid is suspended a little over four and half feet above floor level and a small stone pyramid about three feet high is positioned immediately below the inverted one so that their tips almost touch.

"Q" Document

The Da Vinci Code

Biblical scholars have noted for years that the gospels of Matthew and Luke have many points of similarity, with many identical phrases and wording. Though some of these are also found in the Gospel of Mark, which scholars consider to be one source for Matthew and Luke, others aren't. These observations have led many to believe the gospels to be based in part on a second source, a hypothetical "Q" document that was lost long ago. (Q is short for "Quelle," German for "source.") Some speculate that it was a document of Jesus's teachings, written in his own hand. There is no historical evidence to support the existence of such a document, so it remains a hypothetical source.

Red Room

Deception Point

The Red Room in the White House originally served as the president's antechamber for the Cabinet Room or the President's Library. During the James Madison Administration (1809–1817), the antechamber was a drawing room used for Dolley Madison's fashionable Wednesday-night receptions, and was bright yellow. It remained yellow until 1845, when First Lady Sarah Polk furnished the room in crimson and ruby and it became known as the Red Room. It was redecorated several times, retaining the red color scheme, and in 1971 was furnished in the Empire style of 1810–30 that is seen today. Refurbished in 2000, the Red Room is used as a parlor or sitting room.

Reliquary

Angels & Demons

A reliquary is a container, such as a coffer or shrine, for keeping or displaying the holy relics of saints, or other sacred objects of the Christian religion. The reliquaries may contain remains of saints, such as bones or clothing fragments, and are often designed in shapes that reflect the nature of their content or the shape of the original body part. For example, fragments of the True Cross are often in cross-shaped reliquaries, a skull in a head-shaped box, etc.

Retina scan

Angels & Demons

A retina scan (usually referred to as a retinal scan) uses a low-intensity light source and a delicate sensor to analyze the unique pattern of blood vessels at the back of the retina to identify a person. This method of identification requires the user to remove his glasses and keep his head still and eye focused for ten to fifteen seconds. It is very difficult to counterfeit since there is no known technology to fake a retina and the retina from a dead body would deteriorate too fast to be useful. In the field of biometrics, which develops ways to identify unique individuals, retinal scanning is the most accurate identification available, far more precise and reliable than fingerprints.

The first retinal scanner was made available for commercial use in 1984, and they are used almost exclusively in high-end security applications.

Rhyolite satellites

Digital Fortress

Rhyolite satellites were the first generation of SIGINT (signals intelligence) geostationary satellites developed for the CIA and NSA in the mid 1960s and deployed in orbit in the early to mid-1970s. The satellite system was designed to monitor and intercept communications transmissions and missile telemetry from the Soviet Union and China.

Consisting of three to five satellites, the Rhyolite system may have first been used during the Arab-Israeli war of 1974, then again to monitor local conflicts in Vietnam, India, and Pakistan. When the name Rhyolite was revealed to the public in an espionage trial, the name was changed to Aquacade.

Roman Carabinieri

Angels & Demons

The Carabinieri is the nickname for the Arma dei Carabinieri, which serves both as an Italian military corps and a police corps. The word Carabinieri comes from carabiniere, a cavalry soldier armed with a carbine rifle.

Created in the early nineteenth century by King Victor Emanuel I of Sardinia, the Carabinieri have fought in every conflict in which Italy has been involved. They are highly decorated for gallantry, earning the nickname the Meritorious. Oddly enough, though the Italian people view the Carabinieri with affection and pride, they stereotype them as stupid and use them as the butt of jokes similar to those about blondes in the United States.

Roman Coliseum

Angels & Demons

The Coliseum in Rome started construction under Emperor Vespasian, circa 75 AD, and was finished in 80 AD by his son Titus. It was built at the site of the Domus Aurea, Nero's palace. Originally known as the Flavian Amphitheater, the name Coliseum comes from the nearby colossus, a 130-foot statue of Nero, which was remodeled by his successors into a likeness of Sol, the sun god.

The vast, four-storied oval amphitheater seated about fifty thousand spectators in tiers of marble seats and was roofed by a canvas-covered network of ropes that sloped toward the center and provided a breeze for the audience. The vomitoria (aisles or passageways) were designed so that the huge structure could fill in fifteen minutes, and be evacuated (spewed out) in five.

The Coliseum hosted large-scale games that included gladiatorial contests, fights between animals, contests between people and animals, and executions. The area could even be sealed off and flooded to enact mock sea battles. Historians report that 9,000 wild animals were killed during the 100 days of its grand opening, and it has been estimated that between 500,000 and 1,000,000 people died in the games there.

The Coliseum was struck by lightning and damaged by fire in 217, then restored in 238. Games continued until Emperor Honorius banned gladiator duels in 404, and it was subsequently used for various purposes such as animal hunts until 524. Earthquakes in 442, 508, 847, and 1349 caused great damage to the structure and in the fifteenth century, it was cannibalized of its marble to construct other buildings in the area, notably Saint Peter's Basilica and private palazzi. Pope Benedict XIV put an end to quarrying in 1749 by consecrating the building to the Christian martyrs thought to have perished there. However, there is no proof Christians actually died in this arena; it is believed most perished in the Circus Maximus.

Roman Forum

Angels & Demons

The Roman Forum (*Forum Romanum*) lies in a valley between the Capitoline, Palatine, Velia, Quirinal, and Esquiline Hills in Rome. It was the political and economic center of Rome during the seventh century BC, where commerce, business, trading and the administration of justice took place, and was used as such well into the imperial period. The Regia was constructed as the residence of the kings, the Curia was the meeting place of the Senate, the Comitium and the Rostra held public meetings, and the basilicas hosted commercial and judicial activities.

Though the importance of the Forum as a political center diminished in imperial times, it remained a focus for commerce and religious life. Religious monuments included temples to Antoninus and Faustina, Vespasian and Titus, Castor and Pollux, Jupiter, Saturn, and Vesta. Honorary monuments included the arches honoring Augustus, Titus, Tiberius, and Septimius Severus as well as the Column of Phocas, the last structure built in the Forum.

Political strife often centered around the Forum, which received repeated damage and destruction from the battles and fire. Most of the buildings were destroyed completely in 410 at the hands of invaders and it was abandoned, lying buried under debris during the Middle Ages, until it was eventually used as a quarry and cattle field.

Though earlier efforts were made to excavate the site, serious excavation didn't begin until early in the nineteenth century, and was completed in the twentieth.

Roman plague of 1656

Angels & Demons

After the plague killed one hundred thousand people in Naples, Rome tried to keep out the plague, but it began in 1656 in the city's Trastevere slum and Jewish ghetto. Officials literally walled off the districts in an attempt to contain the epidemic and later confined plague victims to the horrifying lazzaretto, the public plague hospital on Tiber Island. It did little good—about ten thousand people in Rome succumbed.

Roosevelt Room

Deception Point

The windowless Roosevelt Room in the White House's West Wing was the original site of the president's office when the wing was built in 1902. In 1909, the West Wing was expanded and the first Oval Office was built, turning this room into a waiting area. In honor of Theodore Roosevelt who built the West Wing and Franklin Roosevelt who expanded it, President Nixon named it the Roosevelt Room in 1969. Today, the space is used as a conference room.

Rose Line

The Da Vinci Code

Discovering the meaning of the origin of the term Rose Line is confusing. Most seem to agree that the Rose Line indicates the longitudinal line of the prime meridian in Paris before it was moved to Greenwich in 1884, the rose referring to the navigational compass rose. Others (including the characters in Dan Brown's novel) have insisted that the gnomon in the Church of Saint Sulpice is called a Rose Line because of its copper color and because it lies on the Paris meridian. The problem with this is that it doesn't lie on the meridian and the gnomon was an astronomical device constructed to show the summer and winter equinoxes and determine the exact date of Easter.

Another story says that Rosslyn Chapel is part of the Rose Line, whence it got its name. The chapel certainly has a lot of roses, but the meridian doesn't run through it, and the name Rosslyn comes from the Celtic ross (meaning promontory) and lynn (pool), relating to the physical features of the glen. Other beliefs about the Rose Line are that it is either one of a series of telluric ley lines crisscrossing the country, or that it refers to the north-south meridian that runs through Glaston- bury and Rosslyn (though the two aren't on the same longitudinal line) and marks King Arthur's Isle of Avalon, or that it is the bloodline descended from Jesus and Mary Magdalene.

Rosslyn Chapel

The Da Vinci Code

Rosslyn Chapel (sometimes spelled Rosslin) is located about seven miles south of Edinburgh, Scotland. It was originally built in 1446 as the Collegiate Chapel of Saint Mathew by William Sinclair (or St. Clair), Third Earl of Orkney, who is linked in legend to the Scottish Knights Templar. It took forty years to build, but the original vision of the church—a much larger cruciform structure with a tower at its center—was never finished. The current chapel was intended to be the choir, but construction of the larger structure stopped in 1484 after Sinclair died; he is buried in the chapel's foundation.

Rosslyn Chapel has been used and abused many times over the cen- turies, and was rededicated in 1862 by the Bishop of Edinburgh. Reno- vations are currently underway to halt its deterioration.

Though it is copiously decorated with mysterious symbols and icons, there is no Star of David in the floor as Dan Brown says in his novel. The chapel has long been the subject of speculation regarding its possible link to Freemasonry and has also been rumored to hold a number of treasures in its secret vaults, including the Holy Grail, the Ark of the Covenant, the mummified head of Christ, a Black Madonna, lost scrolls from the Temple of Jerusalem, the Holy Rood, and the trea- sures of the Knights Templar. Researchers hope to use scanning, mag- netic resonance imaging, and ultrasound technologies to view the vaults to put speculation to rest and discover exactly what is inside, if anything.

Roswell incident

Deception Point

The city of Roswell, New Mexico, is located in the southeastern quarter of the state. On July 2, 1947, a loud explosion was heard and a strange object reportedly crashed outside the city. The next day, rancher William Brazel (see Brazel, William) went out to investigate and found a large quantity of strange debris with unfamiliar physical properties scattered widely over his property. The local military base allegedly announced at first that a flying disk had crashed, then later said it was a weather balloon.

Roswell has been a focus of alien and conspiracy theory ever since. Some believe an alien craft crashed there and that alien bodies were recovered and autopsied by the government, which hushed up the incident. Others believe the debris belonged to the secret Project Mogul weather balloon that blew up during a test flight, or that the incident was the result of a broken arrow, and the intelligence office released a story about a flying disk rather than admit to an accident with a nuclear weapon. Whatever the true explanation, Roswell has capitalized on the incident to attract numerous tourists interested in UFOs.

Rotary Rocket Company

Deception Point

Dan Brown's book mentions the Rotary Rocket Company as one of the private aerospace firms that offered bribes to Senator Sexton to put space exploration in the hands of the private sector. Located in the Mojave desert in California, the Rotary Rocket Company was to build a single stage from which to orbit reusable manned spacecraft with an unusual helicopter design. An atmospheric test vehicle successfully flew three test flights in 1999, proving the concept, but in early 2001 the venture did not attract sufficient funding and Rotary Rocket was forced to close.

Royal peculiar

The Da Vinci Code

A peculiar is a church not under the jurisdiction of the local bishop. A royal peculiar is a church that is either under the direct jurisdiction of the British monarch, or is closely associated with the monarchy. The concept dates to Anglo-Saxon times and developed as a result of the relationship between the Norman and Plantagenet kings and the English Church, allowing a church to ally itself with the monarch and therefore not be subject to the bishopric of the area. The most common form of royal peculiar today comprises the Chapels Royal, although the most famous is Westminster Abbey (see Westminister Abbey).

Royal Staircase

Angels & Demons

The Royal Staircase (the Scala Regia) in the Vatican connects the papal apartments with St. Peter's Basilica. Constructed by Bernini between 1663 and 1666, this majestic marble baroque staircase starts at the base of Constantine's equestrian statue, ends at the threshold of the grand entrance hall, and is lined by a double row of Ionic pillars.

Saint Agnes in Agony

Angels & Demons

Saint Agnes was a beautiful thirteen-year-old virgin of the Roman nobility in 304 AD who had dedicated her soul to God, so she refused an offer of marriage from the prefect's son. There are different versions of the story, but in many of them, she was stripped of her clothes and forced to stand outside (or serve inside) a house of ill repute. The legend says her long blond hair grew miraculously to cover her nakedness, and her virginity was preserved.

Though condemned to death for refusing to marry the prefect's son, her shackles fell from her wrists. They attempted to burn her at the stake, but the fire would not light. In frustration, her persecutors cut off her head. She is the patron saint of chastity, gardeners, young girls, engaged couples, rape victims, and virgins.

In 1652, the Church of Sant'Agnese in Agone was commissioned by Pope Innocent X and designed by Baroque architect Francesco Borromini. It was built on the site of her martyrdom in the Circus of Domitian, now the Piazza Navona in Rome. However, "Agone" doesn't refer to the agony Agnes experienced; *in agone* was the ancient Greek name of Piazza Navona, referring to the site's being used as a stadium for athletic games, the Greek *agone*. In agone was gradually corrupted into its current usage at Navona.

Saint Peter's Basilica

Angels & Demons

Saint Peter's Basilica, located in the Vatican in Rome, is possibly the largest Christian church building in the world, though others contend that the Basilica of Our Lady of Peace of Yamoussoukro is larger (still disputed). Saint Peter's Basilica stands on the site where it is believed Saint Peter was crucified in Nero's circus (see Peter, Saint) in 64 or 69 AD. Saint Peter was buried on or near the same spot where he was martyred and his successor, Pope Anacletus, built a small *memoria* over the Apostle's tomb.

In 324, Emperor Constantine replaced the *memoria* with an altar and built a basilica centered around Saint Peter's tomb, in the area which housed a pagan and Christian cemetery. When the Saracens pillaged the basilica in 847, Pope Leo IV surrounded it with a wall and towers, the ruins of which are still visible in fragments in the Vatican gardens.

The basilica's floor was raised in the sixth century, making the grave accessible by two stairways that came down into the circular hall of the crypt. The basilica had deteriorated drastically by the fifteenth century, so Pope Nicholas V hired Bernardo Rossellini of Florence to replace the basilica with a church in the plan of a Latin cross (where the vertical bar is longer than the horizontal bar). Construction halted soon after, due to the pope's death.

In 1506, Pope Julius II continued the reconstruction of the basilica, commissioning Bramante to do the design in the form of a Greek cross (with all four arms of equal length). Construction began in 1506 and when Bramante died in 1514, Giuliano da Sangallo, Fra Giacondo da Verona, and Raphael continued his work, but all died within the next six years.

Debate continued on whether to continue the design in the Greek cross or change it to a Latin cross. Antonio da Sangallo and Baldassari Peruzzi attempted several experiments, but they were stopped when Michelangelo was put in charge around 1547. He returned to Bramante's Greek cross plan, and designed the dome above the basilica. Michelangelo didn't live long enough to see the dome completed, but his student, Giacomo della Porta, followed his plan and finished it in the 1590s. In 1606, Pope Paul V decided to extend the church into the form of the Latin cross and hired Carlo Maderno to construct the facade. Bernini took over when Maderno died in 1629 and turned it into a baroque monument.

From Bramante to Bernini, the construction of St. Peter's Basilica took over 120 years through the reign of 23 popes and the commission of ten architects. It cost around $48 million to build.

Though most papal ceremonies take place at Saint Peter's due to its convenience, the Basilica di San Giovanni in Laterno is the actual cathedral of the Bishop of Rome, mother and head of the Catholic churches.

Saint Peter's Square

Angels & Demons

Saint Peter's Square (or Saint Peter's Piazza) lies in front of Saint Peter's Basilica at Vatican City in Rome and is actually more of a ellipse, symbolizing the church's embracing arms. Pope Alexander VII commissioned Bernini in 1656 to build the piazza to hide the irregular buildings around the basilica and enable a larger crowd to view the pope and receive his blessing, which he gives from a library window overlooking the square. The square can hold about three hundred thousand people.

The perimeter of the piazza is marked by two huge colonnades supported by four rows of colossal Doric columns sixty feet tall that frame the elliptical area and the trapezoidal entrance area. A granite obelisk from Heliopolis made in the thirteenth century BC marks the center. It was brought to Rome in the first century by Caligula, who had it set up in the circus where Saint Peter was crucified; Pope Sixtus V moved it in 1586 to Saint Peter's Square. The circular stones installed in 1817 mark the obelisk's shadow as the sun enters each of the signs of the zodiac, making the obelisk a gnomon. Two fountains lie in the oval, one by Carlo Maderno who designed the facade of St. Peter's Basilica, and the other by Bernini.

The long avenue of approach to the square, the Via della Conciliazione, was built by Mussolini in 1936 to honor the "conciliation," the Lateran Treaty that conceded the independent sovereignty of Vatican City.

Saint Peter's Throne

Angels & Demons

Saint Peter's Throne, held aloft in the apse of Saint Peter's Basilica, is a gilded bronze monument, richly ornamented with bas-reliefs, designed by Bernini. It is said to hold the relic of the Episcopal chair of Saint Peter himself.

The chair was encased in Bernini's glorious bronze enclosure in 1666 and remained hidden from sight until 1867 when it was removed so the public could view it. Descriptions from that time tell us the chair has four large rings attached to it, which were used to carry it in processions. The oak framework is much older than the rest of the chair, which was probably repaired around the time of Charlemagne, reinforced by acacia wood and iron bands. The front and back are overlaid with square ivory plaques depicting, among others, scenes from the Labors of Hercules.

Though some are convinced it is Saint Peter's original chair, others believe the wooden chair enclosed in Bernini's bronze throne was of Byzantine origin.

Saint Peter's Tomb

Angels & Demons

Tradition holds that Peter the Apostle was crucified upside down in Nero's circus in 64 or 69 AD and was buried nearby in a vault below ground. In the first century, his successor, Pope Anacletus, built a *memoria* in an upper chamber above the vault, then it was enclosed in the structure known as the Trophy of Gaius in the second century. Saint Peter's remains (or possibly only his skull) were probably moved to the Catacombs of Saint Sebastian for safekeeping in the third century when Emperor Valerian started the persecution of the Christians and forbid them the use of the cemeteries.

Peter's remains were returned at a later date to the original vault (though the skull may have been removed to the Lateran church) and in 324, Emperor Constantine built up the area around the tomb to make the area level. He built an altar above the Trophy of Gaius and constructed the first basilica around that (see Saint Peter's Basilica). That's why the tomb is so far below ground today.

Vatican excavations undertaken in the 1940s found the bones of a sixty- to seventy-year-old vigorous man buried there, which they believe to be those of Saint Peter.

Sala Clementina

Angels & Demons

The Sala Clementina is a gigantic hall, two stories high, on the second floor of the Vatican Palace at the entrance to the papal apartments. Built by Pope Clement VIII in 1595, this magnificently decorated hall serves as a waiting room and a reception hall. This is where Pope John Paul II's body lay in state before his burial.

Saint Peter

(see Peter, Saint)

Salle des États

The Da Vinci Code

This is a gallery in the Louvre museum in Paris featuring Italian paintings from the sixteenth century. The *Mona Lisa* has been displayed here since 1950, but was moved to the Grand Gallery from 2001 to 2005 (the time in which Dan Brown's book is set) while the Salle des États was being remodeled.

Salon Carré

The Da Vinci Code

The Salon Carré (square salon) is a room in the Louvre museum in Paris. The Salon Carré became the official exhibition space for the world's greatest masterpieces in the early eighteenth century and was also the site of the prestigious government-sponsored exhibition the annual Paris Salon, until 1850. This is where the *Mona Lisa* resided when she was stolen in 1911 (see *Mona Lisa*).

Sangreal

The Da Vinci Code

The word Sangreal (or Sangraal) was used to refer to the Holy Grail in early grail romances. Some say that when translating from the old French, separating the word in two different places yields two different meanings: San Greal meaning Holy Grail and Sang Real meaning Royal Blood. However, others say that this is a false etymology and that the old French doesn't translate this way. In addition, they say this theory of the two meanings wasn't common until the later Middle Ages, so its being used to refer to the bloodline of Christ as the the Sangreal is doubtful.

Santa Maria del Popolo

Angels & Demons

Santa Maria del Popolo (Our Lady of the People) is a church in Rome. A chapel was originally built on the spot in 1099 over the tombs of the Domitii family by Pope Paschal II and funded by the people of Rome, hence its name—popolo. It was enlarged and consecrated as a church by Pope Gregory IX in the early thirteenth century, then rebuilt by Pope Sixtus IV in 1477, making it one of the first examples of the Renaissance style in Rome.

Much of the church was designed by Bramante in the sixteenth and Bernini in the seventeenth centuries. It also contains frescoes by Pinturicchio, two paintings by Caravaggio, and the Chigi Chapel designed by Raphael (see Chigi Chapel). The statues of *Daniel* and *Habakkuk and the Angel* are by Bernini.

Santa Maria della Vittoria

Angels & Demons

Santa Maria della Vittoria (Saint Mary of the Victory) is a Baroque church in Rome that houses Bernini's *Ecstasy of St. Teresa*, mentioned as the third altar of science in Dan Brown's novel.

Carlo Maderno started construction on the church in 1608, and it was originally dedicated to Saint Paul. However, the Catholic victory at the battle of the White Mountain at Prague in 1620 was attributed to the Virgin Mary because of the image of the Nativity worn around a priest's neck. In gratitude, the name of the church was changed to Saint Mary of the Victory in 1622.

The image and part of the church was destroyed by fire in 1833 but later restored. A replica of the painting worn by the priest now hangs above the high altar.

Santi, Raphael

Angels & Demons

Raphael Santi (1483–1520) (also Raphael Sanzio, Raffaello Santi, or Raffaello Sanzio) was an Italian Renaissance painter known primarily by his first name. Though he died at an early age, on his thirty-seventh birthday, he left behind many incredible works of art, including large-scale frescos in the Vatican, ten tapestries for the Sistine Chapel, and a number of paintings. When Bramante died, Raphael took over as chief architect of the Vatican, continuing work on Saint Peter's Basilica as well as designing a number of mansions, palaces, and churches.

Sarah

The Da Vinci Code

Legends say that, after Jesus's crucifixion, Mary Magdalene traveled to Gaul (modern-day France) with a party including a young girl named Sarah. Some believe Sarah was Mary's child by Jesus—the Sangreal (see Sangreal) she took with her to France.

Another theory is that Mary fled first to Egypt, the traditional place for Jewish asylum, then later went to Gaul. In Les Saintes-Maries-de-la-Mer in France, there is a festival every May to honor Saint Sarah the Egyptian, a "Black Queen" who accompanied Mary Magdalene to France and is revered because of her royal bloodline. The theory is that the Gauls assumed she was dark skinned because she was Egyptian (literally meaning born in Egypt), and that her darkness is symbolic of her hidden nature.

According to the legend, Sarah grew up in the south of France and had children of her own, carrying on the bloodline that eventually reached the French royal family of the Merovingians.

Seahawk

Deception Point

The Sikorsky Seahawk is a single-main-rotor, twin-engine, medium-lift helicopter manufactured by the United Technologies Corporation.

Basing its design on the UH-60 Black Hawk fielded by the United States Army in 1979, the Navy fielded the SH-60B Seahawk in 1983 and the SH-60F in 1988. It is an assault helicopter used for anti-submarine and anti-ship warfare, drug interdiction, search and rescue, cargo lift, and special operations. The SH-60B is based aboard cruisers, destroyers, and frigates, and the SH-60F is carrier based.

Seahorse mating

Deception Point

Seahorses are the only known species on the planet in which the male gets pregnant. Seahorses mate for life, and they will even mate across different seahorse species. The female packs the male's breeding bag with nutrients, then snuggles up close to deposit orange-colored eggs inside for the male to fertilize. When mating, they link their tails together and do a kind of dance.

Gestation is only two or three weeks, resulting in the live birth of between fifteen and one thousand five hundred baby seahorses! Luckily, they don't have to take care of that many babies—the kids are on their own as soon as they are born. Amazingly, seahorses can get pregnant again almost immediately.

SEALs

Deception Point

The SEALs take their name from the elements in which they operate (sea, air, land) and are the United States Navy's most acclaimed special operations unit. The origins of the SEALs lie back in 1943 when volunteers from the Naval Construction Battalions (SeaBees) were organized into Navy Combat Demolition Units (NCDUs) as an advance force to clear the way for amphibious landings.

Successfully used in World War II and the Korean conflict, these personnel were formed by the Navy into separate units called SEAL teams in 1962, to conduct unconventional warfare, counter-guerilla warfare, and clandestine operations in water environments.

SEAL teams go through arguably the toughest military training in the world, testing their stamina, leadership, and teamwork to build men of character, physical ability, and technical know-how.

Seasonal ice

Deception Point

Seasonal ice is a floating mass of sea ice in the Earth's polar regions, called seasonal because it expands during the winter and melts during the spring and summer.

Secret Vatican Archives

Angels & Demons

The Secret Archives of the Vatican (Archivio Segreto Vaticano), home to many pivotal documents of Western history, is the central repository of papal acts, correspondence, and diplomatic materials. The Vatican archives consist of hundreds of thousands of documents in thirty miles of shelving, dating back to the thirteenth century.

Spotty documentation is available prior to that century, and all documents prior to the eighth century have disappeared. Some of the earlier documents include Henry VIII of England's request for an annulment of his marriage to Catherine of Aragon (denied), a letter from Michelangelo requesting wages for the guards of Saint Peter's who hadn't been paid in three months, and the record of Galileo's trial for heresy (see Galilei, Galileo).

The Vatican secret archives began with documents collected by Pope Innocent III in 1198. Pope Sixtus IV founded the Vatican Library in the fifteenth century and the archive has been damaged and reduced over the years as it followed popes to various papal seats around the world, was involved in conflicts, and was temporarily transferred by Napoleon I to Paris.

The secret documents were removed from the Vatican Library in the seventeenth century by Pope Paul V and remained closed to outsiders until the late nineteenth century, when they were opened by Pope Leo XIII to scholars.

Because of the extent of the documents, many have not been fully indexed, and only a heavily edited index has been published. Those who wish to consult the archive cannot simply browse it. Scholars must be graduate students with a knowledge of archival research, must apply in writing, ask in advance for the precise document they wish to see, use only graphite pencils for taking notes, and must visit the Vatican in the morning hours between September 16 and July 15. Documents after 1922 are still secret and cannot be accessed.

Another secret archive that cannot be accessed is the Apostolic Penitentiary, containing papal documents, canon law, and other unknown documents.

Sènèchaux

The Da Vinci Code

Sènèchaux is French for seneschal, meaning "old servant." It is a medieval title for the steward or majordomo put in charge of a noble's domestic arrangements and administration of servants, and often the rest of their estate. Some were given additional responsibilities, including dispensing of military command and justice.

Seracini, Maurizio

The Da Vinci Code

Maurizio Seracini, a native of Florence, is an internationally renowned expert in high-technology art analysis. As Dan Brown discussed in his novel, Seracini used infrared reflectography and thermographic and ultraviolet scans to look below the visible layers of Leonardo Da Vinci's painting *Adoration of the Magi*. Seracini discovered that, though the sketch beneath the painting was indeed by Leonardo, the paint applied to the canvas was by an inferior, clumsier hand. In fact, the painter changed Leonardo's vision in many places.

Seracini has been looking for Leonardo's largest work, the fresco titled *Battle of Anghiari* (*Battle of Angiers*) for over thirty years. It may be Leonardo's most important work, but hasn't been seen since 1563. We know it existed at one time because writers of the time mentioned it and other artists reproduced the central scene of the mural using Leonardo's drawings.

Using techniques such as radar, x-rays, and ultrasound, Seracini found a narrow cavity in a wall behind a fresco by Georgio Vasari, the *Battle of Marciano*, in Florence's Palazzo Vecchio. Intriguingly, the Vasari fresco features a flag with the inscription "Search . . . find!" It's possible that Vasari, who admired Leonardo, intentionally created the space to preserve the lost fresco.

However, historians know that Leonardo had problems with the fresco and its paint not drying properly, so even if it is found concealed behind the wall, it may have deteriorated beyond salvation. But even if only parts of it have survived, *Battle of Angiers* could be one of the greatest art discoveries in a hundred years.

SETI

Deception Point

SETI (Search for ExtraTerrestrial Intelligence) is the name given to a number of independent programs whose purpose is to search for communications from life on other planets. SETI efforts started in 1959 when Cornell University physicists Giuseppi Cocconi and Philip Morrison suggested using microwave radio signals to communicate with extraterrestrial civilizations.

The first SETI program, Project Ozma (named for the Queen of Oz in L. Frank Baum's fantasy books), was conducted by astronomer Frank Drake at the National Radio Astronomy Observatory in Green Bank, West Virginia, in 1960. He focused on the nearby stars Epsilon Eridani and Tau Ceti but had no results.

A 1971 NASA-recommended "Project Cyclops" program to search the skies never got off the ground, and in 1992, the High Resolution Microwave Survey (HRMS) was initiated to use radio telescopes around the world in a ten-year search. In 1993, it was also halted by inadequate funding, but privately raised funds were used in 1995 by the SETI Institute to generate Project Phoenix, to conduct a search of nearby stars.

More than fifty searches have been conducted to search for extraterrestrial life, but none have been successful . . . so far.

Seville Cathedral

Digital Fortress

The Cathedral of Seville, whose formal name is Catedral de Santa María de la Sede (Cathedral of Saint Mary of the Siege), is the largest of all medieval Gothic cathedrals. It is built on the site of the former Almohad Mosque, which was Christianized in 1248. In 1401, Seville made the decision to build a cathedral to replace the mosque and demonstrate the city's wealth. Construction began in 1402, and additions and embellishments were added into the sixteenth century.

The cathedral's interior is lavishly decorated with copious amounts of gold. The main altarpiece is the largest and richest in the Christian world, and the Capilla Mayor features the lifework of Pierre Dancart: forty five carved scenes from the life of Christ. The cathedral also holds the purported tomb of Christopher Columbus (see Columbus, Christopher).

Sfumato style

The Da Vinci Code

The sfumato style of painting overlays translucent layers of color to blur or soften sharp outlines by the subtle and gradual blending of one tone or color into another so there is no perceptible transition.

Sfumato means a smoky blend, and was coined by Leonardo Da Vinci to describe the hazy style of painting he uses in the *Mona Lisa*.

Shekinah

The Da Vinci Code

Shekinah (or Shechinah, Shekhina, Shechina), meaning dwelling or presence, is a Hebrew word used to indicate the presence of God among

His people. In some works, the Shekinah is treated as God's consort, or the feminine aspect of God, or the feminine Holy Sprit. Shekhina represented the compassion that tempered Yahweh's stern nature.

SIGINT

Deception Point

SIGINT is an acronym from the United States meaning signals intelligence. It consists of intelligence gathering by interception of communications, electronic, and foreign instrumentation signals, or the intelligence derived from such signals.

Sigisbert

The Da Vinci Code

In the novel, Dan Brown refers to Sigisbert, meaning Sigisbert IV (born 676), son of Merovingian king Dagobert II. Dagobert was killed in 679, and many historians believe Sigisbert died either before or concurrently with his father.

Others say he escaped to a village called Rennes-le-Château in France and assumed the name Plantard, continuing the Merovingian bloodline.

Singularity

Angels & Demons

In astrophysics, a singularity is a point in space-time at which matter has infinite density and infinitesimal volume. Most cosmologists believe the Big Bang was a singularity and theorize that we live in the aftermath of the resulting giant explosion that began billions of years ago.

Other cosmologists, such as Stephen Hawking, reject the thought that the universe spontaneously exploded into existence from cosmic nothingness. They believe the universe is completely self-contained and has no boundary.

Sir Gawain and the Green Knight

The Da Vinci Code

Sir Gawain and the Green Knight is a late-fourteenth-century story in which Sir Gawain, one of King Arthur's knights in Camelot, journeys to Hautdesert Castle to fulfill a promise to meet the Green Knight in battle. Despite the fact that he believes he will die, Gawain refuses the advances of the Green Knight's wife three times, thereby establishing his honor and chivalry, resulting in the Green Knight's rewarding him with his life.

Sistine Chapel

Angels & Demons

The Sistine Chapel in the Vatican is north of Saint Peter's Basilica and is named after Pope Sixtus IV, for whom it was built. Designed by Baccio Pontelli and constructed under the supervision of Giovannino de Dolci between 1473 and 1484, the chapel has the same dimensions as Solomon's Temple.

The chapel is magnificently decorated, with paintings by Perugino, Pinturicchio, Botticelli, Ghirlandaio, Rosselli, and Signorelli, as well as tapestries by Raphael and the famous *Last Judgment* fresco and ceiling by Michelangelo. The controversial restoration of Michelangelo's work began in the 1980s and '90s, with some decrying and others lauding the bright colors revealed.

The Sistine Chapel is the setting for the most solemn ceremonies of the Holy See, including conclave and some papal coronations.

Sistrum rattles

The Da Vinci Code

A sistrum was a musical instrument used in ancient Egypt for religious ceremonies and rites, especially those associated with Hathor. Shaped like a "U" with a handle, the wooden or metal sistrum had small metal

disks that rattled when the instrument was shaken. The sound was supposed to please the gods and goddesses.

Skipjack

Digital Fortress

In cryptography, Skipjack is a classified encryption algorithm developed
by the United States National Security Agency (NSA) and originally
intended for use in the controversial Clipper chip. The algorithm uses
an eighty-bit key to encrypt sixty-four-bit data blocks of data, making it
very tough to crack. The controversy was not about the Clipper chip's
effectiveness, but because the chip contains a back door that would
allow government agents to access the secret key, defeating the purpose
of the encryption. It was declassified in 1998.

Skyquakes

Deception Point

Skyquakes are earth-shaking booming sounds, often described as
sounding like cannon fire. Louder than thunder or the sonic booms
created by aircraft, they often occur on bright, sunny days and are unaf-
fected by weather.

Skyquakes have been witnessed all over the world and throughout
history, including by the Lewis and Clark expedition in 1808. Though
scientists postulate that some skyquakes are caused by the testing of
secret aircraft or meteors disintegrating in the atmosphere, there is still
no definitive answer as to what they are.

Smart car

The Da Vinci Code

The Smart car is a tiny two-passenger car, one of the most fuel-efficient,
gas-powered cars on the planet. Produced in an eco-friendly manner,
the Smart car is compact on the outside, but surprisingly roomy on the

inside since the engine is located below the passengers. Developed to be convenient, comfortable, and safe, it minimizes the impact on the environment with low fuel consumption. Most Smart cars average forty-nine miles per gallon, with some models getting up to sixty-five miles per gallon in Europe.

Nicholas Hayek of Swatch watches developed the design in the early 1990s with Mercedes-Benz (now Daimler-Chrysler) and the cars debuted in 1998. These brightly colored "Swatchmobiles" are sold at Smart centers throughout Europe, where they are stacked in towers like toy cars in a display case.

Smart car has recently come out with four-passenger and electric versions as well, and plans a Sports Utility Vehicle in 2006.

Sol Invictus

The Da Vinci Code and Angels & Demons

Sol Invictus (the unconquered sun) was a religious title applied to three separate divinities. The first was under the Roman emperor Heliogabalus, who tried to impose the worship of Elagabalus Sol Invictus, the sun god of his native Syria. The cult ceased with the emperor's death in 222 AD.

Roman emperor Aurelian introduced an official cult of Sol Invictus in 270 AD, borrowing many features from Mithraism (see Mithras), with which it is often confused. Christian orthodoxy had much in common with the monotheistic cult of Sol Invictus, so in the interests of unity, Constantine deliberately chose to blur the distinctions among Christianity, Mithraism, and Sol Invictus. The cult of Sol Invictus continued to be a cornerstone of pagan religion until the triumph of Christianity.

Solomon

The Da Vinci Code

King Solomon (circa tenth century BC), his name meaning "peaceful," was a biblical figure and son of King David and Bathsheba. King Solomon succeeded King David to the throne, becoming the third king of Israel. Solomon is famed for his legendary wisdom and many architectural projects, including the magnificent Solomon's Temple in Jerusalem, which housed the Ark of the Covenant. He was also known for his power and wealth, as well as his hundreds of wives and concubines, including the daughter of the pharaoh of Egypt. Solomon's resulting decadence and idol worship led to his decline and fall in the eyes of his people in the second half of his forty-year reign, and a prophet foretold that his kingdom would be split into two (Israel and Judah) after his death.

Solomon's Temple

The Da Vinci Code

Solomon's Temple was the first Jewish temple in Jerusalem, built on Mount Moriah, most likely on the same site as the temple that Hadrian erected to Jupiter, where Herod later built his temple and where the Dome of the Rock is now. According to tradition, King David provided Solomon with the temple site and a large amount of gold and silver with which to build the temple. The construction began in the fourth year of Solomon's reign and took seven and a half years to complete. Hiram, King of Tyre, provided assistance, and the project employed thousands of laborers and artisans.

Inexplicably, the temple remained unused for thirteen years, then the Ark of the Covenant was brought from the Tabernacle tent where David kept it and Solomon consecrated the temple to God, followed by a feast of dedication that lasted seven days. The Temple of Solomon was pillaged many times and finally destroyed in 586 BC when the Jews were exiled.

Space America, Inc.

Deception Point

Dan Brown's novel mentions Space America, Inc. as one of the private aerospace companies that offered bribes to Senator Sexton to put space exploration in the hands of the private sector. This Alabama-based private company worked on a low-cost launcher and planned to offer commercial launch capability but had to close its doors when the commercial launch market collapsed a few years ago.

Space Frontier Foundation (SFF)

Deception Point

The Space Frontier Foundation, founded in 1988, is a space advocacy organization that seeks to move the exploration and development of space from a government-owned bureaucratic program to more involvement from the private sector. The foundation is often openly critical of NASA.

With membership and advisors ranging from space activists to engineers, scientists, media, entertainment, politicians, and business entrepreneurs, the SFF has as its goal achieving the permanent settlement of space through the use of free enterprise.

Space Industries of Houston

Deception Point

Dan Brown's novel mentions Space Industries of Houston as one of the private aerospace companies that offered bribes to Senator Sexton to put space exploration in the hands of the private sector. In the 1980s, Space Industries of Houston offered to launch a mini-space station for NASA at a price tag of $750 million that would go into operation a decade before NASA's nearly $100 billion station. NASA declined, wanting to own its own facility. Space Industries of Houston has since merged with Veridian.

Special Ops Forces

Deception Point

United States Special Operations Forces (SOF) are elite, specialized military units that are organized, trained, and equipped to conduct and support special operations, many of them clandestine. SOF activities, which require more proficiency and specialization than is found in most conventional military units, include short-duration, small-scale offensive actions such as raids, hostage rescues, strikes, and ambushes; clandestine operations in enemy territory to gain intelligence; and supporting local insurgent and resistance groups operating in the territory of a common enemy. Though each force is highly trained in general combat and small unit tactics, each specializes in particular types of missions.

Special Ops Forces include the Army Special Forces (sometimes called the Green Berets), Army Rangers, Delta Force, and Navy SEALs. Acceptance into the units is highly competitive and very difficult, and those who are accepted undergo very demanding training.

Sphyrna mokarran

Deception Point

Sphyrna mokarran is the scientific name for hammerhead sharks. Their common name comes from their characteristic hammer-shaped head, and they have widely spaced eyes at the ends of the "hammer." Gray-brown with an off-white belly, the sharks have sharp, serrated triangular teeth that are constantly replaced as they fall out. There are nine different species of hammerhead sharks, ranging from three feet in length to twenty. Found in warm water near the coastlines, they are the only species of shark that travels in schools.

Stealth Bomber

Deception Point

The Stealth Bomber, or any stealth aircraft, is designed to absorb and deflect radar, making the planes more difficult to detect than conventional flight technology. Some of the methods used to avoid detection are covering the aircraft with radar-absorbing material, using a shape that deflects radar signals away from the origin of the signal, decreasing the infrared signature, painting them dark, and reducing their noise level.

However, several methods have been developed to spot stealth aircraft, including detecting the turbulence they leave, and using signals from cellular phone towers to create a picture of where they might be, though the practicality of this method is questionable.

Stealth aircraft have been used in Operation Desert Storm, Operation Allied Force, and the 2003 invasion of Iraq to strike high-value targets that were either too heavily defended or too far out of range for conventional aircraft.

Steve Jackson Games

Angels & Demons

Steve Jackson Games, founded in 1980 by Steve Jackson, publishes books, games, and magazines for game fans. Best known for the GURPS role-playing system, Car Wars, Bavarian Illuminati (see Bavarian Illuminati: New World Order), Ogre, and Toon, the company also publishes two online magazines.

Substitution cipher

The Da Vinci Code

In cryptography, a substitution cipher is a method of encrypting a message so that it can't be easily read, using a system of letters or symbols to replace the cleartext and convert it into ciphertext. The receiver can decipher the ciphertext by performing a reverse substitution.

If the cipher uses single-letter substitutions, it is called a simple substitution cipher; one that uses larger groups of letters is called polygraphic. However, this method of encrypting text is easily broken, since frequency analysis allows the code breaker to deduce the probable meaning of the symbols that appear most often and associate them with the most commonly used letters of the alphabet.

Sully Wing

The Da Vinci Code

The Sully Wing, one of three wings in the Louvre museum in Paris, is situated to the west of the Pyramid. The Sully Wing contains French paintings and drawings, the Crown diamonds, Egyptian antiquities and art, and the medieval Louvre.

SWATH twin-hull ship

Deception Point

The Small Waterplane Area Twin Hull (SWATH) is a hull form invented by Canadian Frederick G. Creed in 1938. With catamarans used as a basis for their design, the ships are large but not heavy, with a distinctive bulbous twin hull design that allows them to displace less water and ride lower in the water, so that smaller vessels can run steady in rough seas. They were first used in the 1960s and 1970s as oceanographic research ships or submarine rescue ships.

Swiss Guard

Angels & Demons

The Swiss Guards are Swiss mercenaries who fought in various European armies from the fifteenth to the nineteenth centuries. The Swiss constitution of 1874 forbade recruitment of the Swiss by foreign powers, making a single exception for the Vatican police force, the armed corps of the Vatican state.

The Vatican Swiss Guard, founded in 1506 by Pope Julius II, is limited to 100. To serve in this force, guards must be Roman Catholic males of Swiss nationality in the military, between nineteen and thirty years of age, and at least five feet nine inches tall. They serve between two and twenty-five years.

The official dress uniform consists of pantaloons gathered below the knee; a full-sleeved jacket with broad yellow, red, and blue stripes; a beret; a halberd; and a sword. This distinctive uniform dates to 1914 and though its design is popularly attributed to Michelangelo, it was really designed by a commandant of the guards. The more practical working uniform consists of blue coveralls and a black beret.

Tarot

The Da Vinci Code

The origins of tarot cards are obscure, but they date back to at least the fourteenth century. In *The Woman with the Alabaster Jar,* by Margaret Starbird, Starbird postulates that Jesus and Mary Magdalene were married and had children, founding his bloodline, the sangraal or Royal Blood/Holy Grail. She believes that the tarot was a way of teaching and sharing this alternate secret version of the grail.

The tarot consists of a minor arcana with fifty-two cards in four suits (where modern-day playing cards originated) and a major arcana (or trumps) of twenty-two cards. Starbird contends that the pictures on the trump cards in the Charles VI or Gringonneur deck used symbols to express the story of Jesus's bloodline and those who protected the secret.

Temple Church

The Da Vinci Code

The Temple Church in London is located between Fleet Street and the River Thames. It was established by the Knights Templar in the twelfth century as their headquarters in England and contained residences, military training facilities, and recreational grounds for the knights, monks, and others who served the order. Built from Caen stone, the Temple church was consecrated in 1185 by Heraclius, Patriarch of Jerusalem.

The church building has two separate sections. The original nave is called the Round Church; its design is based on the Church of the Holy Sepulchre in Jerusalem. The adjoining rectangular section, built fifty-five years later, was added when King Henry III expressed a desire to be buried in the church. The choir was pulled down to build the Chancel and Henry attended the consecration in 1240. However, he altered his will before his death and is buried, in accordance with it, in Westminster Abbey.

The temple was used by noblemen of the realm as a bank to keep their valuables, often in defiance of the Crown. For example, when Hubert de Burgh, Earl of Kent, was imprisoned in the Tower, the king demanded his treasure be turned over to the Crown. The Master of the

Temple refused, saying it would not be delivered to the king without de Burgh's consent.

After the dissolution of the Templars in 1307, the church passed into the hands of the Knights Hospitaller who rented the property to two colleges of lawyers who moved to the city to attend the royal courts in Westminster. The two sections are known collectively as the Inns of the Court and individually as the Inner and Middle temples. When Henry VIII abolished the Hospitallers in 1540 and confiscated their property, the temple returned to the Crown. The Inns were unhappy with the arrangement and in 1608, they persuaded King James I to sign a Royal Charter giving them use of the temple in perpetuity. They are still governed by this charter, which requires them to maintain the church.

Though undamaged by the Great Fire of London in 1666, the church was restored afterward by Sir Christopher Wren, who added an organ. Smirke and Burton completed further restorations in 1841. During the Battle of Britain in 1941, incendiary bombs greatly damaged the church. It was restored and rededicated in the 1950s.

On the floor of the church repose nine medieval knight effigies, representing some of those buried in the church.

Thermocline

Deception Point

A thermocline is a layer in a large body of water that separates regions greatly differing in temperature. The top layer of a large lake or ocean absorbs sunlight and the wind distributes it across the top, making the temperature uniformly warm for the first hundred feet down. Below that, the temperature drops very rapidly over the next 500 feet or so. This transition area between the warmer surface water and the colder deep water is the thermocline. Below the thermocline, the temperature continues to drop, but far more gradually. Ninety percent of the water in the oceans is below the thermocline. The thermocline is important in submarine warfare, because it can reflect active sonar.

Thrombophlebitis

Angels & Demons

Thrombophlebitis is the inflammation that occurs in a vein (phlebitis) when a clot (thrombus) forms and blocks the flow of blood. Symptoms may include tenderness over the vein, pain in the calves, skin redness or inflammation, swelling of the extremities, and limping.

Tiber Island

Angels & Demons

Tiber Island (Isola Tiberina) is a small (about 330 yards by 100 yards) boat-shaped island in the southern bend of the Tiber river in Rome. Legends say that after the death of the cruel, despised ruler Lucius Tarquinius Superbus (Tarquin the Proud) in 510 BC, the angry people threw his body into the Tiber River, where dirt and silt accumulated around it to form the island. Another version says they threw his wheat and grain into the river to form the foundation of the island.

Because of this, the island was considered a place of ill omen and used to imprison criminals until 293 BC when there was a great plague in Rome. To appease the gods, the sibyl instructed the Roman Senate to build a temple to Aesculapius, the Greek god of medicine and healing. The senators obtained a statue of Aesculapius, and as they were returning to Rome up the Tiber River, they saw a snake (Aesculapius's symbol) swim from the ship over to the island. Taking this as a sign, they built his temple there.

In memory of the event, the island was modeled to resemble a ship, using travertine marble (see travertine marble) to simulate a ship's prow and stern, with an obelisk in the middle to symbolize the ship's mast. Only small fragments of the original travertine are still visible on the east end of the island, and pieces of the obelisk are in a museum in Naples.

A small church founded in the tenth century, Saint Bartholomew, was built over the remains of the ancient Temple of Aesculapius. The western section of the island became the site of a hospice, run by monks, which slowly grew into a real hospital, founded in the sixteenth century. This hospital, Fatebenefratelli Hospital, is still in operation and is one of Rome's best known medical establishments. Apparently, this is where the fictional Langdon recuperated after his fall into the river.

The island is connected to the mainland by two ancient bridges; the Cestius Bridge, which connects the island to the Trastevere district; and Fabricius Bridge, which connects to the Ripa district.

Tingley, Tyler

Angels & Demons

Dan Brown lists Tyler Tingley in his novel as a conspiracy theorist. In real life, Tyler Tingley is the principal of Phillips Exeter Academy where Dan Brown graduated from; Tingley's appearance in the book is a cameo.

Titan 4 Rocket

Deception Point

The Titan rocket family was established in 1955 when the Lockheed Martin was awarded an Air Force contract to build an intercontinental ballistic missile (ICBM) that became known as the Titan I, the nation's first two-stage ICBM. The Titan II was a more powerful version of the Titan I. Titan III development began in 1961 and evolved into the Titan IV.

The Titan IV family (including the IVA and IVB) of space boosters was launched by the United States Air Force from Cape Canaveral Air Force Station, Florida, and Vandenberg Air Force Base, California. In August 1998, a Titan IVA space launch vehicle exploded approximately forty seconds into powered flight. Two seconds later, range officials sent destruct signals to further break up the rocket so that debris fell over the ocean. The loss was estimated at $1.35 billion.

The lost rocket's cargo was the third in a series of National Reconnaissance Office electronic eavesdropping satellites code-named Vortex 2. The Titan IV was retired in 2005.

Titulus

The Da Vinci Code

On some depictions of the Catholic crucifix, there is a stylized plaque, called a Titulus or Title, with the letters INRI. This is an acronym for the Latin *Iesus Nazarenus Rex Iudaeorum* (Jesus of Nazareth, King of the Jews).

During crucifixions, a small sign, the titulus, stated the victim's crime and was placed on a staff and carried at the front of the procession to the crucifixion grounds where it was later nailed to the cross. Pilate had the INRI inscription placed on the cross to identify Jesus' "crime"—he claimed authority he didn't possess.

Top Secret Umbra

Digital Fortress and Deception Point

The United States security classification system starts with three levels: Confidential, Secret, and Top Secret. Top Secret is applied to information or material whose unauthorized disclosure could cause exceptionally grave damage to United States national security. A code word such as Umbra further clarifies the type of information being classified. Top Secret Umbra then, refers to Top Secret communications intelligence.

Toulos Restaurant

Deception Point

This restaurant is a creation of Dan Brown's, though a number of "power breakfast" restaurants do exist on Capitol Hill. Among the most notable are the Jefferson Restaurant (in the Jefferson Hotel) and the Old Ebbitt Grill, which has been in business and serving the city's (and the country's) power brokers since 1856. Some of Teddy Roosevelt's old hunting trophies decorate the place, and antiques all around add to the ambience.

Traforo, il

Angels & Demons

Il traforo is a giant spiral ramp in Castel Sant'Angelo that led to the area where funeral urns were kept when it was a mausoleum (see Castel Sant'Angelo). The ramp starts at the first floor and winds about four hundred feet to the mortuary chamber, which was originally covered in marble and paved with mosaic.

Transept

The Da Vinci Code

In Roman and Gothic Christian church architecture, the transept is the area set crossways (at right angles) to the nave in a cross-shaped building, separating the nave from the sanctuary. It can also refer to the two lateral arms of the area.

TRANSLTR

Digital Fortress

TRANSLTR, the NSA code-breaking supercomputer featured in Dan Brown's novel, is a fictional creation.

Travertine marble

The Da Vinci Code

Travertine marble, used extensively by the Romans, is a form of massive calcium carbonate, resulting from the deposits of mineral springs, with extensive deposits at Tivoli, near Rome. A beautifully colored and banded marble, it is also called onyx marble, Mexican onyx, and Egyptian or Oriental alabaster. The Roman Colosseum was the largest building constructed of travertine, and in contemporary times the Getty Center in Los Angeles, California, uses travertine imported from Tivoli.

Tribe of Benjamin

The Da Vinci Code

The tribe of Benjamin (meaning "son of my right hand") is the twelfth tribe of Israel, founded by Benjamin, son of Jacob and Rachel. As recorded in the Bible, the other eleven tribes attacked the tribe of Benjamin and defeated it, killing all of the Benjamite civilians, including women and children, and vowed never to let their women marry Benjamites. However, so as not to exterminate a tribe of Israel, they provided the surviving Benjamite men with four hundred virgins raided from another town. Later, after their exile, the tribe of Benjamin joined with the tribe of Judah to form the Kingdom of Judah, which gave their name to the Jews.

Some scholars speculate that Mary Magdalene belonged to the tribe of Benjamin, which they call royal because Israel's first king, Saul, was a Benjamite. Others say there is no historical evidence for Mary Magdalene belonging to this tribe.

Triton Fountain

Angels & Demons

The *Triton Fountain*, commissioned by Pope Urban VIII and carved by Bernini, is located in the Piazza Barberini in Rome. The base consists of four dolphins whose tails support a giant shell on which stands Triton, a sea god of ancient Rome, who is blowing into a conch shell. According to legend, visitors who throw a coin into the fountain will guarantee their return to Rome.

Triton submersible

Deception Point

The Triton, a United States Submarines submersible, is a lightweight minimum-volume configuration designed specifically to deploy from megayachts. This small luxury submarine has excellent visibility and stability, leather seating, and full air conditioning, with easy piloting controls. Different models can submerge from 220 to 400 meters. Delivery includes personal instruction on how to operate it.

True Cross of the Crucifixion

The Da Vinci Code

According to Christian tradition, the True Cross is the cross upon which Jesus was crucified and died. As a symbol of his sacrifice, it naturally became the object of veneration and worship.

Since Jerusalem was laid waste in the wars of the Romans, the places consecrated by the death and burial of Christ were profaned and deserted. However, after Emperor Constantine made peace with the Catholic church, he had Macarius, Bishop of Jerusalem, excavate Jerusalem's holy sites in about 327 AD to find these holy places.

As the story goes, Saint Helena, Constantine's mother, assisted in identifying Calvary and the Holy Sepulchre, and uncovered three crosses nearby as well as the titulus and the nails that pinned Christ to the wood. Believing one was the cross upon which Jesus died, and the other two held those who died with him, they set about to identify which one Jesus died on. Placing each in turn on a deathly ill woman, they found she recovered at the touch of the third, which they determined to be the True Cross. Helena took the nails back with her to Constantinople along with part of the cross. The rest was enclosed in a silver reliquary and given to the bishop of Jerusalem, who exhibited it periodically to the faithful.

Some historians find these stories of questionable authenticity, though it is clear that the Basilica of the Holy Sepulchre was completed by 335 and that relics of the Cross were being venerated there by the next decade. When the Sassanian Khosrau II of Persia captured Jerusalem in 614, he removed the Cross as a trophy. Heraclius defeated him in 628 and took back the relic, which he eventually returned to Jerusalem. Around 1009, Christians hid the Cross and it remained hidden until its rediscovery (as a small fragment of wood embedded in a golden cross) during the First Crusade in 1099. It was captured by Saladin in 1187 and subsequently disappeared.

Before that time, fragments of the True Cross had been broken up and widely distributed; everyone seems to have gotten a piece of it. It is likely that many of the alleged pieces of the True Cross are fakes, created by traveling merchants in the Middle Ages who made a thriving trade in manufactured relics. In fact, by the sixteenth century so many churches claimed to possess a piece of the True Cross that John Calvin remarked that there was enough wood in them to fill a ship. However, Rohault de Fleury made a study of the relics in 1870 and determined that if all the alleged fragments of the Cross were brought together again, they wouldn't fill a third of the original cross. Then again, no scientific study has been done to see if any of these relics are even made of the same kind of wood.

Tuileries Gardens

The Da Vinci Code

The Tuileries Palace (the name is derived from the tile kilns that used to occupy the site) was begun in 1564 by Catherine de' Medici. The southeast corner of Tuileries joined the Louvre, and the palace was greatly enlarged in the 1600s. King Louis XIV stayed there while Versailles was under construction and his landscape architect, André Le Notre, laid out a patterned flower garden for the Tuileries in 1664. After the king left, the building was virtually abandoned, used only as a theater.

However, when Louis XVI, Marie Antoinette, and their children were expelled from Versailles during the French Revolution in 1789, they were forced to live at the Tuileries Palace under house arrest. They tried to escape in 1791, but were captured at Varennes because a peasant recognized Louis' likeness from his coin, and they were returned to the Tuileries.

The Tuileries Palace was stormed in 1792 by the Paris mob, who overwhelmed and massacred the loyal Swiss Guards as the royal family fled through the gardens and took refuge at the General Assembly hall. The "Commune," the first government of the people, was established after that.

Under Napoleon I, the Tuileries was the official residence of the first consul and later the imperial palace. In 1808 Napolean I began constructing the northern gallery, which also connected to the Louvre. The Tuileries Palace served as the royal residence after the Bourbon Restoration in 1814, then was attacked and occupied for a third time by supporters of the Paris Commune, in 1830. King Louis Philippe took up residence there until 1848 when the people invaded it once again in a revolt and sacked it. This time, the Swiss Guard, remembering what had happened to their predecessors, abandoned the palace.

Though never again used as a royal residence, the Tuileries was restored under Napoleon III as a sumptuous palace. It burned in 1871 during yet another communard confrontation. Twelve years later, the burnt-out shell was demolished and the present gardens, formerly west of the palace, extended.

The current Tuileries Gardens, covering about sixty-three acres, are surrounded by the Louvre, the Seine, the Place de la Concorde, and the Rue de Rivoli. They still closely follow the design laid out by Andre Le Notre in 1664.

Tyrrhenian Sea

The Da Vinci Code

This is an arm of the Mediterranean Sea off the western coast of Italy between the Ligurian Sea, the Italian peninsula, and the islands of Corsica, Sardinia, and Sicily. The Strait of Messina connects it with the Ionian Sea.

The sea is named for the Tyrrhenoi, an ancient Greek name for the Etruscans who were emigrants from Lydia led by the prince Tyrrhenus. The chief ports are at Naples and Palermo.

Universi Dominici Gregis

Angels & Demons

The Universi Dominici Gregis is a Catholic Apostolic Constitution issued by Pope John Paul II in 1996. Its title, meaning "the Lord's whole flock," is taken from the opening statement. The document deals with the vacancy of the papacy and how to conduct conclave.

According to this new constitution, four votes (two in the morning and two in the afternoon) are held daily, requiring two-thirds vote plus one to elect a pope. However, the document allows for an absolute majority vote after thirty-three or thirty-four votes if no pope has been elected. In addition, it does away with two methods of electing a pope which have not been used in several hundred years: acclamation and election by compromise committee.

The constitution enjoins strict secrecy and allows the cardinals to be housed more comfortably in Domus Sanctae Marthae, a building with dormitory-type accommodations, built within the Vatican City. Previously, the cardinals were housed in uncomfortable improvised accommodations within the Sistine Chapel. Another change is that the method by which a pope takes office is not regimented; he may choose the Papal Coronation—the old enthronement ceremony, or the Papal Inauguration, so long as some form of formal ceremony takes place. The papal election of 2005 used this new system to elect Pope Benedict XVI.

Uranium 235 and 238

Digital Fortress

In the novel, Dan Brown uses the difference between the uranium isotope numbers of the atomic bombs used at Hiroshima and Nagasaki in 1945 as the kill code for Tankado's virus. Since this is the penultimate moment of the novel, it's disappointing that he got it wrong.

The uranium isotope used on the bomb at Hiroshima, nicknamed "Little Boy," was indeed uranium-235. Uranium naturally occurs in three isotopes: uranium-234, uranium-235, and uranium-238. Though all three are radioactive, only uranium-235 is fissionable; uranium-238 could not have been used. In fact, the bomb dropped on Nagasaki, nicknamed "Fat Man," used plutonium-239.

Urban VIII

Angels & Demons

Florentine Maffeo Barberini (1568–1644) served as Pope Urban VIII (1623–44). A very active pope, he canonized many saints, instituted new orders, continued the reformation of the church, was the last pope to extend the papal territory, established an arsenal in the Vatican and an arms factory at Tivoli, and fortified Civitavecchia harbor, Castelfranco, and Castel Sant'Angelo.

Though he sanctioned the second condemnation of Galileo for supporting the heliocentric theory of the universe, he later freed him. Friend to many artists, writers, and scholars, Urban built and decorated extensively in Rome, and was the first to employ Bernini, who built many prominent structures in the city. When Urban stripped the bronze girders and decorations from the Pantheon to make the baldachin and cannon, the populace quipped that "what the barbarians did not do, the Barberini did."

USS *Charlotte*

Deception Point

The USS *Charlotte* (SSN-766) is a Los Angeles-class submarine and is the fourth ship of the United States Navy to be named for Charlotte, North Carolina. The first three were a schooner, a cruiser, and a frigate. Launched in 1992 and commissioned in 1994, the fourth USS *Charlotte* is a nuclear-powered attack submarine based in Pearl Harbor, Hawaii.

Vasoconstrictor

Deception Point

A vasoconstrictor is any agent that causes a narrowing or constriction of a blood vessel, such as nicotine, epinephrine, norepinephrine, angiotensin, vasopressin, etc. Vasoconstrictors are also used clinically to increase blood pressure or reduce blood flow.

Vatican City

Angels & Demons and *The Da Vinci Code*

Vatican City is an independent papal state on the west bank of the Tiber River in Rome. The Vatican (which takes its name from Mons Vaticanus, the Vatican Hill—see Vatican Hill) was first used as a papal residence in the fifth century, when Pope Symmachus built the Lateran Palace near Emperor Constantine's basilica for Saint Peter. The pope has usually resided there ever since, except for a time in the fourteenth century when the papal seat moved to Avignon, France.

Vatican City became an independent state in 1929 when Pope Pius XI and Victor Emmanuel III of Italy signed the Lateran Treaty. It has its own citizenship, issues its own currency and postage stamps, and has its own flag, diplomatic corps, newspaper, railroad station, and broadcasting facilities.

The pope maintains complete legal, executive, and judicial powers. The government is run by a lay governor and council, who are appointed by and responsible to the pope.

Vatican Grottoes

Angels & Demons

Below Saint Peter's Basilica in Vatican City are grottoes built by Renaissance architects to bury numerous popes and some royalty. It also has various monuments and architectural fragments from the former basilica built on the same site. The Necropolis (see Necropolis), an enormous underground cemetery, was discovered below the Vatican Grottoes.

Vatican Hill

Angels & Demons

Vaticanus Mons (Vatican Hill) is the ancient name of a hill in northwestern Rome from which Vatican City gets its name. It lies west of the Tiber River opposite the traditional seven hills of Rome. Because Emperor Constantine brought in material to level the area when he built Saint Peter's Basilica, the hill is now higher than it was in ancient times.

Vatican Museums

Angels & Demons

The Vatican Museums (Musei Vaticani) are the public art and sculpture museums in Vatican City that display works from the extensive collection of the Roman Catholic Church. The museums' origin is in 1503 when

Pope Julius II placed a statue of Apollo in the internal courtyard of the Belvedere Palace. The *Laocoön* was added to the collection in 1506 and scores of artwork and artifacts were added throughout the next two centuries.

The collections were eventually reorganized in the eighteenth century and today are a complex of different museums and galleries, among them the Egyptian Museum, Chiaramonti Museum, Museum of Popes Clement XIV and Pius VI (Pio-Clementino), Gregorian Museum of Etruscan Art and Profane Art, Christian Museum, Missionary Museum of Ethnology, Antiquarium Romanum, Vase Collection, Biga Room, Gallery of Tapestries, Gallery of Maps, Gallery of Candelabra, Sobieski Room, Room of the Immaculate Conception, Raphael's Rooms and Loggias, Apartment of Pius V, Chapel of Nicholas V, Sistine Chapel, Borgia Apartments, Vatican Pinacoteca, Missionary-Ethnological Museum, Collection of Modern and Contemporary Religious Art, Vatican Historical Museum, Carriage and Automobile Museum, Apostolic Library, and Vatican Picture Gallery.

Vatican Observatory and Library

The Da Vinci Code

The Vatican Observatory (Specola Astronomica Vaticana) is the astronomical research and educational institution of the Holy See. The current headquarters of the observatory are at Castel Gandolfo, the summer residence of the pope. The observatory operates a telescope atop Mount Graham.

Vatican II

The Da Vinci Code

The Second Vatican Council, held from 1962 to 65, is popularly called Vatican II and was the twenty-first ecumenical council. Convened by Pope John XXIII and continued under Paul VI, its purpose was to spiritually renew the Church and consider its position in the modern world. Pope John XXIII said, "I want to throw open the windows of the Church so that we can see out and the people can see in." He invited other Christian churches to send observers to the council, including Protestant and Orthodox churches. All told, the council issued four constitutions, nine decrees, and three declarations.

Though the basic doctrines of the Church didn't change, the council enacted profound changes that liberalized and modernized practices in the Church, such as encouraging the use of the vernacular language in the celebration of the mass and bringing laymen into closer participation in the church services, which resulted in Bible study groups, marriage encounters, social action organizations, and the charismatic renewal movement.

Venus de Milo

The Da Vinci Code

The Venus de Milo is an ancient Greek marble statue that stands slightly larger than life-size at eighty inches high. It dates to about 130 BC and was found in 1820 in two pieces on the Aegean island of Melos, also called Milo. Though missing its arms and plinth, it is generally believed to be a statue of Venus. Since a fragment of a forearm and hand holding an apple were found near the statue, it is believed they are remnants of its arms and that the statue was the work of Alexandros of Antioch.

The statue earned its fame in the nineteenth century when France, which had looted the Medici Venus from Italy, had to return it following Napoleon's downfall. The French promoted the Venus de Milo as an even greater treasure and, because of its great beauty, the propaganda worked.

Virgin of the Rocks, The

The Da Vinci Code

(see *Madonna of the Rocks, The*)

Vitruvian Man

The Da Vinci Code

The Vitruvian Man is a famous drawing with accompanying notes made by Leonardo Da Vinci around 1490 in one of his journals. It depicts a naked male figure with his arms spread apart and differs from other Vitruvian versions because the figure is shown simultaneously in a circle and square to create one image and solve the problem of disproportionate limbs.

According to Leonardo's notes in the accompanying text, done in his famous mirror writing, it was made as a study of the mathematical proportions of the human body as described by the ancient Roman architect Vitruvius. This rediscovery of ancient Roman knowledge is considered one of the great achievements leading to the Italian Renaissance.

The drawing is often used to show the essential symmetry of the human body, and Leonardo believed his drawing to be an analogy for the workings of the universe. The drawing, done in pen, ink, and watercolor over metalpoint, is part of the collection of the Gallerie dell'Accademia in Venice.

Wallops Island

Deception Point

Wallops Island, where Rachel Sexton meets the United States president in the novel, is a six-square-mile island off the coast of the state of Virginia. Established in 1945, this NASA flight and rocket test complex is one of the oldest rocket launch sites in the world. Over fourteen thousand launches have taken place since it opened, most of them of sounding rockets, which are expendable rockets designed to record scientific data to study the atmosphere and space.

Washington Monument

Deception Point and The Da Vinci Code

The Washington Monument is a tall obelisk located in Washington, D.C., to honor George Washington, the first president of the United States. In 1783, congress passed a resolution approving an equestrian statue of George Washington, but he objected to the idea. After he died in 1799, plans for a memorial were discussed but not adopted until 1832, when the private Washington National Monument Society was formed and started collecting money to build a monument.

The original design by Robert Mills was for an obelisk with a nearly flat top designed to hold a statue of Washington, the obelisk to be surrounded by a circular colonnade holding statues of thirty prominent Revolutionary War heroes. But the $1 million price tag made the society hesitate. It decided to start building the obelisk in 1848 and leave the question of the colonnade for later, hoping for further donations. In 1849, states and territories were encouraged to donate blocks of stone to be incorporated in the monument's interior walls.

Unfortunately, donations ran out in 1854, when the obelisk had only been completed to a height of 152 feet. In 1876, Congress agreed to appropriate another $200,000 to resume construction, and it was agreed to dispense with the colonnade and construct the obelisk using classic Egyptian proportions. Construction began again, with the second stage visibly apparent as a difference in the shading of the marble. The base was completed in 1880, the marble capstone was added in 1884 with an aluminum tip (which was a scarce metal at the time), and the monument was opened to the public in 1888.

Though many of the donated tribute stones carried inscriptions irrelevant to a memorial for George Washington, all 193 memorial blocks were incorporated into the interior and can be read on the inside of the monument.

Made of marble, granite, and sandstone, the Washington Monument stands 555 feet high and is reflected in the Reflecting Pool, a rectangular pool extending eastward toward the Lincoln Memorial. It was the world's tallest structure until 1889 when the Eiffel Tower was finished in Paris. The monument underwent renovation from 1997 to 2000.

West Ponente

Angels & Demons

The West Ponente (West Wind) medallion is Dan Brown's second Altar of Science, representing air. The medallion lies in Saint Peter's Square in Vatican City and depicts a man with wavy hair blowing a gust of wind.

The oval medallion is just one of a number of markers that show the cardinal directions and the signs of the zodiac, placed in a circle around the obelisk, which acts as a gnomon to tell the seasons. Since they weren't placed there until 1817, it's doubtful they were designed by Bernini.

Westminster Abbey

The Da Vinci Code

Westminster Abbey is a Gothic church on the scale of a cathedral, located in Westminster, London, to the west of Westminster Palace. According to tradition, a fisherman saw a vision of St. Peter on the site in 616 AD and a shrine was built on the site by Ethelbert, king of Kent. Westminster Abbey was first built on the site by Edward the Confessor, who had failed to keep his vow to go on a pilgrimage and built the abbey as penance. Constructed from 1045 to 1050 and consecrated in 1065, the original abbey was designed to house Benedictine monks.

It was enlarged and rebuilt in the Gothic style between 1245 and 1517, then closed by Henry VII in 1539 and 1540, becoming a cathedral until 1550. The Benedictines returned under Queen Mary, but were ejected again by Queen Elizabeth I in 1559. Twenty years later, she re-established Westminster as a royal peculiar (see royal peculiar). The two western towers were built in the eighteenth century by Sir Christopher Wren and Nicholas Hawksmoor, and extensive renovation took place in the late nineteenth century under Sir George Gilbert Scott.

William the Conqueror was crowned in Westminster in 1066 and nearly every English king and queen has been crowned there since then. It is the burial place of eighteen monarchs, and England's most notable statesmen and distinguished subjects have been buried in the abbey since the fourteenth century, including great English writers (see Poets' Corner).

Westminster Palace

The Da Vinci Code

Westminster Palace accommodates the Houses of Parliament in Westminster, London, on the west bank of the Thames River. The oldest extant part of the Palace, Westminster Hall, dates to 1097. The complex served as the monarch's chief London residence until a fire destroyed part of it in 1529. The Model Parliament, the first official Parliament of England, met in the palace in 1295. Since then, it has been adopted as the assembly place for the House of Commons and the House of Lords.

Westminster Palace was rebuilt from 1840 to 1860 by Sir Charles Barry to replace buildings devastated by fire in 1834, though Westminster Hall was one of the few portions of the palace to survive intact. The palace was burned by incendiary bombs in the Battle of Britain in 1941, but has since been completely repaired.

The palace includes over one thousand rooms on four floors, including the Chambers of the House of Lords, the Chambers of the House of Commons, committee rooms, libraries, lobbies, offices, and dining facilities. One of the Palace's most famous features is the Clock Tower, a popular London tourist attraction that houses Big Ben (see Big Ben).

White House

Deception Point

The White House is the official residence and principal workplace of the president of the United States and his family, located in Washington, D.C. The site was chosen by the first United States president, George Washington, and Washington's city planner, Pierre L'Enfant. The building, which has always been white despite rumors to the contrary, was designed by Irish-born architect James Hoban (see Hoban, James). Originally known as the "President's Palace," the "President's House," or the "Executive Mansion," it is the oldest public building in Washington, its cornerstone having been laid in 1792.

The first president to reside in the White House was John Adams, who moved into the residence after it was completed in 1800. The White House was burned and gutted in 1814 by the British during the War of 1812, but was rebuilt. It was attacked again in 1841 when enraged Whig Party members rioted outside the White House.

The public popularly referred to the building as the "White House," and the name became official when President Theodore Roosevelt had it engraved on his stationery in 1901. The West Wing, which now houses the president's office and those of his political staff, was built by Theodore Roosevelt as a temporary office building in 1902, and in 1909, President William Howard Taft reconstructed the president's office, and changed its shape to oval (see Oval Office), placing it in the center of the West Wing. The West Wing was damaged by fire in 1929 and expanded in 1933, when Franklin D. Roosevelt became president. Disliking the lack of windows in the Oval Office, he had it reconstructed in the southeast corner, which also allowed more privacy.

The East Wing, which contains additional office space and often houses the offices of the first lady, was added to the White House in 1942 to hide the construction of an underground bunker. A few years later, the building was found to be structurally unsound and President Harry Truman moved to Blair House while the White House was repaired. First lady Jacqueline Kennedy remodeled the interior of many rooms in the 1960s and subsequent first ladies have remodeled additional rooms.

The White House covers 55,000 square feet of floor space, with 134 rooms and 35 bathrooms on 6 floors. There are also 412 doors, 147 windows, 28 fireplaces, 8 staircases, and 3 elevators, with a tennis court, bowling lane, movie theater, and jogging track. The grounds cover about 18 acres.

Winged Victory

The Da Vinci Code

The *Winged Victory of Samothrace*, also called the *Nike of Samothrace*, is a marble sculpture of the Greek goddess Nike (Victory) that stands eleven feet high atop the prow of a ship. Sculpted by an unknown artist, it is missing its head and outstretched arms, and is thought to date somewhere between 288 BC and 180 BC.

Nikes such as this were created by the Greeks to celebrate naval victories and it is believed this one honored the Rhodian conquest of Antiochus III. It was discovered in 1863 on the island of Samothrace by French consul and amateur archaeologist Charles Champoiseau. Broken into 118 fragments, the statue was pieced together at the Louvre in Paris, where it now stands at the head of the great staircase leading to the upper galleries.

Witches' Hammer

The Da Vinci Code

The *Malleus Maleficarum* (*The Witches' Hammer*) was first published in 1486 and served as a guidebook for inquisitors during the Inquisition to aid in the identification, prosecution, and elimination of witches. Written by James Sprenger and Henry Kramer, the *Hammer* remained in use for three hundred years and is one of the most blood-soaked works in human history.

The authors claimed that witches flew through the air on broom-sticks, caused lightning and hail storms, changed from humans into animals, become invisible, ate or killed children, etc. They set forth many of the misconceptions and fears concerning witches and witch-craft that are still believed today.

The book was used extensively as a reference by judges, the clergy, and torturers during witch trials, specifying rules of evidence and the procedures by which suspected witches were tortured and put to death. Tens of thousands of people (primarily women) were falsely accused and murdered as a result of the procedures described in this book.

Woman with the Alabaster Jar, The

The Da Vinci Code

Roman Catholic scholar Margaret Starbird read *Holy Blood, Holy Grail* (see *Holy Blood, Holy Grail*) and set out to debunk its hypothesis that Jesus was married to Mary Magdalene and had children with her. Instead, Starbird's research into European history, symbolism, medieval art, heraldry, mythology, psychology, and the Bible led her to believe that the hypothesis—the "Grail heresy"—was true and the sacred femi-nine has been denied through time. She published *The Woman with the Alabaster Jar* (referring to the jar that contained ointment with which Mary Magdalene anointed Jesus) to summarize her findings.

Worm

Digital Fortress

The word "worm" comes from *The Shockwave Rider*, a 1970s science fiction novel by John Brunner. A computer worm is a self-replicating computer program that can spread rapidly from one computer to another over a network. It is similar to a virus, but while a virus attaches itself to and becomes a part of another executable program, a worm is self contained and does not need to be part of another program to reproduce itself. They are often designed to exploit the automatic file sending and receiving capabilities found on many computers, and may delete files or send spam or other documents via e-mail. They often vastly increase network traffic simply by reproducing rapidly.

Wren, Sir Christopher

The Da Vinci Code

Sir Christopher Wren (1632–1723) was an English astronomer, mathematician, and architect who is best known for designing many London baroque buildings.

He served as professor of astronomy at Gresham College and Oxford and was one of the founding members of the Royal Society, but his architectural career began in 1661 when Charles II appointed him assistant to the Royal Architect. Wren studied architecture in Paris, and after the Great Fire of 1666 he designed many new buildings, the greatest of which is Saint Paul's Cathedral. He was named Royal Architect in 1669 and retained the post for more than forty-five years.

His elegant works are numerous, including fifty-two London churches, as well as other distinguished buildings such as chapels, theaters, libraries, hospitals, government offices, palaces and castles, private residences, scientific buildings, and schools and colleges.

Wren was knighted in the 1670s and served as a member of Parliament from 1685 to 1688 and from 1702 to 1705. He is buried in Saint Paul's.

X-33 space plane

Deception Point and Angels & Demons

The X-33 space plane, which Dan Brown's characters use in two of his novels to get somewhere fast, came about as a result of the VentureStar, a reusable space shuttle designed by Lockheed Martin for NASA. The X-33 was a scaled-down version that could fly up to Mach 13–15 and was designed to reduce the turnaround time for flights. Unfortunately, the program was cancelled by NASA in 2001 when the prototype was only 85 percent complete due to a long series of technical difficulties.

So, obviously, CERN does not own an X-33 space plane; this was a bit of literary license by Dan Brown, who wrote the books before the X-33 program was scrapped.

Yin and yang

Angels & Demons

The ancient Chinese concepts of yin and yang are two opposite yet complementary forces in the universe. Yin is the feminine, dark, passive, negative force; and yang the masculine, light, active, positive force. Everything can be described as either yin or yang, but nothing is completely one or the other. Each contains the seed of its opposite and they can change and flow from one to the other. For example, cold (yin) can turn into hot (yang). One cannot exist without the other, and the wise person seeks a balance between the two.

Z-particle

Angels & Demons

A Z particle or Z boson is an elementary particle that is identical to the photon in all respects except mass. Its mass is one hundred times that of the photon, and it is one of the elementary particles that mediate the weak nuclear force.

CERN discovered W and Z particles in 1983 after building its particle accelerator. The Z particle was jokingly given its name because it was said to be the last particle to need discovery and because it has zero electric charge.

BIBLIOGRAPHY

Answers.com

About.com

Encyclopaedia Britannica Online

Wikipedia.com

Dan Brown's Official Website

Dan Brown Biography, Bookbrowse.com

Dan Brown Biography, Answers.com

The Unofficial Dan Brown Biography, Lisa Rogak (2005).

"News of Surveillance Is Awkward for Agency," *New York Times* (December 22, 2005).

"Interview with Dan Brown," Claire E. White, Writerswrite.com (May 1998).

"A Conversation with Dan Brown," Bookbrowse.com (2001).

"*The Da Vinci Code*, the Catholic Church and Opus Dei," © 2005, Information Office of Opus Dei on the Internet (2005).

"Q & A with Dan Brown," Readinggroup.com (2005).

"New Hampshire Book Tourism Thrives in Robert Frost Country," www.VisitNH.gov.

"A *Da Vinci Code* Tour: Travel the Roads Taken by Characters in the Best-selling Novel," Chris Culwell, Fodors.com.

Darrell Bock, "Breaking the Da Vinci Code: Answers to the questions everybody's asking," Nelson Books (2004).

Dan Burstein, editor, "Secrets of the *Code*: The unauthorized guide to the mysteries behind *The Da Vinci Code*," CDs Books (2004).

James Garlow, "Cracking Da Vinci's Code: You've read the fiction, now read the facts," Cook Communications (2004).

Sharon Newman, *The Real History Behind "The Da Vinci Code*," Berkley Trade (2005).